Endorsements for
The Magnificent Obsession

In *The Magnificent Obsession*, Anne Graham Lotz has sensed that the God who guided Abraham one step at a time is now guiding her life. This should be carefully read by all who are diligently seeking God's will.

— Dr. Henry Blackaby, author of *Experiencing God*, founder
and president emeritus of Blackaby Ministries International

⌐∽⌐

Anne has a unique gift of making God's word extraordinarily real. She has again done that through this book, and I, with humility and pleasure, heartily recommend *The Magnificent Obsession* to anyone who is interested in understanding and growing in their faith.

— Ron Blue, president, Kingdom Advisors

⌐∽⌐

These life lessons are written by a woman of God: a dear friend who lives what she writes and writes what she lives, in order that others may live life to the full! . . . We are not left guessing how to love God with our whole hearts when we have finished reading this book.

— Jill Briscoe, author and teacher

⌐∽⌐

Anne Graham Lotz invites lucidly, speaks powerfully, and lives consistently with deep devotion and passion. It is not surprising therefore that she loves the story of Abraham, the friend of God.

— D. Stuart Briscoe, author and speaker

⌐∽⌐

This is without question Anne Graham Lotz's finest work. Her faith and wisdom both shine from the pages. . . . I am astonished by how powerful these words are, and humbled by the challenge she offers.

— Davis Bunn, bestselling author of *The Centurion's Wife*

We don't often think of Abraham as our contemporary, but in this powerful and profound book Anne Graham Lotz shows the relevance of Abraham for today.

— GEORGE CAREY, Archbishop of Canterbury 1991 – 2002

⚬

Anne Graham Lotz is proof that her dad, Billy Graham, is not just a wonderful preacher, but what a daughter he helped raise! As she relates her own life to the trials of Abraham, ancient text becomes vital and relevant. Anne's magnificent obsession may be just the key to discovering your own path.

— ALAN COLMES, FoxNews

⚬

Anne Graham Lotz is an engaging writer with a powerful message for the church.

— CHUCK COLSON, founder, Prison Fellowship Ministries

⚬

The Magnificent Obsession is a true blessing, reflecting her deep spirituality and inspirational life of eternal significance. How timely!

— ELIZABETH DOLE, former United States senator, North Carolina

⚬

This book is tremendous. It has given me a different perspective on Abraham, but it has also caused me to look differently at my own life — and that is the mark of something special.

— TONY DUNGY, head coach of the XLI Super Bowl Champion
Indianapolis Colts, and author of *Quiet Strength*

⚬

The Magnificent Obsession brings you to a moment of truth of how badly you want a God-filled life. What are you willing to do and leave behind to embrace your magnificent obsession? Read the book. You won't be able to put it down.

— DR. TONY EVANS, senior pastor of Oak Cliff Bible Fellowship,
president, The Urban Alternative

⚬

Anne Graham Lotz, as only she can do, gently leads us through a timeless spiritual journey that powerfully inspires and awakens our own understanding of God.

— KARYN FRIST, author of *Love You, Daddy Boy*; and BILL FRIST, MD,
former Majority Leader, U.S. Senate

With characteristic candor Anne Graham Lotz follows the pilgrimage of Abraham, questioning all the way what messages lie in his journey of discovery for each of us today who dares to believe that the God of the universe speaks — to us — and very much cares about how we respond.

> — GLORIA GAITHER, author, lyricist, speaker

For anyone that has ever had a desire to know God in His fullness, this is a must read!... It will encourage you to pursue a God-filled life and experience your own magnificent obsession. Thank you, Anne, for allowing me to share in this journey.

> — SYLVIA RHYNE HATCHELL, Hall of Fame head coach of Women's
> Basketball — University of North Carolina

I pray for God's touch on lives as people read and absorb the challenges of *The Magnificent Obsession*. It is a deeply penetrating practical application of Abraham's journey of faith.

> — DAVID H. HICKS, chaplain (major general) U.S. Army retired

Cravings. Cravings for power, approval, the corner office, the loudest applause. We crave. But behind these yearnings is a deeper one — a craving for God. In these pages, Anne identifies this longing and shows us how God and only God can satisfy it. Thank you, Anne, for this, and a lifetime of words that point us in the right direction.

> — MAX LUCADO, pastor and bestselling author

Don't mistake Anne Graham Lotz's *The Magnificent Obsession* for just another Bible study or you'll miss out on a lump-in-the-throat read, not to mention a rollercoaster ride between the Old Testament and today. With the precision of a surgeon, incisive Bible teacher Anne dissects the life of Abraham and invites us along on her quest to embrace the God-filled life.

> — JERRY B. JENKINS, novelist, coauthor of the Left Behind series,
> and owner, Christian Writers Guild

Anne Graham Lotz has given us a unique genre that weaves thorough, thoughtful Bible study with her own spiritual journey. With an engaging style, she models both expectant exploration and sincere responsiveness.

— TIMOTHY S. LANIAK, Th.D., dean and professor of Old Testament,
Gordon-Conwell Theological Seminary

∽∾

This book came to me during a time of great pain and struggle. Anne Graham Lotz's words lifted me, fixed my eyes upon the Lord, and renewed my passion to trust Him heart, mind, and soul in every circumstance. Our God is worthy! He is magnificent.

— FRANCINE RIVERS, author of *Redeeming Love*

∽∾

Abraham's fame is that God called him "friend." Anne Graham Lotz's personal obsession with the God of Abraham will spill over into your heart as she walks you through a life that finds meaning and fulfillment in a vibrant friendship with God.

— JOSEPH M. STOWELL, president, Cornerstone University

∽∾

Whether teaching, speaking, or writing, Anne Graham Lotz communicates her love for God and people with great passion and conviction. Her own stories of struggle and faithfulness and her biblical insights into Abraham's journey will challenge you to seek God with great encouragement and hope.

— RAVI ZACHARIAS, author and speaker

THE
MAGNIFICENT
OBSESSION

Other Books by Anne Graham Lotz

The Vision of His Glory

God's Story

Daily Light

Just Give Me Jesus

Heaven: My Father's House

My Jesus Is ... Everything

Life Is Just Better with Jesus

Pursuing MORE of Jesus

Why? Trusting God When You Don't Understand

The Joy of My Heart

I Saw the LORD

Into the Word

THE
MAGNIFICENT
OBSESSION

EMBRACING *the* GOD-FILLED LIFE

ANNE
GRAHAM
LOTZ

foreword by
RICK WARREN

ZONDERVAN.com/
AUTHORTRACKER
follow your favorite authors

ZONDERVAN

The Magnificent Obsession
Copyright © 2009 by Anne Graham Lotz

This title is also available as a Zondervan ebook. Visit www.zondervan.com/ebooks.

This title is also available in a Zondervan audio edition. Visit www.zondervan.fm.

Requests for information should be addressed to:

Zondervan, *Grand Rapids, Michigan* 49530

This edition: ISBN 978-0-310-33010-3 (softcover)

Library of Congress Cataloging-in-Publication Data

Lotz, Anne Graham, 1948-
    The magnificent obsession : Embracing the God-filled life / Anne Graham Lotz.
        p.   cm.
    Includes bibliographical references.
    ISBN 978-0-310-26288-6 (hardcover, jacketed)
    1. Abraham (Biblical patriarch) 2. God (Christianity) — Knowableness.
  3. Intimacy (Psychology) — Religious aspects — Christianity. 4. Spirituality.
  5. Bible. O.T. Genesis — Criticism, interpretation, etc. I. Title.
  BS580.A3L68 2008
  222'.11092 — dc22   2008013130

Published in association with the literary agency of Alive Communications, Inc., 7680 Goddard St., Suite 200, Colorado Springs, CO 80920. www.alivecommunications.com

Cover design: Studio Gearbox
Cover photography: Photos.com
Interior design: Beth Shagene

Printed in the United States of America

10 11 12 13 14 15 16 /DCI/ 25 24 23 22 21 20 19 18 17 16 15 14 13 12 11 10 9 8 7 6 5 4 3 2 1

If . . .

If you are a member of the younger generation who sometimes feels the traditional church is irrelevant . . .

If you are a member of the older generation who sometimes feels excluded by the contemporary church . . .

If you are a member of my generation who has been raised in the church and has been burned by the hypocrisy within . . .

If you have been a seeker of God but have been hurt by those who call themselves by His name . . .

If you consider yourself a Christian but are not actively involved in, or even currently attending, a church . . .

If you attend a home church, seeking God outside the mainstream . . .

If you are a believer in exile . . .

If you are a liberal who is uncomfortable with the God of the religious right . . .

If you are a conservative who is uncomfortable with the God of the progressive left . . .

If you are a member of another religion but feel dissatisfied and unfulfilled in your relationship with God . . .

If you just have a restlessness in your spirit, believing that there must be something more to life than you are experiencing . . .

this book is dedicated to you.

Contents

Foreword by Rick Warren 15

My Magnificent Obsession 17

1. Leave Everything Behind 21

2. Let Everything Go 51

3. Entrust Everything Completely 81

4. Pursue Everything Patiently 109

5. Lift Everything Up 133

6. Cast Everything Out 163

7. Lay Everything Down 187

8. Mourn Everything Hopefully 213

9. Pass Everything On 227

Epilogue 263

Modus Operandi 265

Notes 267

A Very Special Thank-You 283

For this reason
I kneel before the Father,
From whom his whole family in heaven
and on earth derives its name.
I pray
that out of his glorious riches
he may strengthen you with power
through his Spirit in your inner being . . .
that you may be filled
to the measure
of all the fullness
of God.

— EPHESIANS 3:14 – 16, 19

You Are About to Begin the Adventure of a Lifetime

The Bible is extremely clear about the importance of living by faith: "Without faith it is impossible to please God" (Hebrews 11:6); "The just shall live by faith" (Romans 1:17); "Whatsoever is not of faith is sin" (Romans 14:23). Learning to love and trust the loving God who created you and sent His Son, Jesus, to die for you is what life is all about. My dear friend Anne calls it "the magnificent obsession."

Magnificent is the perfect description! The faith life unlocks amazing resources you may have never imagined. Jesus says, "According to your faith, it will be done to you" (Matthew 9:29). For just a second, think about the implications of this truth. Jesus says, "You get to choose how much I use and bless your life. It's all based on how much you choose to trust Me." Intimacy with God is a choice. You decide how much God gets to work in your life and how close to God you are. If you feel far from God right now, guess who moved? You're only a decision away from reconnecting.

For this reason, I am thrilled you have picked up Anne's book. Anne Graham Lotz is God's woman with God's message of faith for all of us today. I read everything Anne writes, and you should too. She has a passion for God's Word that shines through on every page, and because of her faith in His Word, God has given her a unique ability to hear His voice through Scripture and then communicate it in a clear and compelling way.

The great model of faith in the Old Testament is, of course, Abraham. He is the father of faith. You cannot fully grasp the life of faith God intends for you to live without understanding the lessons of Abraham — both his successes and his failures. Abraham shows us why we are often full of faith one day and full of doubt the next. In this book Anne shows us how an obedient faith must be lived out step-by-step and day-by-day. You need new faith for each new day. To enjoy the life God intends for you, you must daily lay everything down and let everything go in surrender to Him. You release everything — and then you receive more than you ever imagined!

Here's what I urge you to do with this book. Don't just read it. Buy several copies and start a reading group with some friends. At Saddleback we call these groups "Connection Groups." Share your struggles and admit your doubts. Get your fears out in the open and watch them vanish when held up to the light of truth. Pray for each other. Then create some practical ways that you can help each other practice the transforming truths of a God-filled life.

I am excited for you. You are about to begin the adventure of a lifetime! After you've completed this book, let us hear how you are moving forward in *your* magnificent obsession. You can write Anne, or me, or both of us! We'll be praying, *in faith*, for you!

Dr. Rick Warren
author, *The Purpose Driven Life*

My Magnificent
Obsession

I was raised in a home where God was not only believed but loved, obeyed, and served. As I was growing up, it never occurred to me to question or doubt His existence because His presence permeated our family's life. Yet it wasn't until I was older and able to think through some of the larger issues of life for myself, such as who am I and why am I here and where am I going, that I was struck by the fact that my parents had not just taught me the truth by their words but, even more powerfully and effectively, by their own example.

And what an example it has been! With my mother's heartfelt support, my father preached the gospel face-to-face to over 220 million people around the world. He shared his faith in God with presidents, kings, queens, emperors, popes, dictators — every conceivable world leader — as well as masses of ordinary people for over six decades. In so many ways he has lived out his faith on a world stage. What I saw in private was totally authentic and completely synchronized with the public figure.

While I cannot emphasize enough the impact my parents' faith has had on my own, I must admit that Billy and Ruth Graham are not the primary ones who shaped my own personal magnificent obsession. Instead, I can trace my passionate embrace of the God-filled life to someone I have never met in person, someone with whom I have little else in common. He lived in a long-ago time, in a foreign culture, in a patriarchal society, in an idolatrous home. His life was full of twists and turns, riches and losses, deceit and redemption, failure and success. Nevertheless, he has become a spiritual mentor to me.

The person who has motivated me to pursue a God-filled life, the person whose own magnificent obsession is as powerfully contagious today as it was four thousand years ago when he first embraced it, is Abraham. His name means "father of nations." And even though he was a wanderer, he was the founder of the Israelites, Ishmaelites, and Edomites. Even more interesting, while he claimed no religion, he is claimed as the patriarch of three: Judaism, Islam, and Christiantity.

Let me tell you how we met . . .

In the spring of 1976 I established Bible Study Fellowship, a weekly lay Bible school in my hometown, because I wanted to be in it. A group of 150 women joined me in the small church chapel as I stumbled my way through teaching a six-week class on the New Testament book of Ephesians. After a three-month break, the class reopened, doubling in size to the capacity allowed by the national headquarters, and I plunged into teaching the first book of the Bible, Genesis. After wrestling with the mind-expanding, controversial, fundamental first eleven chapters, I was unprepared for what happened next. The text blossomed into the biography of Abraham — and my life was forever changed.

As I saturated myself in the text, Abraham walked off the pages and into my life — a very ordinary man who became extraordinary for one primary reason — he made the critical choice to embrace a God-filled life, to pursue knowing God and making Him known through living a life of obedient faith. His initial choice was then followed by a series of choices that were worked out on the anvil of his life. Each subsequent choice not only reinforced the first one but became the stepping-stone for the one that would follow. Like a hammer striking steel, Abraham made choice after choice after choice until he forged an intimate relationship with God that God acknowledged as a friendship.

I decided that Abraham's goal would be mine, and I began a passionate pursuit of embracing the God-filled life. Choice after choice after choice. Knowing Him has become the magnificent obsession of my life that grows and intensifies with each passing moment. I want to know God as He truly is . . . and make Him known . . . *to you.*

A few years after I had set knowing God as my life's goal, I was confronted by a contemptuous public rebuttal to a message I had given. I had done my best to point people to Jesus, but I was informed emphatically and somewhat condescendingly that we all have our own gods! I was told that some may call him Buddha, some may call him Muhammad, some may call him Allah, some may call him Messiah, some *may* call him Jesus.

I remember thinking, But I don't want to know God like that. I don't want to know the names other people call Him. I don't want to know Him as someone says He might be like, or thinks He might be like, or was told He might be like. If there is a God at the center of the universe, I want to know Him as He is. Surely He has a name He calls Himself. I want to know that name. I am not content with religion. I want to know God personally. And there's a big difference.

Since that moment on the platform so long ago, I have noticed a similar attitude to that of the emcee, but within the evangelical church. It's an attitude I have heard bestselling author Dr. Henry Blackaby describe as "evangelical idolatry": Christians who worship and serve a god they have made up. A god who meets their needs. A god who serves them. A god who is convenient. And comfortable. A god they can market and promote and politicize for their own agendas. A god they can use to justify their prejudice and oppression and greed and selfishness and shallowness and sin. A god who bears no real resemblance to the Creator of the universe, the God of Abraham, Isaac, and Jacob, the Father of Jesus Christ. A god of religion.

I don't want to know God like that. I don't want to know God as *I* want to know Him, as my imagination conceives Him. I don't want to know Him as others say they know Him. I want to know God *as He is.* For myself.

I want to know God . . .

> as Noah did . . . in His salvation from judgment.
>
> as Moses did . . . in His liberating power.
>
> as Elijah did . . . in His still, small voice.
>
> as Isaiah did . . . in His glory.
>
> as Jeremiah did . . . in His faithfulness.
>
> as David did . . . in His shepherding care.

I want to know God as Ezekiel did . . . seated on the throne as the Son of Man.

I want to know God...

> as Mary did... in His humanity... and in His deity.
>
> as Peter did... in His forgiveness.
>
> as Mary Magdalene did... in His authority over demons.
>
> as Lazarus did... in His resurrection life.
>
> as Lazarus's sisters did... in His tender compassion.
>
> as Paul did... in the sufficiency of His grace.

I want to know God as the apostle John did... seated on the throne as the Son of God.

Summed up, I want to know God as Abraham did... as His friend. As *His* friend. The Bible reveals an astonishing fact when it describes Abraham as God's friend.[1] The designation "friend" comes *from God's perspective.* What an achievement! It would be one thing if I told you the president of the United States was my friend. You might smile rather skeptically. But it's an entirely different matter if the president were to say, "Anne Graham Lotz is my friend." The president's personal perspective would make all the difference in how seriously such a relationship would be viewed.

Likewise, Abraham did not claim to be God's friend. It was God who stated that Abraham was His friend. And since the Bible also says that God does not change, that He is the same yesterday, today, and forever,[2] then I decided if I don't know God as Abraham did, nothing is wrong with God... there must be something wrong with the way I am living out my Christian life.

It was this thought process, triggered by my first in-depth study of the life of Abraham, that redefined my life as I made the initial choice to pursue...

> Knowing God and making Him known.
>
> Receiving His blessing to be a blessing.
>
> Fulfilling all the potential He has for my life.
>
> Living a life of step-by-step obedient faith.
>
> Embracing the God-filled life...
>
> ... a life of eternal significance.
>
> *This is my magnificent obsession...*

Anne Graham Lotz

∽ ONE ∽

Leave Everything Behind

Genesis 12:1 – 13:4

The Bible doesn't tell us exactly what prompted Abraham's desire to know God. Perhaps the desire began when he witnessed the miracle of human birth and marveled, *This baby is so perfectly and wondrously made, there must be a Maker somewhere.* Or was it when Abraham observed the migratory habits of the birds and the way the sun came up every morning and went down every evening, and he reflected, *These things must be more than just an accident or a coincidence.* Was it when he entered into a business deal and refused to cheat even though he could have profited personally if he had? Did he walk away, shaking his head and wondering, *What's wrong with me? Why did cheating make me so uneasy? How did I know that it was wrong even if I could have gained by it?* Did he come away from the worship of idols empty and dissatisfied with his religion, restless in his spirit, increasingly convinced that it was as man-made as the objects of wood and stone on which it focused?

Although I don't know the tantalizing details that surrounded Abraham's launch into the adventure of knowing God, it's clear that something stirred in his heart. The small candle of his conscience must have been lit, his spirit must have sought to draw near to the one true living God, because God leaned out of heaven and invaded Abraham's life.[1] Abraham was not some random selection on a divine whim. He had been carefully chosen by God. Why? Why out of all the people living

21

on the planet did God lean down out of heaven and call Abraham to follow Him
in a life of faith? Was it just *because*? Because God loved Abraham? Because God
discerned that Abraham, deep down in the secret recesses of his soul, longed to
know Him "in spirit and in truth"?[2]

It was that last assumption that captured my thoughts and resonated with my
heart. Because deep down, in the secret recesses of my soul, I too long to know God
in spirit and in truth. I yearn for God to fill my life, saturating me with Himself.

But how does a person today even begin to pursue knowing God? Does a
person . . .

> Go to church every time the door opens?
>
> Do more good works than bad works?
>
> Meditate in a monastery in some remote mountain village?
>
> Walk barefooted over fiery coals?
>
> Pray facedown five times a day?
>
> Chant repetitious phrases in unison with others?

How does someone even take the first step in God's direction?

For me, the process began with a small desire in my heart, a small thought in
my mind, a small light in my eye, a small turning of my spirit when I observed the
example of someone else who pursued God. Nothing really big and flashy.

Like Abraham, do you want to know God? Could Abraham serve as the example for all of us? Has the magnificent obsession begun in your heart and mind and
eye and spirit for the simple reason that you have chosen to read this book? Maybe
the small spark of desire has been fanned into flame by what you have observed
in the created world around you or by your conscience within you.[3] I do know that
if you and I ever truly know God, it will not be an accident. It will be because we
have pursued with focused intentionality. It will happen when, like Abraham, we
abandon every other goal, every other priority, and embrace the God-filled life
until He becomes our magnificent obsession.

LEAVE BEHIND THE FAMILIAR

So who *was* Abraham? As I delved into his life, I discovered he was the son of Terah, a wealthy man living in the Mesopotamian city of Ur, an internationally recognized center of culture and trade. Terah was also a worshiper of idols, which makes me wonder what the trigger was that fired the faith for which Abraham has been so well known for four thousand years. And because it was his home, he must have been comfortable in Ur; it was very familiar territory. It was the land of his father, the city in which he had been raised, the values he had lived by, the culture that had shaped him, the attitudes he had adopted, the religion he had followed.

Ur was not only familiar to Abraham, Ur was a habit. To my knowledge, he had never known anything else. Yet when God called him out of that familiar place, Abraham leaped to obey, making the choice to take steps that began a journey that lasted a lifetime.

Abraham's willingness to leave *everything* behind arrested me, challenged me, convicted me. Would I be willing to do the same? Could I ever really know God if I didn't choose to leave everything behind? If I clung to some things, small things, hidden things, past things, *anything*?

What Abraham did in the Old Testament, the apostle Peter did in the New Testament. In response to Jesus' invitation, Peter climbed out of his fishing boat, put his feet on the surface of the stormy sea, and walked on the water to Jesus. As Peter stepped out in faith, we have to step out in faith.

As we begin this journey of faith together, let me ask you:

> What is the familiar territory of your life?
> What values have you lived by?
> What culture has shaped your thinking?
> What attitudes have been molded by your social or educational
> or political environment?
> What religious experience has formed your concept of God?

My familiar territory is the southeastern United States, where magnolias bloom and NASCAR reigns and neighbors still know each other by name. I love the varied beauty of North Carolina, my home state. I love the friendly authenticity of the people who surround me. I love the down-home atmosphere that is still felt in even the larger cities. I love pig-pickin's and shrimperoos and Silver Queen corn and homemade ice cream. I love fried chicken and fried fish and fried hushpuppies and fried green tomatoes and fried anything, actually.

But my familiar territory is also the land of cultural Christianity. It's the buckle of the Bible Belt, where there's a church in every neighborhood and sometimes on every corner. It's a land where many people believe they are Christians because they were born that way, have gone to church all their lives, were baptized in the river at age twelve, have gone to church youth camp, and have even been on a missions trip. They can quote Bible verses, recite the Apostles' Creed, sing the second and sometimes third verses of most hymns from memory, and weep during the visiting preacher's revival sermon.

These are some of the familiar components of my home territory, my background, my "country." I love it here, and it's hard to leave. It's hard to shed the comfort of assuming that of course I'm a Christian because, after all, it's my culture. I'm a church member, and I'm a southerner.

Surely Abraham, after a virtual lifetime in Ur, must have felt just as strongly about his country and his culture as I feel about mine. So I can imagine the impact God's command must have had on him. "Leave your country" were the exact words that God leaned out of heaven and spoke into Abraham's life (Genesis 12:1).* How they must have reverberated through Abraham's heart and mind, ricocheting off his attitudes, values, perceptions, culture, and religion until his entire world shook with the personal command: "Leave your country." In other words, "Abraham, you must choose to leave your comfort zone and your familiar territory."

A Personal Command

Seventeen times in the first three verses of Genesis 12, God used the personal pronouns *I* or *you* or *your*. I have no doubt that God was speaking to Abraham personally, commanding him to leave all that was familiar.

But I can't help wondering what Abraham was doing when God called him to embark on the magnificent obsession. Maybe he was running an errand for his wife, or striking a business deal for his father, or attending the funeral of his brother, or just sitting in the courtyard of his home, contemplating the meaning of life.

---

*Throughout this book, Scripture references in parentheses refer to the book of Genesis.

And then it hit me: God shows up in the ordinariness of our day, doesn't He?

He doesn't show up *only* when He parts the Red Sea with a powerful wind, or in the banquet hall with handwriting on the wall, or on Mount Sinai with thunder and lightning, or on the Mount of Transfiguration in radiant glory.[4] He shows up in everyday situations, as we are going about our everyday responsibilities in our everyday routines.

Moses was shepherding his flock at Mount Horeb. Gideon was threshing wheat by the winepress. David was looking after his father's sheep. Elisha was plowing with twelve yoke of oxen. Nehemiah was serving wine to the king. Amos was tending his flock and his sycamore-fig trees. Peter and Andrew were casting their fishing net into the sea. James and John were mending their nets. Matthew was collecting taxes. The Samaritan woman was drawing water from the well. Saul was in the midst of a "business trip."[5]

All of these people were simply living their ordinary lives when God invaded, interrupted, and turned their world inside out.

When has God's Word come to you in a personal way? What were you involved in at the time? What difference has it made?

I remember when God spoke to me through His Word, calling me to step out of my familiar territory, teach a Bible class for women in my city, and begin pursuing Him through a life of obedient faith. I was riding in the front seat of our family station wagon, which my husband was driving from New York City to Hyannis on Cape Cod. His parents were in the backseat, and our three children were crawling all over the seats (long before the requirement of infant car seats or even seat belts). In the midst of the chaos, my sweet mother-in-law was reading the Bible aloud to no one in particular. Suddenly my ears tuned in to her voice. I asked her to pass her Bible to me in the front seat, and I read out loud the verses she had just read. As I read them, they seemed to be lit up with my name on them. No one else was listening, but I was: *Anne, "I know your deeds. See, I have placed before you an open door that no one can shut. I know that you have little strength, yet you have kept my word and have not denied my name."*[6]

During the ordinariness of a family vacation, God leaned out of heaven and called me to leave the familiar territory of cultural Christianity, reject what seemed to be a mediocre pew-warming faith, and plunge into the magnificent obsession. I chose to obey — but also discovered there was more to the command.

I had to leave my extended family and do something no other woman in my family had done. I had to be willing to break with family tradition.

Thousands of years earlier, Abraham had perceived the same call. God commanded him to leave "your people and your father's household" (12:1). If leaving his country and familiar territory was hard, it must have been even harder to contemplate leaving his loved ones behind.

And it *is* hard. While I didn't have to physically leave my family, I know from personal experience how hard it can be to leave them in other ways — psychologically, emotionally, and culturally. When I began the Bible class in my city, both of my parents opposed what I was doing. Although my grandmother was a trained nurse, the traditional role of women in my family had been one of stay-at-home mother. My parents gave me loving, firm counsel; they commended my desire but stated clearly that my role was at home as wife and mother.

My husband also resisted my efforts because he knew how tired I stayed throughout the day tending three children ages five and younger. He couldn't imagine my taking on added responsibility. He also knew that by nature I'm shy and have an inferiority complex. How could I possibly train and disciple leaders, much less stand in front of hundreds of women to give a forty-five-minute weekly lecture?

At that point in my journey, I did not recognize that I was embracing the magnificent obsession. All I knew was that I wanted to fulfill the potential God had for me. I wanted everything He wanted to give me, and I knew I was missing something. I instinctively knew that what I was missing was an authentic life of faith. I wasn't living it. At least I wasn't living on the cutting edge of it. And that's what I wanted. At the time, I described myself as being homesick for God as I had known Him as a little girl. Because of the busyness of young motherhood, I had neglected Him and I wanted Him back in the center of my life.

It was hard to shed the comfort of assumptions: Of course I'm a Christian; after all, it's my culture; I'm a church member; I grew up in the church; I've been baptized. And yet I felt a deep, compelling conviction that if I wanted to really know God and experience all that He had for me, I had no other option but to leave that comfort zone.

A Radical Promise

Abraham walked out of Ur of the Chaldeans not only challenged by God's personal command but also encouraged by God's radical promise to saturate him in blessings. Five times in Genesis 12:2 – 3 God distinctly promised to bless Abraham. Thousands of years later, we see how those promises were fulfilled:

"I will make you into a great nation."

Today's Jews and Arabs descend from Abraham.

"I will bless you."

At one hundred years of age, Abraham fathered Isaac, the longed-for desire of his heart.

"I will make your name great."

No name in all of human history is greater than the name of Abraham, except the name of Jesus Christ.

"You will be a blessing."

Abraham not only longed to receive God's blessing, he began to long to impart it to others . . . and he has for the past four thousand years.

"I will bless those who bless you, and whoever curses you I will curse."

God would so fill Abraham's life, so identify with him, that the way others treated him God would consider to be treatment of Himself. God blessed Abraham's friends and destroyed his enemies.

"All peoples on earth will be blessed through you."

Through Abraham's descendants, God gave the world the sacrificial system and the ceremonies that instructed people on how to approach Him and reconcile with Him. He gave the law that taught people how to live a life that not only worked but would be pleasing to Him. He gave the historical record of His interaction with His people that revealed not only the glory of His character but also the fact that He was involved in the details of their lives. He gave the prophets, whose writings revealed He was in charge, working out a divine plan for His people that would climax in the coming of the Messiah. And ultimately, He gave the Messiah, His own Son, as the sacrificial Lamb who died to take away the sin of all people and open heaven to forgiven sinners. God's blessings were poured out on Abraham in order for him to be a channel of God's blessing to the entire world.

These were God's radical promises. They were promises to enlarge the scope of Abraham's life beyond anything he could have thought to ask for.

God desires to enlarge each of our lives, usually beyond what we can imagine, if we are willing to let Him. I could never have envisioned how God would enlarge my life. But as I look back over more than thirty years since that first BSF group, I realize the size and scope of my life have grown beyond imagining.

It's also important to understand what is meant by "God's blessing." God's blessing is not the same thing as wealth, health, prosperity, and a problem-free life. I know this personally too! My son has had cancer and has been through a devastating divorce; my daughters each have painful and chronic physical problems; my husband is struggling with the long-term effects of adult-onset diabetes, including increasing blindness, renal failure, neuropathy, heart disease, and much more. Yet in the midst of it all, I know the blessedness of the presence and peace and power and provision and pleasure of God in my life.[7]

Yes, I firmly believe God has blessed me! And the primary blessing in my life that makes all the others pale in comparison is that through it all I have indeed come to know God. I don't know Him as well as I would like to, or as well as I should, but I know Him now much better than I knew Him when I first began to observe Abraham. And I know Him better today than I did yesterday.

God's promise to me, like His promise to Abraham, was radical, yet it was fulfilled more abundantly than I could have ever imagined. Which leads me to wonder ... what blessing are you missing because you refuse to leave behind the familiar "country, your people and your father's household"?

It's time to leave. Maybe not physically, but emotionally and spiritually and mentally and psychologically and culturally. It's time for you to get out of there!

Leave Behind the Fence-Sitting

Abram left, as the Lord had told him (12:4).[8] The fascinating thing about Abraham's journey is that although Abraham left Ur bound for Canaan, he stopped in Haran. He seemed to sit on the fence of compromise, halfway to where God wanted him to be.

Starting Out to Pursue God

The first hints about why this happened are given in the previous chapter of Genesis.

God commanded Abraham to leave Ur[9] and all that was familiar, including his father's household, but we see that he initially heeded only part of God's command. He left Ur with his father, nephew, and wife, and when they came to Haran, they settled there. We can only guess why this happened, but perhaps Abraham shared the news with his family, and his family decided it was a great idea. I can hear his father, Terah, reacting with something like this: "Abraham! That's amazing! I've been thinking myself lately . . . I could easily sell the family business and retire at this stage of my life. In fact, your brother Haran's death has been harder on me than I would have thought. I just can't seem to get over the grief. It would be really good to have a change of scenery. So . . . we'll all go with you!"

I don't know why Abraham's family accompanied him. I don't know if Abraham invited them and they accepted his invitation — or if they decided to come along and he failed to stop them. But I can see by what happened that Abraham was not clear and decisive about fully following God's call. I assume he must have struggled with whether to leave his family. Maybe he straddled the fence . . . offered a compromise in how he followed God's directive. He would leave his country, but he would bring his family with him.

If I could have warned Abraham, I might have said, "Abraham! God said to leave Ur *and* your people *and* your father's household! He did *not* say to leave your country but take your family with you! What on earth are you doing with Terah and Lot and all of their servants and belongings?"

I wonder if he might have answered, "Anne, it's easier this way. You just don't know how hard it is to leave my country and all that's familiar in Ur. Having my family around will take the sting out of the separation and some of the sacrifice out of the commitment. Plus, I just couldn't hurt my father's feelings by leaving him when he's still in mourning for my brother. It just isn't a good time to begin to pursue God on my own."

What has caused you to think this isn't the right time in your life for you to embrace the magnificent obsession? Does it have something to do with your family? Have you refused to pursue God until you can get your family to join you?

The problem for Abraham, besides his disobedience to God, was that when his family stopped before reaching the destination, so did he. And as a result, he postponed experiencing the God-filled life for as long as he delayed going all the way.

Stopping Halfway through Compromise

If Ur represented all that was familiar and comfortable in Abraham's life, Haran represented the place of compromise. It was six hundred miles from Ur but still approximately two hundred miles from the outskirts of Canaan. It was the place where Abraham tried to do things God's way — and also his way. The place where he tried to force what he wanted and what God wanted into a synchronized plan. And it just didn't work. Compromising with God never does.

What is your place of compromise? Did you start out on a journey of authentic faith, then stop halfway because of the demands of your job? Or the birth of a baby? Or the opinions of those you love or want to impress? Are you living in Haran, halfway to real discipleship? Halfway to a vibrant, personal relationship with God? Halfway to the fullness of all He wants to give you?

As you read this, are you acutely aware that God did call you to follow Him in a life of genuine faith years ago? Is His call to you in the past tense?

There is no record that God called Abraham twice. And God may not call you again. What will it take to get you to resume the journey?

As Abraham observed his aged father grow more and more frail, as he stood by his father's bedside in Haran and watched him breathe his last breath, as he said his farewell and placed Terah in the tomb, was he overwhelmed with the brevity of life? Did he begin to question life's purpose? Did he wonder if there was something more to his own life than just being born, living from day to day, working to support himself and Sarah, then dying and being buried in an earthen grave where his body would return to the dust from which it had come? Was there more to life than maintaining a degree of comfort through compromise? What *was* the meaning to life, after all?

As I have observed my own father grow more and more frail, I have been forcibly struck by the biblical truth that "all men are like grass, and all their glory is like the flowers of the field; the grass withers and the flowers fall, but the word of the Lord stands forever."[10] And as gloriously significant as my mother's life was on this earth, like the grass, her beloved body withered away, died, and was buried. And someday my father's body will complete the same earthly journey. Despite all the accolades and honors they collected during their earthly lives, the only thing that matters at the moment of their death is what they did in obedience to God's

Word, according to His will, and carried out in His way. Everything else, without exception, will be no more.

I wonder if Abraham began to examine his own life and started wondering what in the world he was doing in Haran. Or maybe his compromise and fence-sitting had been nagging at his spirit for years. His father's death may have been a relief in a way, setting him free to embrace the God-filled life, to pursue the magnificent obsession.

The only thing that seems obvious is that Abraham resumed his journey to pursue God when his father, Terah, died. Which triggers these thoughts . . .

> Who has to die to get you to resume your journey?
>
> What will it take to wake you up to God's call in your life?
>
> What will God use to push you off the fence of compromise?

Thousands of years after Abraham, Jesus would admonish the people crowding around Him with words that even now seem to echo throughout the "Harans" of our lives: "Any of you who does not give up everything he has cannot be my disciple."[11] Jesus made it clear: you and I must — it's not an option — we *must* give up everything, not *half* of everything, if we want to truly know and follow Him.

Abraham was seventy-five years old when he finally left Haran and resumed his pursuit of God. I can only imagine how hard it was for him to organize and close down his business, to pack up his wife and his belongings, to make a clean break with all that was familiar, to put one foot in front of the other, having no clear idea of where God was leading him.[12]

Do you think you're too old and it's just too hard to embrace the magnificent obsession? Are you even now wishing you had been given this challenge ten or twenty years ago? Are you feeling too tired, too weak, too slow, too dull, too forgetful to leave everything behind and begin? Or . . . do you think you are too young? Are you even now thinking that you will read this book, yet you won't really take it to heart until after you graduate from school, get settled in a good job, marry and establish a family?

Remember that God's timing is perfect.[13] He knows what time it is in your life, and He is issuing this challenge to you right now. If you want to truly know Him in a vibrant, personal relationship, then you must leave everything behind, including that which is familiar, the places of fence-sitting compromise, and your fear of living a life that will be very different from the people around you . . .

Leave Behind the Fear

Once again, Abraham found himself leaving a place that had become familiar. Surely he must have felt some fear as he set off into the unknown. Once again, he left with an entourage, which still included at least one questionable person, his nephew Lot. But this time, Abraham went all the way. "He took his wife Sarai, his nephew Lot, all the possessions they had accumulated and the people they had acquired in Haran, and they set out for the land of Canaan, and they arrived there" (12:5).

He had left Ur not knowing where he was going; yet when he got to Canaan, he knew he had arrived. He had the deep assurance and conviction that he was exactly where God wanted him to be. His heart must have been filled with overwhelming joy and peace. After a lifetime of being everywhere else, he had finally arrived in the center of God's will. He had begun the adventure of stepping out of his comfort zone in order to truly experience God in a personal, authentic, vibrant relationship.

What a thrilling adventure that is. I recently spoke with a young mother who felt God had called her to accept the incredible challenge to write. As she prayed about it, He confirmed again and again through His Word what she was to do. And so in fear and trembling, she stepped out of all that was familiar and began to put her thoughts on paper. As she related her experience to me, she described the thrill of "stepping into the flow of His will and knowing I am exactly where I am supposed to be, doing exactly what I am supposed to do." The intensity of joy in her voice revealed that she too has embarked on the magnificent obsession as she experiences God outside of her comfort zone.

The Fear of Standing Out from the World around You

Abraham arrived in Canaan and "traveled through the land as far as the site of the great tree of Moreh at Shechem." But the joy he felt in arriving there was surely dampened by the fact that "at that time the Canaanites were in the land" (12:6). The Canaanites! The biblical and historical record indicates they were among the vilest, most obscene and pornographic people ever to inhabit planet Earth.[14] They indulged in prostitution and human sacrifice as part of their religious worship! And now they surrounded Abraham. They were the majority of many while he was the minority of one. He must have stood out in stark contrast to them in every facet of his life: his looks, his dress, his behavior, his relationships, his attitude, his values, his priorities, his speech . . . everything!

I have discovered that as I pursue knowing God, I too have found myself in the minority. I am surrounded by others who seem so different from me in their values and priorities. Canaanites today are those the Bible describes as worldly. Their pattern of behavior is based on what everyone else is doing, on what feels right to them, on what seems to work for their advantage. Their preoccupation is with personal pleasure. Their priority is "me first." And their lives are so fast paced they have no time for God or for their neighbor. Yet many of them are very religious, like the Canaanites, worshiping a god of their own making.

It's easy to be deceived by the fact that "Canaanites" are religious because the world assumes religion is the way to know God — when the truth is exactly the opposite! Think about just a few examples: The priests of Baal who worshiped the Canaanite gods were the ones who led Israel into idolatry and provoked the judgment of God.[15] The Jewish religious leaders turned Jesus Christ over to the Romans for crucifixion.[16] The religious people of the first century persecuted the early Christians, putting many of the disciples of Jesus to death.[17] In fact, during the two thousand years of church history since Christ, religion has been a prime source of division, hatred, war, injustice, and prejudice. It has been religious people, often within the organized church, who have been the most critical of and even hostile to my relationship with God. It was religious people from the board of deacons who voted to remove my nine-year Bible class from their church facility. It was religious people who voted with applause to remove my husband from a church leadership position.

It's reasonable that you and I should stand out from those around us. Absolutely. Obviously. Is that what you're afraid of? Are you afraid of being so different that you draw the stares of your coworkers? That you provoke whispers behind your back? That someone will raise an eyebrow, curl her lip, and leave you off the social register in your community?

Abraham was surrounded by Canaanites, but I can see no evidence that he felt any fear at all at this point in his journey. He probably felt empowered and encouraged because the Lord appeared to him and said, "To your offspring I will give this land" (12:7). I wonder if Abraham's lack of fear was because he kept his focus on God. This seems likely, because just the opposite happens at the end of this chapter when Abraham loses his focus. He was so filled with fear when surrounded by the Egyptians that he instructed Sarah to lie on his behalf.

The best way for you and me to overcome our fear of those people so unlike us who surround us in our everyday lives is to keep our focus on the Lord and cultivate an awareness of His presence in our lives. We need to learn to be more aware of *Him* than of *them*. And the best way to cultivate an awareness of His presence in our lives is to read our Bibles every day, listening for His voice to speak to us.[18]

Not too long ago, I found myself sitting in a select group who were very religious, very self-assured, very articulate — and very unsettling to me. As we began our discussion, the sun came through the window, and I could feel it warming my face, almost blinding my eyes. When the conversation began to deteriorate into personal attack, I heard the still, small voice of God speaking to my heart: *Anne, "God is light; in him there is no darkness at all. If we claim to have fellowship with him yet walk in the darkness, we lie and do not live by the truth. But if we walk in the light, as he is in the light, we have fellowship with one another, and the blood of Jesus, his Son, purifies us from all sin."*[19] I knew God was affirming that I was in the light … literally and figuratively. I was acutely aware that He was with me in the midst of the "Canaanites," and my fears melted.

The Fear of Speaking Out to the World around You

Right in the midst of the Canaanites, God spoke to Abraham, saying, "To your offspring I will give this land." Abraham responded with the equivalent of a gospel presentation to the world around him: "He built an altar there to the LORD, who had appeared to him" (12:7).

I can imagine the Canaanites rather curiously and cynically gathering around Abraham, laughing, mocking, questioning him as he gathered the stones for the altar, piled the wood on the top, and sacrificed an animal:

"What did you say your name was? Abram? What do you think you're doing?"

"I'm building an altar to the Lord."

"What Lord is that? Here in Canaan, we have lots of lords and many gods. Which one is yours?"

"My God is the one true living God. The Creator of the universe and all that is in it."

"That sounds pretty narrow-minded to us. So what's with the altar?"

"God has said the only way we can be reconciled with Him, the only way we can enter into His presence, is through the sacrificial blood of a lamb. I'm worshiping God as He requires."

"Didn't I tell you he was narrow-minded? I've never heard of anything more intolerant or exclusive — not to mention weird. We need to keep our eye on this stranger in our midst."

When have you presented the gospel to the people around you? Who has seen your "altar"? When have you told others that you have been reconciled to God through the blood of His Lamb, and that they can be too? Are you afraid, in our politically correct, increasingly pluralistic, multicultural society to exalt Jesus as . . .

the unique Son of God,

the sinner's Savior,

the captive's Ransom,

the Breath of Life,

the Centerpiece of all cultures,

the One who stands in the solitude of Himself, by His own authoritative declaration, as "the way and the truth and the life"?

Jesus said, "No one comes to the Father except through me."[20] So don't be afraid. Build your altar!

When Abraham built his altar "there to the LORD," right in front of the Canaanites, what impact did it have on them? Was anyone converted? Did anyone turn from darkness to embrace the light of truth? No, not that we know. So what difference did it make?

It may not have affected the Canaanites at all, but I think it made a difference in Abraham's life. It must have strengthened his faith. It must have been very freeing for him to live his life openly, unafraid of what others would say. It must have sharpened his focus as he lived out the genuineness of his relationship with God regardless of where he was or who was watching. Instead of being a spiritual chameleon who changed behavior/attitudes/values according to the whimsical dictates of those around him, Abraham lived a life of consistent worship.

One year I was invited to attend an international gathering where two thousand world business and political leaders came together to discuss ideas and to network with each other. I was asked to lead two dinner discussions, one of which was on happiness and how to find it. I was preceded in the concluding presentations by an internationally acclaimed sex therapist who said happiness could be found in sexual pleasure and orgasm. Then it was my turn!

When I stood up with knocking knees and thumping heart, I felt everyone's eyes on me with mocking amusement, knowing who I was and wondering what in the world I would say after that. A ripple of laughter passed through the room. So I smiled as though I got the "joke," nodded toward the woman and thanked her for her opinion, but said I couldn't disagree more. Happiness is to be found in relationships, the first of which is our relationship with God. Then I presented the gospel to the best of my ability in the brief time I had been assigned.

Although the rabbi seated at my table gave me a thumbs-up, as far as I know, no one's life was changed. I did have some very interesting, thoughtful conversations afterward. But I was blessed and strengthened, knowing I had nothing to hide or be ashamed of. I had spoken the truth as the Bible reveals it.

The situation reminded me of our son, Jonathan, when he was a teenager attending the large public high school. One afternoon when he came home, he said he had been changing classes when another student rudely bumped into him, then verbally assaulted him, using profanity to curse Jonathan — and Jesus. Jonathan described how he grabbed the kid by the front of the shirt, threw him up against the locker, leaned in about an inch from his face, and said firmly, "Listen, buddy, you're talking about my Savior, the One who died to take away my sins and yours. Watch your mouth."

Then he let go, and the kid crumpled to the floor. When Jonathan told me this story, there was a big grin stretched across his face. He concluded with, "Mom, it felt so good!"

It *does* feel good to boldly identify with God . . . right in the face of those who use His name in vain!

Stuart Briscoe, one of my very favorite preachers and authors, relates that when he told a family friend he was joining the Royal Marines, the friend, who was a captain in the Royal Artillery, replied, "You will of course nail your colors to the mast." When Stuart inquired what he meant, the friend explained that in the

Royal Navy, the sailors *nailed* the sovereign's flag to the ship's mast as they sailed into battle so that it could not be hauled down and replaced with the white flag of surrender.

The friend applied the Royal Navy's practice to Stuart's life by challenging him to let those around him know immediately that he was a Christian.

By building his altar right there, in the midst of the Canaanites, Abraham was nailing his colors to the mast. He was refusing to surrender to popular opinion or personal intimidation or political pressure ... or his own fears.

Where have you built your altar? Have you built it where it's safe and comfortable, in the midst of like-minded people? Or have you built it *there*, in front of your unbelieving neighbors? Worship God *there*, and you will overcome your fears.

In his teens, my husband was a highly recruited basketball star from Long Island, New York, who signed a coveted four-year scholarship with the University of North Carolina. As he left his home in New York, his parents told him to make sure he prayed and read his Bible every day, regardless of who was his roommate or what the other guys were like on his hall.

The very first night in the dorm, he waited until all the lights were turned off, then he quietly slipped out of bed and knelt beside it to pray. But almost as soon as his knees hit the floor, the lights were switched back on, and his astonished roommates confronted him. "Danny, what's wrong? What in the world are you doing on the floor?" they asked.

Danny sat on the edge of the bed and, until the wee hours of the morning, explained his faith to his roommates. Were they converted? No. But they never questioned or bothered Danny again when, on a daily basis, he read his Bible and prayed. Danny had nailed his colors to the mast, right in front of his unbelieving roommates.

The Fear That God Is Not Present with You in the World

After boldly building his altar, Abraham continued to travel within the land God had promised to him: "From there he went on toward the hills east of Bethel and pitched his tent, with Bethel on the west and Ai on the east. There he built an altar to the Lord and called on the name of the Lord" (12:8). God had appeared to him when he had built his altar earlier in Shechem. This time, still in Canaan, as he built his altar and called on the name of the Lord, God did not appear.

Abraham was learning that sometimes when he built his altar, he would hear God's voice and see His face. And at other times when he built his altar, he would not hear His voice and he would not see His face. Abraham was learning to walk and work and worship by faith.

The disciples were taught this same lesson of faith in dramatic fashion after the resurrection of Jesus. As they gathered together in the upper room, suddenly Jesus was with them.[21] The disciples who walked along on the Emmaus Road found that suddenly Jesus walked with them, then just as suddenly, as they broke bread, He disappeared.[22] When the disciples went fishing on the Sea of Galilee, they suddenly saw Jesus on the shore fixing breakfast for them.[23] Perhaps Jesus was teaching His disciples that He was present in their lives whether or not they could see Him. He was teaching them to live by faith.

Sometimes when I open my Bible to read, a verse leaps off the page and I know God is speaking to me. Sometimes I read and nothing seems to be illuminated. Sometimes I pray and have the keen sense that He is listening to every word and will answer me. Sometimes when I pray, I have no awareness that He's anywhere around. Sometimes when I go to church or draw aside for some quiet reflection, I have the overwhelming sense that Jesus is right beside me. At other times in the exact same settings, I have no conscious awareness of His presence at all. And I know by each experience — as I read my Bible and pray and work and worship — that He is teaching me to live by *faith*, not by my feelings.

As Abraham took the initial steps to embrace the magnificent obsession, he had one more lesson to learn, and again he would learn it the hard way. In order to pursue knowing God, he had to leave everything behind: his familiar, comfortable territory and family, his place of compromise and fence-sitting, his fear, and also his failure ...

Leave Behind the Failure

At the same international gathering I spoke of earlier, I missed several opportunities to exalt Jesus because I was afraid. I was unsure as to what was considered appropriate participation for a newcomer at such a prestigious gathering. I had been informed by former attendees that evangelical Christians were viewed with great skepticism; therefore, my instructions were not to further the negative perception by saying something "stupid." To make sure I complied with their advice, I just didn't say anything at all.

While compliance seemed the best course at the time, it later caused me great misery. I desperately wished to have a do over.

Unintentional Failure

I've never heard of anyone deliberately deciding to fail. People often seek me out for counsel or relate to me their struggles, but no one has ever confided the following: "Today I'm going to fail." "Today I'm going to backslide." "Today I'm going to wreck my Christian life and witness." "Today I'm going to wander away from God."

We all do those things, but I've never met anyone who did them intentionally.

Abraham's failure was not intentional either. As he traveled through the land God had promised him, he simply kept going. He knew he had "arrived" where God wanted him to be, but then, unexplainably, he "set out and continued toward the Negev" (12:9).

The Negev was not where God wanted him to be, so why did he keep going? Maybe he was just excited about the journey, thrilled with the adventure of living by faith, and in the flush of enthusiasm ran ahead of the Lord.

Sometimes I cringe as I observe and listen to new believers who are so bold in their witness they are almost brash, so aggressive in sharing the gospel they are almost offensive, so confident in their relationship with God that they are almost foolish about practical matters. I know they are headed for a rude awakening. They're charging ahead without waiting for God's guidance. They are so enthusiastic about their God that they don't take time to discern His still, small voice whispering into their hearts. They're doing what *they* want to do on His behalf rather than what *God* wants them to do. I believe that's how Abraham ended up in the Negev.

I wonder if you began a journey of faith but ran ahead, as Abraham did, until you too were rudely awakened by failure in your life. Does that even now make you very apprehensive about beginning again? Is there a longing in you to embrace the magnificent obsession, but your past experience warns you that you can't? Then keep tracking with Abraham...

Shortly after heading to the Negev, he ran into trouble. He came up short when "there was a famine in the land" (12:10). Not only was there an obvious lack of physical necessities but there seemed to be a lack of spiritual necessities as well. There is no record that God appeared to Abraham or spoke to him in the Negev. Nor is there any record that Abraham prayed or spoke to God while he was there.

Failure in my life almost always begins with a famine of God's Word and prayer. Without them, I'm left to make my decisions based on my own logic or circumstances or feelings or the counsel of others. And that's never a good place to be. Solomon exhorted God's people in Proverbs 3:5 to "trust in the LORD with all your heart and lean not on your own understanding." But Abraham did not have Solomon's wisdom to direct his faith. Instead, he leaned on his own understanding, logically concluding that if there was a famine where he was, but there was food down in Egypt, the practical course of action would be to take his family to Egypt. After all, he was responsible for their well-being, and he was accustomed to making decisions for the welfare of those who were with him.

While we may think he did the sensible thing, I can't help but wonder what would have happened if he had prayed about it first. Maybe God would have directed him to Egypt. But if God had, I don't think Abraham would have become as fearful there as he did. If Abraham had prayed first, maybe God would have had him stay exactly where he was and fed him with manna from heaven. Or maybe God would have instructed him to return to Shechem or Bethel, where there may have been some food he didn't know about. Instead, Abraham charged off to Egypt without asking for God's guidance.

The first consequence of Abraham's failure was that he missed discovering how God could have met his needs if he had just trusted Him with all his heart and leaned not on his own understanding. As I have reflected on my failure at the international convention, the most painful consequence has been to wonder what God could have done had I just opened my mouth and talked about Jesus. But Abraham ... and I ... will never know what God could have done because we didn't keep our focus on Him. We failed.

Sometimes, especially in stressful situations, I rationalize that I don't want to bother God with such a small thing, such a small decision, such a small amount of time, such a small thought, such a small action.

Abraham's actions seemed so logical. Surely it would have been a waste of

God's time to be consulted about something that was so obvious. Abraham "went down to Egypt to live there for a while because the famine was severe" (12:10). He went for just a little while.

What "obvious" decision have you made without asking the Lord? Like Abraham . . .

> Have you moved your family to another location . . . without asking the Lord?
>
> Have you changed jobs or a job position . . . without asking the Lord?
>
> Have you chosen a school for your children . . . without asking the Lord?
>
> Have you gone to work part-time . . . without asking the Lord?
>
> Have you purchased new equipment or a new car . . . without asking the Lord?
>
> Have you mapped out your summer vacation or holiday time . . . without asking the Lord?

And have you neglected your Bible reading as well? The combination of a lack of prayer *and* lack of Bible reading is a recipe for disaster.

Miserable Failure

As I left the site of the international gathering, I was acutely aware of my failure. I felt myself spiraling into a state of miserable depression, not knowing how I would be able to complete my next assignment, which was to address a gathering of pastors and evangelists in the capital city of another country. On my flight there, I became aware of a very famous couple seated about ten rows in front of me. They were hard to miss because everyone around me was pointing and giggling and straining to catch a glimpse of them. I put my head on the back of my seat, closed my eyes, tried to block out what was going on around me, and just wallowed in my own misery and guilt.

Similarly, it didn't take long for Abraham's misery to set in. He immediately began to worry: "As he was about to enter Egypt, he said to his wife Sarai, 'I know what a beautiful woman you are. When the Egyptians see you, they will say, "This is his wife." Then they will kill me but will let you live' " (12:11 – 12). Abraham lost his peace, which is one of the hallmarks of someone who is wandering outside of God's will. A child of God who is outside of God's will becomes very insecure and has no confidence of God's presence or protection or provision. Abraham seemed afraid to stay where he was, but then he apparently became terrified to go where he was headed.

What are you worried about? How have you taken matters into your own hands to deal with the problem? Has the situation become worse?

Abraham's fears were well-grounded, because the Egyptians were known to be ruthless with anyone who got in the way of what they wanted. But he handled his fears in a very wrong way. He instructed his wife, Sarah, to "say you are my sister, so that I will be treated well for your sake and my life will be spared because of you" (12:13).[24] Abraham was instructing his wife to lie on his behalf, and God hates lying![25]

Has your worrying led to wrongdoing as you have tried to get yourself out of a jam? Have you lied? Manipulated? Stolen? Lost your temper? Bullied? Have you sinned because you were worried? Abraham did.

The horror of it was that "when Abram came to Egypt, the Egyptians saw that [Sarah] was a very beautiful woman. And when Pharaoh's officials saw her, they praised her to Pharaoh, and she was taken into his palace" (12:14 – 15). Abraham's worry that had led to wrongdoing landed his beloved wife in a pagan king's harem! How would he ever get her out when the famine was over? He had selfishly sacrificed her to save his own skin! Abraham's example shows us that, along with worry, selfishness is another hallmark of someone outside of God's will.

Can you imagine how Sarah suffered? Her name means "princess," which perhaps indicates she either was the literal daughter of a king or chieftain or was raised in a pampered, privileged, protected home environment. I imagine her saddle on the camel's back had plump cushions to recline on and a fringed, draped roof to protect her delicate skin from the sun. Her tents must have been lined with thick woven carpets, her walls hung with elegant linens, her dresses made of the finest, softest fabrics, her skin perfumed with priceless oils, her servants trained to be quietly attentive to her every whim as well as to her every need . . . you get the picture. And because of Abraham's wrongdoing, she endured the humiliation of being dumped into Pharaoh's palace, surrounded by strange people and strange customs and strange language, vulnerable to being defiled by a strange pagan man! Can you imagine the emotional and psychological damage done to Sarah, knowing she was in this impossible, dangerous, terrifying situation because *her husband* had put her there? What was Abraham thinking?!

But if Sarah suffered, Abraham suffered too. He must have been horrified at the sordid turn of events. As he watched his beloved Sarah being surrounded by Pharaoh's guards, disappearing into Pharaoh's palace, with the gate barred shut behind her, what did he think? Did he let out a mourner's agonized cry? Did he crouch in his tent with his head in his hands, unable to speak or think or move? Did he toss and turn night after night as he wrestled with guilt and all the "if onlys" that surely plagued his thoughts?

I can testify through painful experience in my own life that sin almost always leads to suffering. I will never forget sitting beside my husband in the front seat of his truck, with the kids in the back, insisting that he turn left when the road sign in front of us clearly said, "No Left Turn." He did as I instructed ... and plowed right into the side of a station wagon! Almost simultaneously, the family in the other car screamed in fear, my children cried out, Danny buried his head in his hands, horrified to realize what he had done (and even more so when he recognized the driver of the other car as one of his own dental patients), and I wept with shame and remorse because I knew the entire mess was my fault!

The sound of the crunching metal and breaking glass still rings in my ears to remind me of the consequences of my sin. Yet more painful than that memory are the consequences of my parenting sins and selfishness that have caused my children to struggle even as adults. Our sin seems to cause those we love the most to suffer the worst.

Who is suffering due to your sin?

- Has your sin of immorality led to divorce ... and your children are suffering?
- Has your dishonesty led to a job termination ... and your coworkers are suffering?
- Has your obesity led to ill health ... and your spouse is suffering?
- Has your anger led to division ... and your friends are suffering?
- Has your pride led to a critical spirit ... and your church is suffering?

God had told Abraham he would be a blessing to all nations, yet that possibility seems almost impossible to imagine because the first time he steps out, he's not a blessing at all. He's a curse!

Sin leads to suffering, and in Abraham's case, sin also led to a substitute for God's blessing. We're told that Pharaoh "treated Abram well for [Sarai's] sake, and Abram acquired sheep and cattle, male and female donkeys, menservants and maidservants, and camels.... Abram had become very wealthy in livestock and in silver and gold" (12:16; 13:2).

The first time I read that passage, I was surprised. Are you? Does it surprise you that Abraham's sin brought him great wealth? Are you shocked by the fact that Abraham seemed to profit greatly from his scandalous behavior? You and I shouldn't be surprised, because we see it happening every day, don't we? Drug cartels, arms dealers, pornographers, abortionists, and so many others rake in billions of dollars as they profit from their sin. Which tells us that financial wealth and material prosperity are not necessarily an indication of the blessing of God.

Abraham's wealth acquired in Egypt was not God's blessing. In the future it would become the cause of great distress and sorrow. In the midst of Abraham's possessions was a little Egyptian servant girl with whom Abraham would commit the greatest sin of his life. And the possessions themselves became a source of conflict and division within his own home. They also provided an irresistible temptation to his nephew Lot, who, from the time they left Egypt, embraced the world and all it offered, to the ultimate destruction of himself and his family.

The wealth that Abraham had acquired in Egypt was a substitute for the blessing of God. What substitute for God's blessing have you settled for? Instead of the blessing of knowing God, have you settled for devoting yourself totally to your career in order to attain a position of prestige and power? Instead of making Him known, have you settled for the popular opinions of others ... and for making yourself known in a widely recognized reputation? Instead of humbly submitting to His leadership, have you settled for achieving your own goals and dreams? Instead of investing your time in developing your personal relationship with God, have you settled for an extra thirty minutes of sleep in the morning? Instead of following Him all the way to "Canaan," have you settled for going halfway to "Haran"?

Don't settle for less than everything God wants to give you!

I wonder if Abraham, in the midst of his material wealth, finally realized he had settled for a substitute instead of a blessing and cried out in spiritual poverty to God — maybe just a simple cry, "God, help me!" We don't know what prompted the next chapter in his story, but we know *who* caused things to change: "The LORD inflicted serious diseases on Pharaoh and his household because of Abram's wife Sarai" (12:17). Whatever the diseases were, they apparently prevented anyone from physically harming Sarah.[26] God Himself was Sarah's defender and protector as He lowered judgment on all the men.

We're not told how Pharaoh connected the dots, but he did: "Pharaoh summoned Abram. 'What have you done to me?' he said. 'Why didn't you tell me she was your wife? Why did you say, "She is my sister," so that I took her to be my wife? Now then, here is your wife. Take her and go!'" (12:18 – 19).

In the face of such caustic questioning, what could Abraham say? He was silent because there was no excuse for his behavior. He must have hung his head with his face burning crimson as he was rebuked by an unbeliever for something he should never have done. His sin had led to suffering, a substitute for God's blessing — and now to shame.

Have you ever been rebuked by an unbelieving in-law? Or boss? Or neighbor? You're the one who should have known better. You're the one who is embracing the magnificent obsession and embarking on a life of obedient faith. You're supposed to be a Christian! Yet has your behavior been worse than those around you who have no faith at all? Has a totally godless, secular person pointed that out? That's a very bitter pill to swallow, isn't it?

Recently our news was filled with the story of a pastor from a megachurch who repeatedly solicited a male prostitute. The sin of immorality in his life caused his wife and family to suffer, his church to suffer, and him to suffer. But the worst part of it all was the humiliating shame he brought, not only to his own name and that of his family and church but to the name of God. He was rebuked by the news media and every comedian in the nation, who mocked his faith and his God. He was removed from his church's leadership by the other leaders. I pray he will one day be restored. But he will never, ever, regain his credibility in the eyes of the general public. My face is flushed with disgrace and my eyes are moist with tears at the shame of it all, even as I write.

Abraham surely felt even greater shame as he took Sarah and was escorted out of Pharaoh's presence, Pharaoh's palace, and the land of Egypt by armed guards who made sure he left: "Then Pharaoh gave orders about Abram to his men, and they sent him on his way, with his wife and everything he had" (12:20). Pharaoh's parting words, ringing in Abraham's ears, must have sounded something like this: "If you're a God-fearing man, Abraham, I never want to be one. If you're living a God-filled life, I never want to live one. And if your god is God, I never want to know Him. Now get out. You're not good enough to stay in Egypt."

As Abraham retreated from Egypt, he must have reflected on how far he had come — and how far he had fallen. Would you reflect now on *your* spiritual journey? Where are you? Are you in Ur ... the place of comfortable, familiar territory, religiosity, and family? Are you in Haran ... the place of compromise and convenience and fence-sitting? Are you in Canaan ... filled with fear of what others are thinking or saying behind your back, hiding your light under a bushel? Or are you in Egypt ... wallowing in your unintentional but miserable failure, ready to quit before you even really begin to embark on the magnificent obsession?

Don't give up! No matter how far you've fallen, God offers a way to reverse your failure.

Reversible Failure

On my way to my next engagement, as I dozed on the plane, even my unconscious thoughts seemed nightmarish. I just couldn't shake the sick feeling of shame that engulfed me because of my failure during the week. I had confessed my sin and returned to the cross for cleansing many times during the past thirty-six hours but seemed to get no relief from the guilt and pain.

As we neared our destination, the comments of those around me grew louder, and I opened my eyes. The ogling of the famous couple had increased. Then the thoughts began to come: *I wonder if everyone who meets them either grovels at their feet or giggles in their faces or tries to take advantage of them in some way. I wonder if anyone has ever shared the gospel with them.*

As those thoughts lingered on my mind for a moment, I also remembered seeing a television special about the woman in the celebrity couple before I had left the States. She had led a very wicked, immoral life. As I was wishing she could know the Savior, His distinct soft voice whispered in my heart, *Anne, why do you think you're on this plane? Is this a random coincidence? Or could it be by My divine arrangement? You know the gospel. Why don't you share it with them?*

My stomach turned over and fear gripped my pounding heart. *Not me!* I wanted to shout. *I'm a failure!*

But I knew! I *was* on the plane, and I *did* know the gospel, and hadn't I just been wallowing in guilt for having missed opportunities that very week? Was I going to choose to miss this opportunity too? Or would I use this opportunity to turn the corner and put my failure behind me?

Just as I started to tell the Lord I would speak to them, the pilot came on the intercom and announced we were beginning our descent. We were to remain seated with our seat belts fastened. Breathing a deep sigh of relief, I relaxed and prayed, "Well, Lord, You know I would have done it, but now there's no time. If I get up now, the flight attendant will tell me to sit down and I'll cause a scene. If You had just given me some time, I would have done it."

Then, after a moment's pause, I added, "And even now, if You give me the time, I'll do it."

No sooner had I told the Lord I would do it than the pilot came back on the intercom. He said our plane had been put into a holding pattern, and we would be circling for ten minutes. *Ten minutes!* Before I could have another fearful thought, I unsnapped my seat belt, walked quickly up the aisle, and straight into the lavatory!

My knees were knocking, my heart was beating, and then the entire plane started lurching, as though it too felt my panic. As I held on to the safety handles, the warning light flashed, instructing all passengers to take their seats and buckle their seat belts. As I gripped the handles, I told the Lord how embarrassed He and I would be if the plane crashed with me in the lavatory! But I also told Him I was going to stay in the bathroom as long as it took for the plane to settle down, and then I would go speak to the couple.

The plane immediately became calm and the flight smoothed out. I opened the door, took two long strides to the front row where the young couple was sitting, crouched down beside the woman who was seated on the aisle, and asked if I could speak with her. Her eyes widened as she looked at me, but then she nodded yes.

I identified myself, told her where I had been and what I was doing, then looked her straight in the eye and told her that God loved her. In fact, I said, He loved her so much that He had given her Jesus. And if she would repent of her sin and place her faith in Him alone for her salvation, He would forgive her. She would never perish but have eternal life and go to heaven when she died.

As I shared the gospel in a nutshell, her beautiful eyes softened, and I knew she was listening intently. My heart was calm, my manner was gentle, my words were confident, and I was actually filled to overflowing with an awareness of God's love for her. (Her companion sat quietly beside her with his baseball cap pulled down over his eyes. He seemed to be dozing, *but ...*)

I wish I could report that she prayed to receive Christ. Or that she promised to begin reading her Bible. All I know is that she thanked me softly. But I also knew I had turned the corner. I had reversed the downward spiral of my failure. I had rebuilt my altar once again in front of the Canaanites, and it felt good!

Abraham reversed his failure too. He didn't quit. He didn't return to Haran. Or to Ur. Or even to Egypt. "From the Negev he went from place to place" (13:3). My impression is that Abraham was searching for something. For Someone, desperately frantic to find Him once again. His thoughts must have been tumbling over themselves in his mind. *God, where did I leave You? You used to be in my life. I used to know You. You used to appear to me. But somewhere I lost You. I've left You. Please, God, I want to find You again. I want You back in my life. I want the fullness of Your blessing ... I want to be a blessing. Oh God, where are You?*

Abraham kept searching "until he came to Bethel, to the place between Bethel and Ai where his tent had been earlier and where he had first built an altar. There Abram called on the name of the LORD" (13:3–4). I wonder what he called to the Lord? Was his heart's cry something like ...

"God, I'm *so* sorry! I've made a mess! I'm so ashamed. I packed up everything and left Ur because I wanted to know You. My family tagged along and when *they* stopped halfway in Haran, *I* stopped too. But when I buried my father, I remembered Your call in my life, and I got off the fence and resumed my journey. God, I know I arrived where You wanted me to be. I know what it's like to be in Your will. I built my altar in front of the Canaanites. I nailed my colors to the mast! It was thrilling! I was set free in my spirit! I wanted to live for You, love You, serve You, know You! Then ... I just kept going ... wandering ... worrying. I don't know what got into me. I took matters into my own hands when I didn't sense Your presence. I got scared and lied and told Sarah to lie. I just can't believe what I did! I can't believe I landed Sarah in Pharaoh's harem and caused not only her but all the people in the palace to suffer! Now they all despise me ... and they despise You because of the way I've behaved. God, I'm so sorry. I just want to come back to You. I want to get right with You. Please, God. I want to start all over again."

Abraham's search had led him to Bethel, a place of sacrifice, a place that can be understood as an Old Testament picture of the cross. Abraham returned to the cross ... the place where he had last known God's presence in his life. There he called on the name of the Lord ... out loud ... right there in front of the Canaanites. And it must have felt good!

What is your heart's cry? Do you want to start all over again too? Then would you tell God about your sin and your failure? God is so gracious and merciful to sinners. He is full of compassion and loving-kindness. And He has never turned away anyone who comes to Him in humble repentance at the foot of the cross.

Before you can embrace a God-filled life, do you need to return to Bethel? Come back! *Come back to the cross!*

Pray like I've imagined Abraham prayed. Pour out your heart. It doesn't matter if you can't remember how or when or where you began to wander. Just come back to the cross! Right now!

Are you hesitating because you feel ashamed and embarrassed? Because you're not sure God will receive you? He will. *I know!* So ... don't keep Him waiting. Leave everything behind ... the familiar, the fence-sitting, the fear, the failure ... and *run back to Him*!

Let Everything Go

Genesis 13:5 – 18

Following Abraham's repentance at Bethel, I wondered what difference it had made in his life. I've heard that a person's character is revealed by what he does when he doesn't know anyone sees him. And I wanted to know what Abraham was *really* like. When he was at home. In private. Behind closed doors.

It didn't take long to find out. Abraham's character and his determined pursuit of the magnificent obsession came into clear focus as a result of the contrast between him and his nephew Lot.

When God had called Abraham to leave behind Ur of the Chaldeans, along with everything else, and follow Him in a life of obedient faith, Lot also had made the initial choice to leave. He had left behind his own familiar territory and people and father's house.[1] In fact, he is described in the New Testament three times as a *righteous* man who must have established a relationship with God and to some degree desired God's blessing in his own life.[2]

But Lot reminded me of a monkey ...

I've been told that if you want to catch a monkey, the first step to take is to go to the jungle where they live. Take a jar that is shaped like a carafe, with an opening that is smaller than the rest of the container. Place a banana inside the jar, bury it in the ground so that the mouth of the jar is even with the surface of the ground, then quickly hide in the bushes nearby and watch what happens.

Sources say that soon a monkey will come happily along and stop as he carefully sniffs the air. His sniffer will lead him to the hole in the ground, which is actually the top of your jar. He will begin to get excited when he realizes there is a banana down in that hole!

Not to be denied, he will reach down into the jar, swish his humanlike hand around the bottom of it, find the banana, grasp it with his greedy little paw ... and you've caught yourself a monkey! The monkey's fist around that banana is too large now to come out of the small mouth of the jar, and yet he won't let go of the banana!

The monkey may throw up his hind legs and screech pitifully into the air as if to say, "I'm a monkey! I was meant to swing through trees! I want to be free!" But ... he won't let go of his banana. So he remains trapped.

Lot appeared to be a "monkey" who clutched several "bananas" in his hand, refusing to let them go. In the end, they cost him not only the magnificent obsession but also his own family, friends, and future. His life's story is a very solemn one that challenges me to let go of anything and everything, especially the shallowness, selfishness, and sinfulness in my life that hinders me from receiving and experiencing all that God wants me to have.

Lot's life contrasts sharply with that of Abraham, who let everything go with dramatically different results. As we compare Abraham and Lot, I wonder ...

Fellow monkey, what's the banana you're clutching in your hand that is keeping you from embracing the magnificent obsession? You can say how desperately you want to know God, how earnestly you long to receive all that He has for you, how committed you are to making Him known to the world around you ... but you won't let go of your banana. What is it?

LET GO OF YOUR SHALLOWNESS

The first banana Lot seemed to hold tightly in his fist was that of shallowness in his relationship with God. We have to look closely to see it at first, then it becomes obvious. It's there. Lot was one-dimensional in his spiritual life. Flat. Superficial.

Shallowness in Prayer

There is no biblical record that Lot ever built an altar, nor did he ever call on the name of the Lord. The lack of prayer in his life is apparent when we observe the way Lot's Uncle Abraham prayed. When the Lord appeared to him in the midst of the Canaanites, Abraham "built an altar there to the LORD, who had appeared to him" (Genesis 12:7). When Abraham moved on to Bethel from Shechem, "there he built an altar to the LORD and called on the name of the LORD" (12:8). After his miserable failure in Egypt, Abraham returned to Bethel, "where he had first built an altar. There Abram called on the name of the LORD" (13:4). After Lot moved away, "Abram moved his tents and went to live near the great trees of Mamre at Hebron, where he built an altar to the LORD" (13:18).

Prayer was central to Abraham's life. What a simple, fundamental principle that is as necessary today as it was then. In fact, prayer must be central to our lives if we are serious about embracing the magnificent obsession. So ... how's *your* prayer life? Before my study of Abraham's life, mine was pitiful.

Prayer has always been a struggle for me. In fact, I've described it is as the fight of my life. If there is anything consistent about it, it's that I consistently struggle to maintain a quality time alone with God every day. I fail more often than I succeed.

Often, as I begin to pray, I suddenly become so sleepy I can hardly keep my eyes open ... never mind that I have just had eight hours of good sleep! Or as I begin to pray for those on my prayer list, I find my mind wandering into situations that involve them ... and instead of praying for them, I'm holding imaginary conversations with them. Or because I have been traveling quite a bit, I find that when I begin to pray for the practical concerns of my trip, invariably my mind begins to dwell on what clothes I'm going to take! Or suddenly my mind takes off, and I begin to imagine all of the things that could happen, the dangers that are lurking, what people could be saying behind my back, the sickness that could develop into life-threatening illness.

I seem to plunge into thoughts about a situation, conversations about people, or fantasizing about dangers and problems, only to realize, as the time slips away, that I have spent very little time actually talking to God.

From personal experience, I know that my prayer life tends to be very shallow unless I deliberately, intentionally make the effort to deepen and develop it on a daily basis — an effort that Abraham helped to jump-start, just by his example.

I tried to deepen my prayer life by focusing on three areas — consistency (making time every day), content (having a prayer list, a devotional book, and my Bible), and concentration (setting aside a particular place free from distraction, praying out loud, and writing out my prayers).

Not only has Abraham's prayer life been an inspiration to my own but, again and again, I have turned to our Lord's example for motivation and even conviction. Throughout his gospel, Luke gives us a tantalizing glimpse of Jesus' prayer life. Beginning with the baptism of Jesus, Luke tells us that "as he was praying, heaven was opened and the Holy Spirit descended on him";[3] that "Jesus often withdrew to lonely places and prayed";[4] that before He called His twelve disciples, "Jesus went out into the hills to pray, and spent the night praying to God";[5] that "Jesus was praying in private and his disciples were with him";[6] that Jesus "took Peter, John and James with him and went up onto a mountain to pray. As he was praying, the appearance of his face changed, and his clothes became as bright as a flash of lightning";[7] and that "one day Jesus was praying in a certain place. When he finished, one of his disciples said to him, 'Lord, teach us to pray.'"[8]

Every time I reflect on the prayer life of Jesus, my mind wraps and rewraps around the question: If He felt the need to pray, how do I think I can go without it? What is my excuse for not praying?

What's your excuse?

> You don't have enough time?
> You're too tired?
> You don't know how?
> You think it's boring?
> You feel foolish trying?
> He's not going to answer you, so why bother?
> Prayer doesn't really change anything anyway?

I really don't have an excuse, not one that God accepts. I know how to pray; it's just that often I don't do it. God spoke to me very firmly several years ago, letting me know that He was not at all pleased with the shallowness of my prayers. Through His personal letter to the church at Sardis in Revelation 3, He revealed that He was fully aware of all that I was doing in His name, inside and outside my home. But He rebuked me for having "a reputation of being alive" while at the same time I was lifeless in my relationship with Him because I was virtually prayerless.[9] He made it very clear that He was not at all impressed with my résumé or my family connections or my reputation as a messenger from Him. While my spirit squirmed, He shined the light of His Word into my heart: *Anne, I "have not found your deeds complete" because they are not done in total dependence upon Me.*[10]

As He commanded me to repent of my shallowness, I asked Him, *How?* His answer was so practical and simple that I smile even now as I remember it. He instructed me to *Wake up!*[11] I knew exactly what He meant. I was to literally wake up by setting my alarm earlier than I would otherwise need to and spend time with Him before my day began and my household stirred. I remembered what a great Bible teacher from England, Dr. Alan Redpath, once said, that what American Christians needed most was *blanket victory*... victory over those blankets in the morning!

So I repented. I went to the mall, found a gadget store, and bought an alarm clock that was so loud when it went off in the dead silence of the early morning, it scared the wits out of me! My heart would pound, my husband would yell, and there was no chance at all that I was going to roll over and go back to sleep! As my dear friend Jill Briscoe has said, it's better to be sleep deprived than God deprived.

Now, years later, I can testify to the fact that those early morning moments are the most precious of the day. I'm still not as consistent as I want to be, but I'm no longer shallow in my prayer life. And most of the time, I get up now without the need of an alarm.[12]

Shallowness in Bible Reading

Lot's relationship with God was weakened not only by his shallowness in prayer but also by his shallowness in listening for and heeding God's voice. I can almost hear the Lord saying to Lot, "Lot, you have a reputation for being alive. You're Terah's grandson and Abraham's nephew. You left everything behind to pursue Me, but you're spiritually dead on the inside. Your deeds are incomplete because your prayer life is nonexistent. And you never listen to My Word."

While God spoke repeatedly to Abraham, who listened attentively to what He had to say, I can find no record that God ever spoke to Lot. When Abraham was living in Ur, "the LORD had said to Abram ...," but He didn't speak to Lot (12:1).

When Abraham arrived where God wanted him to be, "the LORD appeared to Abram and said ... ," but He didn't speak to Lot (12:7). Following Lot's separation from Abraham, "the LORD said to Abram ... ," but He didn't speak to Lot (13:14). God was silent in Lot's life.

Anyone who has ever had a friend or spouse or child understands that communication is key to the relationship. If one person does all the talking but never listens, or if the other person never says a word so you don't know what he is thinking or even if he has been listening, the relationship is going nowhere. Relationships require communication. And communication requires talking *and* listening.

My relationship with God is no exception to that basic rule. I must communicate with Him by talking to Him in prayer and listening to what He has to say as I read my Bible. Otherwise I will be shallow too.

When do you read your Bible? And when you read it, is it just for facts and information, or do you read it as though you're listening for His voice to speak to you through it?

This past week I became very burdened for a young friend in India who had taken a strong, principled stand in her family. She had spoken the truth in love about a very difficult situation. Her business called her out of town for a few days, and when she returned home she found her furniture had been removed, the doors had been torn off the hinges, and she was ordered to leave without even being allowed to say good-bye to her children. She left with grace and dignity, while I was the one outraged and in tears.

That day when I opened my *Daily Light*, a small volume of selected Scriptures for morning and evening,[13] I read these words:

> My [sisters], take the prophets, who spoke in the name of the Lord [who spoke the truth in love], as an example of suffering and patience....

> Shall we indeed accept good from God, and shall we not accept adversity? In all this Job did not sin with his lips.

> Aaron held his peace.

> It is the LORD. Let Him do what seems good to Him.

> Cast your burden on the LORD, and He shall sustain you.

He has borne our griefs and carried our sorrows. [He knows exactly how it feels to be rejected and thrown out.]

Come to Me.[14]

As I read these words and let their truth envelop my heart and mind and soul, my tears dried, and I had a quiet peace. I knew God had leaned out of heaven to give me His words of comfort and encouragement so that I could be a friend who strengthened my friend. God did not want me to be someone who gives cheap sympathy that would serve as an invitation to a pity party. I know He wanted me to encourage my friend in her faith. So I did my best. Once again, I just bowed my head, face in my hands, and praised God for His written Word!

Because it's His Word that gives me …

encouragement in my despair,

comfort in my isolation,

strength in my weakness,

light in my darkness,

dignity in my humiliation,

joy in my tears,

peace in my turmoil,

purpose in my struggle,

protection in my battle,

wisdom in my decisions.

Because through His Word, *I know Him*, and He gives me acceptance in my rejection, love in my loneliness, grace in my failures, hope in my grief, and a lap to crawl into and a shoulder to cry on plus all spiritual blessings in heavenly places![15]

How could I exist without Him?!

And how could I ever begin to know Him without His Word?!

Shortly after I returned from a trip overseas, I knew I had to start writing this book or I would not make my deadline. But I hadn't seen my parents in about a month, and I was torn as to whether I should make the four-hour drive and spend a couple of days with them. Feeling the stress of wanting to be in two places at the same time, I prayed for wisdom to know what to do. Once again, when I opened my *Daily Light*, these verses seemed to leap off the page:

The word of the LORD came to [Elijah], saying, "Get away from here and turn eastward, and hide by the Brook Cherith, which flows into the Jordan. And it will be that you shall drink from the brook, and I have commanded the ravens to feed you there."[16]

My parents' home is west of mine. I knew God was telling me to turn away from the thoughts of going home, stay east, hide by the brook of living water that is His Word, and drink deeply of it, and He would feed me the thoughts and insights I would need as I wrote. Deep peace enveloped my heart and mind as I relaxed in the will of God, knowing I was exactly where I needed to be — at my desk, in front of my computer, writing this book.

So, repent of your shallowness and start reading your Bible. Now. And as you do, listen for the God of Abraham to speak to you.

Lot never built an altar or called on the name of the Lord, and he never heard the voice of the Lord speaking to him. The result was that his commitment to live a life of obedient faith pleasing to God was shallow also.

Shallowness in Commitment

Lot seemed to live out his relationship with God through Abraham. When Abraham left Ur and then Haran, "Lot went with him" (12:4). When Abraham left Egypt and went back to Bethel, "Lot went with him" (13:1). It didn't seem to matter where they were going or what they were doing, "Lot … was moving about with Abram" (13:5). Lot was just tagging along *with Abraham.* The impression I have is that he seemed to substitute Abraham's relationship with God, and his commitment to Him, for his own.

That shouldn't be surprising because we do the same thing today! As a wife, are you living in the shadow of your husband, who is in a leadership position within your church, and you think somehow if you're just supportive of your spouse, God will credit you with what he does?

As a husband, are you wrapping yourself in your wife's relationship with God, believing that somehow He will credit you with her prayer, Bible reading, and good works?

Are you a church member who believes that going to church, serving in the church, and living a good, moral Christian life is the same as a relationship with God? Are you living out your relationship with God through your church?

As a young girl, I hid spiritually in the large shadow of strongly committed Christian parents and grandparents. From the time I was eighteen months old, my father has been an internationally known evangelist. My mother was a deeply spiritual woman who immersed herself in Scripture, devoted herself to prayer, raised five children as, for all practical purposes, a single parent, and was a widely read author. My grandparents were missionaries to China; when they were forced out of China by the Japanese, they returned to a thriving medical practice in this country while also taking on national leadership within the church denomination of which they were members.

As a girl, whenever I thought of my relationship with God, it was always intertwined with that of my parents and grandparents. But I knew God had no grandchildren, so at the age of eight or nine, after watching a portrayal of the life of Christ on TV, I confessed my sin and asked Jesus to be my Savior and come into my heart. I believe He did, and as a young girl I was assured that I was not only a child of Billy and Ruth Graham, I was a child of God.

Still, I subconsciously assumed that when I stood before God, I would smile and say something like, "You know who my daddy is. He's a world-famous preacher of the gospel. And You know who my mother is. She takes care of all of us so that Daddy can serve You. See all those books? They're best sellers, and my parents wrote them. And I know You know my grandparents. They were medical missionaries to China ... "

But at sixteen years of age I was confronted by the fact that when I stood before God, I wouldn't be held accountable for the way my parents and grandparents had lived their lives, I would give an account for the way I had lived my life. I don't remember anything that triggered the confrontation. I simply experienced a gradual awakening to the fact that I would stand on my own before God.

I remember distinctly one afternoon in my parents' mountain home, kneeling down on the floor beside the window of my upstairs bedroom, telling God I wanted my life to count. I passionately declared that when I stood before Him, I wanted something to show for the life I had lived here on earth. I desperately desired to live a life of eternal significance. And so with the limited understanding of a sixteen-year-old, I surrendered all of my heart, mind, strength, and spirit to the lordship of Jesus Christ. I gave Him my life, surrendered and available for His use.

Shortly after that teenage commitment, God gave me the opportunity to share the gospel in a very relevant way with my best friends, four of whom prayed with me to receive Jesus as their personal Savior. My pastor recognized a sharpened focus in my life and invited me to share my testimony publicly for the first time in our church. He also arranged for me to attend a Christian leadership conference.

And then … I became seriously ill, missed out on my first year of college, met Danny Lotz, married at the age of eighteen, had my first child shortly after I turned twenty-one … and plunged into all the busy, busy, busy responsibilities of young motherhood.

God's time is perfect, but so often it's not our time, is it? I can remember lying awake at night in our small home, with my small children, wondering what had happened to the answer to my prayer. While I'm very convinced nothing is as significant as rearing godly children, I believed I was meant for something more, although I had no idea what it was. When I shared my concerns with my very wise mother, she encouraged me not to "waste my wilderness years." She told me that if one day God called me to serve Him outside my home, I needed to be ready.[17]

So I disciplined myself to pray and study my Bible on a daily basis. I maintained a vibrant personal love relationship with God. And I was ready on the day, years later, when He did call me out.

Lot had no individual relationship with God. He was totally dependent on his uncle in spiritual matters. He was only able to maintain his relationship with God as long as he was with Abraham. But when they separated, his relationship with God was like a mirage and seemed to evaporate into thin air.

If you were severed from your spouse or your family or your church or your best Christian friend or your Bible study group, would your relationship with God remain intact and continue to grow? If you were all alone, stranded on a desert island or placed in solitary confinement, what would the condition of your relationship with God be like within a week? A month? A year?

Several years ago, I felt an intense desire to meet with some of the women who had been in my Bible class during the twelve years I taught. I missed their friendship and just wanted to catch up with what and how they were doing. So I arranged once a month to have lunch with four or five of them at a time. After several months, I stopped the luncheons because I had become so discouraged. While I discovered that some of them were doing well spiritually, others seemed to have disintegrated into pleasant but mediocre, worldly lives. It was increasingly apparent that when they left the Bible class, they had also stopped the disciplined study of God's Word, prayer, and sacrificial service. Their deplorable spiritual condition was illustrated when, at the last luncheon, one of the women carrying her plate of food from the buffet line to the table dropped something — and cursed while she looked straight at me! I tried to keep the look on my face pleasant, but I felt my heart being stabbed with the pain of observing a Christian who had a saved soul but was living a wasted, shallow life!

Lot was a saved soul who lived a wasted life. I wonder if he had deceived himself into thinking he was okay because he had made the initial choice to leave everything behind. I wonder if he just didn't understand that he also had to let everything go . . .

LET GO OF YOUR SELFISHNESS

Lot not only seemed to me to be very shallow, he was also glaringly selfish. Apparently when Abraham acquired great wealth in Egypt, Lot did also, because the Bible says, "Lot, who was moving about with Abram, also had flocks and herds and tents" (13:5). From the story that follows, it's apparent that Lot's head had been turned while he was in Egypt. He must have seen the material luxury, the political power, the financial prosperity, the environmental beauty of all that was in Egypt at that time . . . and longed for it himself. Even while he was wandering around with Abraham, his heart and his mind must have settled on gaining for himself the worldly advantages he had been exposed to.

His opportunity to realize his dreams of power and position and possessions and prestige came more quickly than perhaps he could have thought. Soon after returning to Bethel from Egypt, tension developed and tempers flared between his servants and Abraham's when "the land could not support them while they stayed together, for their possessions were so great that they were not able to stay together" (13:6).

Selfishness in Disputes

The problem that created the tension was an ordinary, practical one that erupts in homes and offices and schools today. There just wasn't enough of what both Abraham and Lot needed to go around. Sharing was no longer an option.

What have you been sharing with someone else that is no longer practical or possible? Are you going through a divorce settlement and what once was enough for two of you to live on together is now not enough to support each of you separately in the way you've been accustomed to living? Is the one computer allotted to you and your coworker no longer sufficient as your workload has increased? Is there only one TV in your home, and both you and your spouse want to watch a different program? Or is there only one remote that controls the TV while there are several "controllers"? Does your small home have one bathroom ... and four teenagers who all need to use it before school in the morning? Does your church have limited classroom space so that not everyone who wants a Sunday school class can have one? Or does it have limited parking so that some members can park next to the church and some have to use a satellite lot?

The practical problem became personal when "quarreling arose between Abram's herdsmen and the herdsmen of Lot" (13:7). Fighting broke out in the home, and the situation rapidly deteriorated into a serious spiritual problem because "the Canaanites and Perizzites were also living in the land at that time" (13:7). The distinct impression is given that the Canaanites and Perizzites were watching what was taking place in Abraham's and Lot's home. I wonder if they leaned in to get a good look, watching how God's children handled their problems. I'm sure there was a lot of fighting in the homes of the Canaanites and Perizzites too. Tension, quarreling, and divorce were nothing new to them. What made this situation so intriguing was that it was happening in the home of people who claimed to have a personal relationship with God ... people who built their altars and prayed and heard God's voice and obeyed what He said.

So Abraham's and Lot's neighbors, including some who were of other religions and some who were the secularists of that day, intently watched to find out what difference a relationship with God made on a practical, personal, day-to-day basis. How *would* Abraham handle this conflict? What *did* go on behind the closed doors of his home when the pressure was on? What a keen disappointment it must have been for his neighbors to discover that initially there really wasn't any difference between their homes and that of Abraham and Lot.

The practical problem that had become a personal problem was now a serious spiritual problem because Abraham's and Lot's testimonies were at stake.

That was a sobering thought! Someone is watching ... *me*?

Who is watching *you* and the way you handle your problems and disputes? Your spouse? Or child? Or coworker? Or employee? Or roommate? Or neighbor? Often it's someone you don't even know is watching. But you and I can count on the fact that one reason God allows us to have problems is so we can demonstrate to a watching world how His children respond.[18]

Maybe the person who is watching is someone you've been talking to about Jesus. And God is giving you the opportunity to show that person the difference Jesus can make in everyday life. What a tragedy when the person looks at you but doesn't see any difference at all.

I can imagine Lot's foreman coming to him early one morning and saying, "Sir, I've got some good news and some bad news. The good news is that your flocks and herds are increasing rapidly. We've got a bumper crop of little lambs and calves. The bad news is, so does your Uncle Abraham. And there's just not enough grass to feed 'em all. Something's got to give or somebody's got to go."

I wonder if Lot stared hard at the man, then put his finger to his lips. "Shhh."

"Sir? What do you mean, 'Shhh'? We've got to do something! There's not enough food for everybody. The herdsmen are already quarreling. Tempers are heating up. It's just a matter of time before fights break out and something ugly happens."

Shhhh ...

Lot didn't do a thing. Maybe he was hoping *his* herdsmen would win. Then, if someone asked where Abraham was, he would just reply, "Poor old man. He just couldn't cut it out here. He's headed back to Haran. Such a shame. He really felt God had led him here, you know. I guess everybody makes mistakes."

Lot's silence revealed to me his selfishness when disputes arose within his home. Somebody needed to give in, to give up, to let go of his rights, but it wasn't going to be the monkey clutching tightly to his bananas.

Once again I closely watched Abraham to see his reaction to the dispute within his home — and then compared it with Lot's response. Once again, a sharp contrast became obvious. Abraham "said to Lot, 'Let's not have any quarreling between you and me, or between your herdsmen and mine, for we are brothers. Is not the whole land before you? Let's part company. If you go to the left, I'll go to the right; if you go to the right, I'll go to the left'" (13:8 – 9). Abraham not only took the initiative to settle matters, he offered an incredibly generous and gracious solution.

What problem would be solved if you and I would initiate a solution, as Abraham did? What problems could you remedy if you just went to the person you're quarreling with and asked, "How can I be right with you?"

Several years ago, my husband and I made the time to go hear a nationally known preacher. He was speaking at a large conference, and we settled into our seats with great anticipation. But as the man began preaching, he said some things that were extremely offensive to us. Instead of being encouraged or blessed, we left feeling very disheartened. I would have dropped the issue entirely except the speaker was told we were in his audience, and he wrote to ask my evaluation of what he said. So I wrote back a very clear, strong rebuke, asking him not to publicly repeat the things we had heard him say. I didn't expect to hear back from him, and I didn't.

A year later, I was invited to speak to a large Christian rally. Before the program began, I was led into the backstage greenroom for prayer with the other platform participants. I looked up to see this same preacher in the circle of people who would be with me on the platform! I quickly scanned my printed program and discovered he was designated to give the invocation. My knees quaked, my heart turned over, my spirit began to panic ... and then my mind began to spin in an almost incoherent prayer that was more like a complaint: *How can I stand on the same platform with this man? How can I get up and give out God's Word when I know I'm not right with the man who will precede me in prayer? God, what am I supposed to do?*

He didn't give me a verbal or audible answer, but as everyone in the room filed out to go to the platform, the man held back until he and I were the only ones left. He graciously motioned for me to go through the door ahead of him. I paused, looked him in the eye, and heard myself asking him, "Are we all right?"

His response was, "Anne, I'm all right if you're all right."

I must have nodded yes, because he kissed me on the cheek, and we went out to serve the Lord together. Had I not timidly initiated a solution by asking him if we were all right, at the very least there would have been tension between us.

Abraham would have been perfectly within his rights if he had stormed into Lot's tent, jerked him up by his robe, thrown him across his carpet, and yelled, "Lot! You little pip-squeak! You've been tagging along ever since I left Ur! You're nothing but trouble! I'm the leader of this expedition. I'm the elder, and God has promised me this land. Now, you beat it before I decide to confiscate all those flocks and herds you obtained because of your association with me. Get out!"

But that wasn't Abraham's response at all. Instead, he yielded to Lot his right of first choice. In essence, he told Lot, "You take first choice, and I'll take your leftovers!"

That's very impressive to me! The only motive he could have had was that he wanted to be right with God more than he wanted to exercise his rights.

While the world exhorts you and me to … insist on our rights, assert our rights, protect our rights, demonstrate for our rights, sue for our rights … would you just let them go?

Sometimes the solution to a problem is just to give up and let go of your right to be right, your right to an inheritance, your right to special attention, your right to go first, your right to a certain seat, or to a certain place, or to a certain privilege, or to a certain position.

Just give it up. Let it go. Don't let selfishness keep you from solving the problem and restoring peace in your home or office or school or church. If you truly desire peace, just let go of your rights.

Lot was helpless to offer any solution when disputes arose because the desires of his heart were saturated in selfishness. When Abraham offered him first choice, "Lot looked up and saw that the whole plain of the Jordan was well watered, like the garden of the LORD, like the land of Egypt, toward Zoar" (13:10). It was as though his uncle had given him an unlimited gift certificate to Home Depot, and he was standing inside the store's big glass doors, just looking up and down at all the stacks of stuff, knowing he could have anything and everything he desired.

Selfishness in Desires

Lot greedily fastened his gaze on all that was before him. The first thing he noticed about the land was how beautiful it was. It looked like "the garden of the LORD" — the garden of Eden. Lush, extravagant, luxurious. His eyes must have traveled slowly over the landscape … tall green grass rippling gently in the breeze, the sparkling water of the Jordan River meandering through the valley, the sunlight glistening off the tops of the whitewashed homes in the cities. Paradise was not lost after all! It was his for the taking!

Maybe Lot thought, *Finally, we can get out of these smelly tents and into one of*

those starter castles on a quiet palm-tree-lined boulevard. Our children can go to
the best private schools, we can join the elite country club, and our names will be
on the social register. I'm going to buy a chariot for myself. I deserve it after riding
hundreds of miles on these ridiculous, irritable camels.

Lot noticed also that the plain before him looked "like the land of Egypt." How
fresh those memories of his brief sojourn there must have been. While Egypt had
been a place of humiliating failure for Abraham, it seems to have been an intoxi-
cating place to Lot, one that had opened his eyes to a whole new, exciting world of
wealth and privilege and power. A place like Egypt, with all its intellectual, social,
financial, political, and educational advantages, was within his grasp ... right
there on the plain near Sodom and Gomorrah. It was sophisticated, civilized, a
place where maybe he could even get involved in civic affairs ... a place where a
man could make a name for himself if he worked hard enough.

What are the desires of *your* heart? The way you answer that question will not
reveal the truth about you but your decisions will. Lot's decisions revealed to me
that he was selfish to the core — selfish in his desires as well as his decisions.

Selfishness in Decisions

Lot was totally oblivious to Abraham's feelings or needs or rights as he made his
decision. He could not have been more inconsiderate when he "chose for himself
the whole plain of the Jordan" (13:11). Whoa, wait a minute! Chose for *himself*?
The *whole* plain? What was Lot thinking?! What about Abraham? Abraham had
given him first choice, but did he mean for Lot to take *everything*?

I was astounded by Lot's inconsideration toward Abraham, and even more astounded by his indifference toward God. Of all the places to live on that broad and
beautiful land, Lot "pitched his tents near Sodom. Now the men of Sodom were
wicked and were sinning greatly against the LORD" (13:12 – 13). Lot seemed to
give no thought whatsoever to the spiritual climate of the place where he chose to
live and rear his children. Maybe he rationalized his decision to move into such
a wicked area by thinking he could somehow be a witness. Maybe he thought he
could change them instead of being changed by them.

Was that how you rationalized joining that club? Moving into that area? Taking that job? Making those friends? Be very careful. Paul wisely admonished the
Corinthians, who were noted for their compromised Christian behavior, to "come

out from them and be separate."[19] The command is for our own good and for our spiritual health because, if we are like Lot and have a weakened relationship with God, more than likely, instead of having a positive impact on others, they will have a negative impact on us.

Lot seemed to move into the area gradually. Genesis chapter 13 says he "lived among the cities of the plain," then he "pitched his tents near Sodom"; but by chapter 14, he is living *in* Sodom (13:12; 14:12). The pull had just been too great. The temptation had been irresistible to such a selfish man. Lot finally gave in and embraced the world. And God let him have it.

Lot reminds me of a little boy who walked into his grandfather's house and saw a jar of jelly beans on the table. He asked if he could have some, and his grandfather smiled and replied, "Yes, son, help yourself."

The little boy shook his head and said, "No, Grandfather, you give me the jelly beans."

The grandfather encouraged his grandson. "Go ahead. You can get some yourself."

Again the little boy protested and asked his grandfather to get the candy for him. Exasperated, the grandfather reached into the jar and grabbed a handful of jelly beans. As he placed them into the little boy's cupped hands, he inquired irritably, "Why on earth wouldn't you get the jelly beans for yourself?"

The little boy grinned. "Because your hands are bigger."

Lot had reached into the jelly bean jar and grabbed what he wanted, which was a lot less than he would have gotten had he let God choose for him.

What are you insisting on getting ... having ... owning ... being ... doing ... achieving ... possessing?

Watch out! If you insist on selfishly getting what you want, you just may get it — and wind up with a lot less than what God wants to give you. For myself, I want all the "jelly beans" God wants to give me. I want the fullness of His blessing. I want a God-filled life!

Lot selfishly chose for himself the whole plain of Jordan, pitched his tents near Sodom, then moved in with nothing held back. Sodom was a very wicked world. A world without any fear of God. A world that made sin look attractive ... and fun ... and politically correct ...

LET GO OF YOUR SINFULNESS

In the end, what difference did clutching a few bananas make? To find out, let's look ahead to the tragic end of Lot's life. It gives a powerful warning to anyone who makes the initial choice to leave everything behind in order to pursue knowing God, but who, because of shallowness, selfishness, and sinfulness, just won't let everything go.

The short- and long-term consequences for Lot were disastrous. The Bible warns, "Do not be deceived: God cannot be mocked. A man reaps what he sows. The one who sows to please his sinful nature, from that nature will reap destruction."[20] That warning was not heeded in Lot's life, and the truth of the warning was dramatically lived out.

In Genesis 19 we find Lot was sitting in the city gate, which meant he had indeed worked his way into civic affairs. He had become, as it were, a member of the city council. Literally, he was a judge. Instead of being separated from the world, he was immersed in Sodom. And although he seemed to have gotten everything he had desired, it had not made him happy. He is referred to in the New Testament as one who "was distressed by the filthy lives of lawless men (for that righteous man [Lot], living among them day after day, was tormented in his righteous soul by the lawless deeds he saw and heard)."[21] Lot was miserable in the midst of a godless, wicked world ... but he still stayed there. He could have gone back to Bethel, or back to Haran, or even back to Ur. But he stayed in Sodom, enjoying the pleasures of sin for a season,[22] even though the guilt gnawed at his spirit and he could never really enjoy anything. If Lot were alive in the twenty-first century, I would expect he would take pills to help him sleep, pills to help him wake up, and all sorts of alcoholic fortifiers just to get him through the day.

Do you know someone like Lot? Someone who looks successful, influential, and wealthy? Someone who holds a powerful position, has a well-known reputation, possesses more wealth than can be spent in a lifetime, and has an entire network of friends to do his bidding? Someone who has lived a life of compromise with sin and who seems to have everything? I do. Like me, are you hurt because your "Lot" seems to be better off than you are? He seems to have everything plus God tacked on to his life. Are you resentful because you've lived a life of obedient faith and have nothing? God is not mocked.[23] Sinfulness may bring momentary pleasures and satisfaction, but it leaves a devastating and lasting impact.

Sinfulness Impacts Your Friends

The sinfulness of Sodom exceeded the patience of God, and He sent angels disguised as men to take a closer look.[24] As they approached the city, they were greeted by Lot, who "got up to meet them and bowed down with his face to the ground. 'My lords,' he said, 'please turn aside to your servant's house' " (19:1 – 2). His invitation was warm and sincere and very intentional. When the men refused, implying they were on business and needed to assess the city, Lot, who knew that the streets in Sodom were not safe at night, "insisted so strongly that they did go with him and entered his house" (19:3).

After dinner, Lot heard a commotion at the door, and when he stepped outside, he discovered a gay demonstration in the street. Men from throughout the city, old and young alike, surrounded his house and demanded that he turn the two strangers over to them for their pleasure. "Lot went outside to meet them and shut the door behind him and said, 'No, my friends' " (19:6 – 7). My *friends?!* Men who wanted to assault his guests were *his friends*?! That's astonishing! How is it possible that Lot, a "righteous man," would call men like these his *friends*? These were the men he did business with? And played golf with? And sat on the city council with? These men were his *friends*?

Then Lot did the unthinkable. He offered his two virgin daughters to "his friends" in place of the strangers who were under the protection of his roof. It's hard to imagine that anyone's standards could fall any lower. As despicable as the offer was, the response of the demonstrators was worse. In a flash, they turned on Lot. " 'Get out of our way,' they replied. And then they said, 'This fellow came here as an alien, and now he wants to play the judge! We'll treat you worse than them' " (19:9).

Who do you call "my friends"? Are they the people that you … grew up with? went to school with? played games with? took vacations with?

Are they the people who … were in your wedding? started their family when you did? lived next door?

Are they in your … tennis club? bridge club? golf club? country club? book club?

Are they on your ... shift? street? staff?

Have you resisted letting go of everything in order to pursue God because you don't want to lose your old friends?

Unless and until you and I are willing to let everything go, including our old friends, we will never discover the friends God wants to give us and the blessings He wants to pour out on us. And who knows? If we let everything go and embrace the magnificent obsession, maybe at least some of our friends will be so intrigued that they will embrace it too.

As much value as Lot had put on his friendship with the men of Sodom, as hard as he had tried to hang on to his relationships with them, they wasted no time at all in turning on him. From one moment to the next, Lot lost his friends.

Sinfulness Impacts Your Family

The angels disguised as men pulled Lot back inside and shut the door, "then they struck the men who were at the door of the house, young and old, with blindness so that they could not find the door" (19:11). In what must have been an incredibly tense moment, with the sound of the blind mob groping for the door, the two men urged Lot to warn everyone in his family to leave quickly because they were going to destroy the city.

I imagine Lot dashed out the back door, sprinted through the city streets, burst into the houses of his future sons-in-law, and, in what surely was a voice choking in panic, urged them, "Hurry and get out of this place, because the LORD is about to destroy the city!" (19:14).

The sons-in-law must have looked at him first in astonishment, then in amusement. "Hey, Lot, settle down," they may have said. "Man, you're all worked up over a little commotion in the street. Go home. Have a drink. Pop one of your pills. Chill out in front of the TV. You'll feel better in the morning." They actually "thought he was joking" (19:14).

Their reaction isn't really surprising. Lot had lived as though God was not that important, so his children grew up to believe that God was not important at all. They didn't even acknowledge that He existed, much less desire to know Him for themselves. What a solemn, costly lesson to learn, that sin in our environment, as well as sin in our lives, impacts our friends, our immediate family, and our extended family members.

Lot must have hurried back to his house breathless with all of the running and the confusion and the panic and the terrifying fear. The two men told him that time had run out. They said, "Hurry! Take your wife and your two daughters who are here, or you will be swept away when the city is punished" (19:15). There could have been no doubt as to the truth of what the men were saying. The fierce look in their eyes, the urgency of their tone of voice, the authority of their words all would have been like a five-bell fire alarm going off. But Lot still couldn't bring himself to let go! He just couldn't let go of all he had worked so hard to achieve and to accumulate — his position and possessions and prestige and power and popularity. He just couldn't let go, so "when he hesitated, the men grasped his hand and the hands of his wife and of his two daughters" and dragged them out of the city (19:16)!

When they had passed the city limits, the two men released Lot, his wife, and his two daughters, urging them, "Flee for your lives! Don't look back, and don't stop anywhere in the plain! Flee to the mountains or you will be swept away!" (19:17).

I would have thought that surely Lot then would have gathered up his robes, grabbed his wife and children, and kept running until he collapsed, like those who ran over the Brooklyn Bridge to escape the smoke and fire and debris of the collapsed Twin Towers on 9/11. I will never forget the look on their ash-covered faces as they walked in business suits and high heels, carrying briefcases and purses, holding handkerchiefs over their noses with one hand while the other hand gripped the arm of the person walking next to them. I don't remember seeing anyone looking back once they got to that bridge. They just kept walking, horrified by what they had been through, numbed by the shock of their experience, relieved that they were alive to just keep walking.

Lot, instead of heeding the instructions of his angelic rescuers, instead of continuing to run or even to keep walking, Lot began to *argue and whine*! Like a drowning man who fights the lifeguard that swims out to save him, Lot unbelievably resisted! In what must have been a sniveling voice, he wheedled, "No, my lords, please!... I can't flee to the mountains; this disaster will overtake me, and I'll die. Look, here is a town near enough to run to, and it is small. Let me flee to it — it is very small, isn't it? Then my life will be spared" (19:18 – 20).

Lot just couldn't let go. He gave the impression that he would rather die than give up his beloved cities of the plain. He just had to have one, just a "very small" one. When the men agreed, it appeared Lot had salvaged something valuable from the destruction and would be able to have at least one city. But from that "very small" city, his wife looked back with what must have been longing for all her friends and things, with resentment toward the men who had dragged her away, with a settled determination that as soon as she could escape, she would head right back to the city she loved. And right there, refusing to let go of everything even as it was all turning to ashes, she came under God's judgment (see 19:26). Lot had not only lost his sons-in-law and other extended family members, he lost his wife. And he was the one who had put her in the position of turning her back on God.

Lot solemnly teaches you and me that if we want our families to be saved from the judgment that is coming, then letting go of everything is not an option. It is a necessity. Jesus warns you and me to "Remember Lot's wife! Whoever tries to keep his life will lose it."[25] Lot's wife teaches us by her miserable example not to despise God's gracious offer of salvation by clinging to our own prejudices and perspective and pride and possessions and position. Just let it go. And make sure you lead your family, to the best of your ability, to the place of God's will for their lives, refusing to settle for just a "very small" compromise.

Sinfulness Impacts Your Fortune

As the sun came up, the fire came down: "Then the LORD rained down burning sulfur on Sodom and Gomorrah — from the LORD out of the heavens. Thus he overthrew those cities and the entire plain, including all those living in the cities — and also the vegetation in the land" (19:24 – 25). Remember when Lot had chosen for himself "the whole plain of the Jordan"? God's record makes it very clear. The entire plain, all those living in the cities, the vegetation, those beautiful green pastures that Lot had selfishly snatched from his Uncle Abraham — it was all gone! Everything Lot had desired for himself, dreamed of possessing, decided to take, devoted himself to get ... all had turned to ashes in his hands. Lot lost his considerable fortune.

My mother used to quip that we shouldn't begrudge an unbeliever his possessions or pleasures, because what he has in this life is all that he's ever going to get. The apostle Peter confirmed that sentiment when he predicted that one day this planet and everything and everybody in it as well as on it would be burned up by fire.[26] There is nothing you can see, feel, taste, touch, or hear that will survive the devastation that is coming. Therefore, there is no logic in acquiring the things of this world as your life's goal. Even if you are on the *Forbes* list of billionaires, what difference does it make in the end? It's often been said that no one has ever seen a U-Haul following a hearse. You came into the world with nothing, and you will take nothing out of it.

Wanting them to live lives that counted for the long term, Jesus instructed His disciples, "Do not store up for yourselves treasures on earth, where moth and rust destroy, and where thieves break in and steal."[27] If you do, it's just a lot of wasted effort. Ask Lot.

Sinfulness Impacts Your Future

The story of Lot actually gets worse. In the end, he left the "very small" city he had bargained so passionately to keep, the place that had cost his wife her life. He went to the mountains as he had originally been told to do, but instead of having an elegant home or even a mountain cabin, he lived in a cave. His two daughters, who had been raised with the morals of the Sodomites, lived with him. Their wickedness is beyond belief; they entered into an incestuous relationship with their father. Lot's children were also his grandchildren, Moab and Ben-Ammi, or Ammon (see 19:30 – 38). Not surprisingly, they grew up to reject God and were therefore rejected by God.

Years later, when God gave the law to Moses, He forbade any descendant of Moab or Ammon, down to the tenth generation, to come into His presence at the temple.[28] Lot lost his future.[29]

The words of Jesus are engraved like an epitaph over this entire sordid story. "What good is it for a man to gain the whole world, yet forfeit his soul? Or what can a man give in exchange for his soul?"[30] It's just not worth getting what I want when it's not what God wants me to have.

What are you clutching that you simply will not let go and give to the Lord? Whatever it is, is it worth missing out on what God wants to give you?

After tracking Lot to his miserable end, I wondered how all of this had affected Abraham. He had let everything go, including first choice of the land God had promised to give him. He impressed me as someone who wanted to be right with

God more than he wanted to insist on his own rights. He wanted to maintain his own testimony more than he wanted to accumulate the world's treasures. He wanted peace in his home more than he wanted property and possessions. And so he had to just let everything go.

When Abraham offered Lot first choice, I wondered if he really believed Lot would take it. Maybe he thought they would haggle a little, in a gracious eastern way:

> Nephew, you take first choice.
>
> No, Uncle, you take first choice.
>
> Nephew, I insist, you go first.
>
> No, Uncle, you're the leader and the elder. You go first.

Was Abraham actually surprised when Lot *took* first choice? When he took *everything*? Was he surprised when Lot walked all over him?

I remember leaving a church building when the rain was pouring down in body-soaking sheets. As I stood under the portico, wondering how in the world I was going to get to my car without being totally soaked, the associate pastor came. He saw my predicament and thoughtfully offered to get my car for me. When I quickly handed him the keys and said thank you, the startled look on his face let me know he had never really intended to get my car. But he did.

Have you ever offered up your rights as a mere courtesy and someone actually *took them*? Did it surprise you? Did you get walked on? Were you hurt? God knows. And He has promised, "Everyone who has left houses or brothers or sisters or father or mother or children or fields for my sake will receive a hundred times as much and will inherit eternal life. But many who are first will be last, and many who are last will be first."[31] Did you give up your right to your own time? Your own money? Your right to be right? God will make it up to you. He says so.

Abraham's choice to let everything go left him in a tent in the desert. I wonder if he was hurt. Disappointed. A little angry and resentful at having been taken advantage of. But it was at that very moment, as Abraham watched Lot leaving — with maybe a gleeful backward glance at his old uncle — and taking everything, that "the LORD said to Abram after Lot had parted from him, 'Lift up your eyes from where you are…. All the land that you see I will give to you and your offspring forever…. Go, walk through the length and breadth of the land, for

I am giving it to you'" (13:14 – 15, 17). I could almost see the divine Hand reaching into the jelly bean jar. What pleasure it must have given God to give Abraham more than Abraham could ever have taken for himself. Reflecting on my original curiosity as to what difference Bethel had really made in Abraham's life, I have concluded that it had made *all* the difference. The outcome was that Abraham received more than he could have ever thought to ask God to give him. Certainly he received much more than Lot had seized for himself.

I will never forget a very dramatic experience God used to teach me this same lesson. I had been invited to give a plenary address at the International Congress for Itinerant Evangelists in Amsterdam, the Netherlands, in the summer of 1986. One of my best friends and her husband were going as volunteer staff, so we worked out an itinerary that included coordinating plane tickets and hotel reservations, then four days of sightseeing in Europe after the congress. My son, Jonathan, and his friend, Jeff, went six weeks in advance to work as part of the setup crew while my daughter Morrow went with me. Well ahead of time, I instructed all three teenagers to save their money for our upcoming European excursion, and they promised to do so.

I delivered my plenary address, "The Evangelist and His Faithfulness," based on the prophet Jeremiah, on Sunday morning, the last day of the congress. Sunday afternoon, Morrow and I returned to the hotel to rest before the evening's concluding message and time of Communion. Morrow was sleeping when the phone rang. I answered to hear my friend's voice. Before I could confirm with her the practical details of beginning our tour together the next morning, she informed me, "Anne, something has come up. My husband and I have been given the opportunity to go to Switzerland. I'm not sure I will ever have this chance again, so we've decided to go. I'm sorry that means we won't be able to take our excursion together, but I hope you have a good time driving through Europe."

I mumbled something like, "I'm so glad you can go to Switzerland. I know how much you love it. Have a wonderful time."

When the phone clicked off, I held the receiver for a moment, not believing what I had heard … trying to will the conversation to go away. Then I dropped to my knees, and the tears began to flow. I could hardly get the words out through the turmoil of my mind and my emotions. But my prayer was something like, "God, I can't believe this! What in the world am I going to do? I can't drive one block in Amsterdam without killing about fifty people with all of these cars and bicycles. Even if I could, I wouldn't feel safe or confident enough to drive three teenagers through Europe by myself. I'm stuck in Amsterdam for four days with three teenagers who think they're starting a wonderful trip tomorrow. They've worked so hard, saved their money, and now, for what? What am I going to do?"

As I prayed, my predicament came more clearly into focus, and my tears flowed harder. "Lord, I've been serving You, and I get left like this? Don't You know? The congress ends tonight! My parents are leaving tomorrow morning. All the workers will be gone. No one can help me. Father God, are You listening? I'm helpless! I mean, totally helpless! I'm a woman with three children stuck in Amsterdam with hotel reservations that run out in the morning and return plane tickets that are scheduled for four days from now. When morning comes, I will be on the street with nowhere to go. All I have is You."

To my mind came that still, small voice that was almost an impression, except that it was much clearer and more distinct than that, saying, *Anne, I am going to do for you more abundantly than you can even think to ask.*

And in my fear and frustration, I replied, "Well, let's just see."

I decided that if God was going to do something, He would have to do it without my help, so I determined not to tell anyone about our situation, except Morrow. When she woke up from her nap, I did tell her that we would not be going on our tour of Europe. Her immediate reaction was one of anger, then tears. I told her what I felt God had said to me, and together we knelt down beside the bed and claimed His promise. Even while we were praying, in my heart, what I was really saying to the Lord was, "How can You stand to have her hurt this way? Please come through, for her sake."

We went early enough to the closing evening service so that I could speak to my son and his friend, telling them the plans had changed and we would not be going on a trip in the morning. In fact, I didn't know what we would be doing. To this day, I can see Jeff, standing there with hands blackened from working the television cables, sweat dripping down his young face, tears filling his blue eyes, saying, "It's okay, Mrs. Lotz. There'll be plenty to do around here. We'll just find a job."

Again, I sent up a little arrow prayer, "Did You hear that, Lord? What are You going to do?"

I got delayed at the conclusion of the congress as many of the evangelists had recognized me from the morning session. Since I didn't think we would be going anywhere Monday morning, Morrow and I stayed late, talking, taking pictures, and just interacting with those who are surely heaven's aristocracy: pastors, missionaries, evangelists who worked on the front lines all over the world, sharing the gospel. We missed our ride and had to walk back to the hotel through a light, misting rain. It was almost midnight.

As we walked through the hotel lobby, we passed the open door to the dining room. My friend was sitting at a long table with her husband and other participants. When she saw me, she called out, inviting me to join them for supper. She was actually the last person I wanted to see at that moment, but neither Morrow nor I had had anything to eat, so we joined her.

I was feeling increasingly tired, depressed, and more and more helpless and hopeless. Across the table from me was a stranger I had met briefly that morning on my way to the congress. As we ordered some soup, he asked, "Anne, when are you going back to the States?"

I almost choked but managed to say in what I hoped was a normal tone of voice, "Thursday."

Then he inquired, "What are you going to do between now and then?" His words stabbed at my heart, and I almost burst into tears but was able to control myself and say through tightened lips, "I'm not sure. My plans have suddenly changed." I quickly changed the subject and tried to divert attention to the other end of the table. But the stranger interrupted the conversation, inquiring, "Anne, why don't you come to London?"

My emotional strength returned as anger welled up within me, so I retorted, "There are many reasons I can't go to London."

When I tried to change the subject again, he persisted. "Anne, why don't you come to London? We're having a wedding! Prince Andrew is marrying Lady Sarah! Come on, you'll have a good time."

In my heart I was feeling more than a little resentful, and my silent prayer was something like, *Do You hear that, Lord? I can't go traveling in Europe. I can't go to Switzerland. Now I can't go to London. I want to know what I can do. And do You know what time it is? It's almost midnight, and then this Cinderella goes back to her rags, a pumpkin, and some mice. Within hours, I'm going to be thrown out of this hotel with three kids! When are You going to come through?*

Outwardly, in what I hoped was a pleasant, sort of bored demeanor, I simply said, "I'm sorry, but I just can't go to London."

But the stranger wouldn't give up. "Anne, tell me *exactly* why you won't go to London."

At that point I was truly irritated to the point of anger and frustration, so in a tone of voice that was meant to put an end to the subject, I stated rudely, "All right, I'll tell you why I can't go to London. There are three reasons. Number one, I don't have the money. I have three children with me and can't possibly afford plane tickets, hotel reservations, taxis, meals, whatever. Number two, as a woman traveling alone with three children, I would not feel safe on my own in an unfamiliar country, even if I did have the money. And number three, I'm too tired to talk about it." Then I deliberately turned my attention away from him and back to the others at the table.

A few minutes later, looking me straight in the eye, the stranger said, "Anne, I will take care of the first two reasons if you will take care of the third."

I stared at him, not comprehending. "What did you say?"

He replied, "I'll have four prepaid plane tickets at the airport for you in the morning. You will fly to London. I'll have my chauffeur-driven private car pick you up at the airport. You will stay in my club, two blocks from Buckingham Palace. And it's a club. Since you don't belong to it, you cannot pay for anything. I will give you and your children all the spending money you need."

I stared hard at this man, letting his words sink in. Then my heart was stirred, and I was genuinely moved by his generosity. At least *someone* cared about my predicament. My voice was warmer as I replied gently, "Thank you very much, but I could never accept such an offer from a stranger."

To which he said, "Anne, the Lord is wanting to do for you more abundantly than you can think to ask!" I almost fell out of my chair! If he had suddenly sprouted wings and worn a halo, I could not have been more shocked! So, the three teenagers and I went to London!

And I learned in a fresh way that I can't outgive God. If I just give up and let go, what He gives me in return makes that banana I had clenched in my fist seem so small and worthless. If I had insisted that my friend hold to our original itinerary, even if she had done it, there would have been an enormous strain in our relationship. If I had insisted but she had gone to Switzerland anyway, our relationship would have been broken. But because, by God's grace, I let go of my right to hold her to our agreement, she had a fabulous trip to Switzerland, and we had an even more glorious time in London. When we met back up on Thursday at the airport in Amsterdam before leaving for New York, we both hugged and shared little souvenirs from our trips, and our friendship was intact.

If you insist on getting what you want, on what you have a right to have, watch out! You may get it! And you may then wind up with a lot less than God wants to give you.

What's keeping you from pursuing the magnificent obsession? By reading this book and sharing my goal, you're saying you want to know God as Abraham did. You're saying you want to receive the fullness of His blessing. You're saying you want to be a blessing. You're saying you want to fulfill the potential He has for your life. You're saying you are embracing a God-filled life. You're saying you want everything He has to give you. But ... what's that I see clutched in your hand? Is that a banana? Which one is it? Is it really worth missing all that God has for you because you won't let it go? Take advice from another monkey: Don't miss out! Let it go! *Let it go! LET EVERYTHING GO!*

THREE

Entrust Everything Completely
Genesis 15

At this stage in Abraham's spiritual journey, he seemed to have a relationship with God that was more fully developed than that of many people I know today who've been going to church all their lives. As I have observed his story unfold on the pages of my Bible, I have seen this relationship blossom into the faith for which he is still known today.

Faith is a familiar term to us, yet one frequently misunderstood. I remember a young Indian couple who came up to me following a message I had given in Cape Town, South Africa. They bowed politely, then asked with intense eagerness, "Ma'am, if we are saved by faith, what is faith?"

In response, I told them this story . . .

One day an acrobat staged a dramatic performance by walking on a tightrope across Niagara Falls. Crowds gathered on each side of the falls, pointing and staring at his daring feat. When he returned to the overlook where his rope was anchored, the crowd applauded enthusiastically. Then, in astonishment, they watched as he took a wheelbarrow and pushed it over the tightrope. When he turned and came back, this time the applause was thunderous. But when he picked up a burlap bag of sand, placed it in the wheelbarrow, and began to push it across the tightrope, many in the crowd thought he was crazy! As they held their breath in suspense, unable to tear their eyes away from such a display of death-defying bravado, he very gingerly completed his walk. The crowd gasped, then burst into applause punctuated by cheers and whistles.

The acrobat bowed dramatically to the crowd, then issued a challenge: "I'd like to do something even more spectacular!" he said. "But first let me ask you something: since the bag of sand weighs the same as an average-size man, how many of you believe I can take a man across the tightrope in a wheelbarrow?"

"We believe you can do that. You can do it! You can do it!" everyone shouted.

Then the acrobat asked, "All right, which one of you will be that man?"

There was dead silence. No one moved. Finally, a shriveled little old man in the back raised his hand as he stepped forward. "I've seen what you've done, and I've heard what you've said. I believe you can push me across, so I'll do it."

He climbed into the wheelbarrow, and the acrobat set out across the tightrope with the brave little man perched precariously inside. Everyone in the crowd held their breath and strained to watch as the wheelbarrow was rolled over the falls ... and back again. On the final return, the roar of the crowd was deafening as the man was helped out of the wheelbarrow. The acrobat gallantly bowed, saluted, smiled broadly, and said, "Thank you, sir, for really believing in me."

As I concluded the story, I drove the point home for the young couple: "Everyone in the crowd at Niagara Falls *said* they believed in the acrobat, but only the old man demonstrated genuine faith. He was the only one who trusted the acrobat so completely he was willing to climb into the wheelbarrow and let himself be pushed across the tightrope."

The story illustrates one of the main criteria for embracing the magnificent obsession. In addition to leaving everything behind and letting everything go, Abraham had to get into the "wheelbarrow" and trust everything completely to God.

TRUST GOD WITH YOUR FEARS

Abraham's complete trust in God was challenged following his separation from Lot. When he "moved his tents and went to live near the great trees of Mamre at Hebron" (Genesis 13:18), Abraham had no way of knowing that this move may have saved him from being attacked when war broke out in the region.

Both Hebron and Sodom were located in one of five satellite provinces ruled by four kings from the Babylonian area.[1] The provinces did not seem to benefit from this rulership; for twelve years they had had to pay stiff annual taxes to these kings from the East. In the thirteenth year, they decided to revolt, gambling that these kings would not bother with five obscure, rebellious provinces located eight hundred miles away. But they lost their bet.

The four kings of the East decided to squash the rebellion. They marched eight hundred miles west and swept through the trans-Jordan area, destroying everything in their path. Those they didn't kill, they captured. What they didn't loot and cart off, they burned. No one could stop them or stand up against them. The five provincial rulers cowered and hid in the tar pits sprinkled throughout the valley. When the eastern kings came to Lot's highly prized cities of the plain, they looted, pillaged, and carried off the inhabitants as slaves, including Lot.

I wondered if Abraham would even care, since Lot had chosen to live in Sodom. But Abraham did.

One afternoon, Abraham was sitting under one of the big trees near Hebron, minding his own business. A man who had obviously been running a long time came hurrying up to Abraham. I imagine the man was filthy dirty and covered with tar. His hair was probably scraggly and his beard stubbly. His dark eyes may have rolled wildly in his head as he blurted out to Abraham that the kings from the East had swept through and destroyed everything.

"Yes, I heard that," Abraham may have calmly responded.

"They took me captive too," the exhausted man may have said.

"I'm sorry to hear that."

"But there were so many captives and so much loot, I watched for my chance to escape. I slipped away during a distraction."

"I'm glad to hear that."

"Abraham, they kidnapped your nephew Lot! He's being taken back to Babylon as a slave."

Did Abraham's eyes narrow with sharpened, steely focus as he stared hard at the man? "You're sure?"

"I saw him with my own eyes."

Abraham would have graciously thanked the man, paid him handsomely for the information, and instructed his servants to see he got a hot bath, some clean clothes, and a good meal before he sent him on his way. Then Abraham must have issued an emergency summons to his three neighbors. While they were hastening to his tent, he gathered together 318 trained, armed men born in his own household.[2] With his men and neighbors at his side, Abraham took off in pursuit of the eastern kings.

Abraham chose to get involved in a political, social, and military issue of his day because it had become personal. In doing so, he taught me that although I may be aware of dozens of very legitimate and worthwhile political and social issues in our day, I can't get involved in all of them. But when the issue becomes personal, that may be God's signal to me to get involved.

More than twenty years ago, my mother asked me to visit someone she had been corresponding with on death row. I got involved in prison ministry, and I'm still involved today. I have a friend who got very involved in our local Pregnancy Life Care Center when her daughter had an abortion. Another friend ran for the local school board when her children were adversely affected by the board's decisions. Abraham got involved in a regional war when he discovered his nephew had been taken captive.

As Abraham, his neighbors, and trained servants traveled during the night, Abraham devised a strategy of attack. His small militia took the undefeated eastern kings by complete surprise while they were relaxed and enjoying the spoils of their victories, and they chased the invaders more than 154 miles north of Hebron. The kings ran like scared rabbits, and Abraham "recovered all the goods and brought back his relative Lot and his possessions, together with the women and the other people" (14:16).

As Abraham triumphantly returned to the ransacked plain of the Jordan River, followed by those he had saved, he was greeted by Melchizedek, the king of Salem, or Jeru-Salem.[3] Melchizedek mysteriously stepped out of the shadows and into history as a "priest of God Most High" who blessed the weary warrior, giving God the glory for Abraham's victory over the eastern kings. Abraham received his blessing, then gave him a tenth of everything, acknowledging the kingly priest's supremacy and greatness (see 14:18 – 20).[4] The blessing must have comforted Abraham's heart. He must have known God had sent this special emissary to commend his enormous, sacrificial effort to save the Sodomites.

However, the beautiful moment was fleeting because about that time the king of Sodom slithered up out of the slime pits where he had been cowering. In brash arrogance, he must have puffed up his tar-smeared chest, stuck his dirt-streaked nose in the air, and said in a voice that dripped with condescension, "Give me the people and keep the goods for yourself" (14:21).

It's surprising that Abraham didn't laugh in his face! Because all the people and all the goods belonged to Abraham by right of conquest. But Abraham refused to touch any of it, explaining, "I have raised my hand to the LORD, God Most High, Creator of heaven and earth, and have taken an oath that I will accept nothing belonging to you, not even a thread or the thong of a sandal, so that you will never be able to say, 'I made Abram rich'" (14:22 – 23). He then gave instructions for an equal share to be given to each of his three neighbors to repay them for their time and trouble before turning the rest back over to the Sodomite king.

Four thousand years later, even I can hear the loud wake-up call that Lot should have heard — let everything go. But he didn't get the message! Unbelievably, instead of letting everything go, he *returned to Sodom* with his friends and neighbors. And Abraham returned to his tent, walking across the stony soil to his location under the trees at Hebron, once again having given up everything. It was in this setting that God taught Abraham the criteria for the magnificent obsession. It was here He taught Abraham to trust Him completely, with everything, including his fears.

God Knows You

I've wondered if Abraham's quick, almost knee-jerk reaction to Lot's capture had placed him in a life-threatening situation. It's easy to imagine that a prickly, panicky, almost paralyzing fear began to rear its ugly head as he thought about what he had just done and where he had just been. His emotional fear must have become a spiritual battle because, as Amy Carmichael wisely observed, "When we are downhearted or fearful or weak, we are saying to everybody . . . , 'After all, the Lord can't be absolutely trusted.'"[5]

But God knew all about the invasion of the kings of the East. He knew about Lot's capture and Abraham's valiant effort to save him and all those who were taken with him. He knew about Lot's ingratitude and the king of Sodom's arrogance and Melchizedek's blessing. God knew that Abraham was once again sitting alone in his tent. God knew all that Abraham had just been through. God knew exactly what time it was in Abraham's life. And so when God spoke to Abraham, He spoke relevantly: "After this . . ." (15:1).

God Speaks Relevantly

What time is it in your life? What is this moment in time *after*? What have you just done? Have you just been in battle with the enemy? Have you taken a stand for God's Word, confronting someone in authority? Have you just initiated a ministry? Taken a bold step of faith? And now, are you terrified of retaliation? Are you afraid of the consequences of having done the right thing? Are you afraid you will lose your job or at least the promotion you had hoped to get? Are you afraid a friendship will be irreparably damaged? Are you afraid your loved one will never be saved? Are you afraid _____? You fill in the blank.

Could it be that you have made the choice to leave everything behind, then followed through with the commitment to let everything go in order to pursue knowing God as Abraham did?

And now you're wondering, What in the world have I done? What is this going to mean in practical terms in the way I spend my time and my money? How will this change my relationships or my business practices? Are you suddenly afraid of abandoning yourself to God? Afraid of becoming too . . .

radical in your lifestyle?

fanatical in your faith?

hysterical in your emotions?

mystical in your thinking?

fundamental in your doctrine?

Maybe you're not afraid of the consequences of *what you've just done*, but of *where you've just been* in your life. Have you been in a hard place? a lonely place? a painful place? a place of sacrificial service?

When God spoke to Abraham, He reminded me that He knows where I am too. Recently, He underscored this truth in my life.

In response to a gracious invitation, I traveled across the country to deliver a message to a large convention. I was housed in an old hotel that wasn't clean, didn't have food services, and was located in an unsafe part of the city. My slot on the program was preceded and followed by completely inappropriate content that seemed to directly clash and oppose what I had said. And my flight out the next day was canceled, forcing me to spend hours waiting in a relatively small, crowded airport and causing me to miss my connections. I was spiritually, emotionally, and physically weary.

When I opened my Bible, the Lord spoke directly to me … "As your days, so shall your strength be…. He gives power to the weak, and to those who have no might He increases strength…. My grace is sufficient for you, for My strength is made perfect in weakness…. I can do all things through Christ who strengthens me…. O my soul, march on in strength!"[6]

His Word gave me comfort and peace as well as the challenge to lean on Him and allow His strength to flow through my weakness. As I relied on Him, I was able to relax, work while I waited, and give genuine thanks from a very grateful heart when I did arrive safely home.

God knew where I was and spoke into my life with sweet relevance. And He knows where you are.

God Speaks Personally

God knew about the place Abraham was in and the place where Abraham had been, so He not only spoke relevantly, He spoke personally as "the word of the Lord came" (15:1).[7] Because this same Word later takes Abraham outside his tent to show him the stars of the sky, the implication is that the Word that came to Abraham was a Person or a Being in visible form. The strong impression given is that the "Word of the Lord" was more than just nouns and verbs, more than just a spoken language. Incredible as it seems, could it have been the pre-incarnate Son of God, whose name *is* the Living Word of God?[8]

The beautifully tender and moving revelation is that the Word of the Lord "came to Abram."[9] We are not told that Abraham called on the name of the Lord, or that he cried out to Him, or that he even whispered a prayer. God is the one who took the initiative to draw near to Abraham and speak personally to him, not in the thunderous voice of the Creator or the authoritative voice of the Lawgiver, but as the gentle Shepherd who knew His sheep and called him by name.[10]

The prophet Isaiah heard this same voice when the Lord said, "Fear not, for I have redeemed you; I have called you by name; you are mine."[11] What thrilling reassurance to know that Abraham's God, and Isaiah's God, is also *my* God. And He speaks personally to you and me too.

God Speaks Clearly

The Word of the Lord not only came to Abraham relevantly and personally but also clearly "in a vision" (15:1). There was no doubt in Abraham's mind as to what *God was saying*.

Sometimes I wonder why I haven't had visions myself. Yet I'm aware of people who, instead of reading the Bible, are so fascinated with visions and dreams that they seek God's guidance in the supernatural or the mystical. While not limiting what God may or may not do, I have decided that it seems unwise and even dangerous to follow such a subjective, uncertain path. And so I want to be very discerning when it comes to attributing to God any communication outside of His Word.[12]

The apostle Peter himself, when he described the thrilling, mind-expanding vision of the glory of the Lord he had had during a quiet retreat on the mountain of the transfiguration, stated emphatically that as thrilling as the supernatural experience had been, the written Word of God held more certainty for him than the vision.[13] If ever you or I have a vision or a dream that we think is meaningful, we need to ask God to confirm it through His written Word, the Bible.

Abraham had no written revelation of God. He had no history of Israel. There wasn't even an Israel in existence. He had no prophets or psalms or indwelling Holy Spirit. When God's Word came to him in a vision, it came to him clearly. He knew exactly what God was saying.

God's Word comes to you and me clearly when we read our Bibles. When you are confused about what God is saying to you, open your Bible and listen as you read.

Every year I lead an advanced four-day seminar called "Filling Up to Overflow" at the Billy Graham Training Center at The Cove, which is nestled in the Blue Ridge Mountains near Asheville, North Carolina. During this annual intensive teaching event, I give six messages and direct nine workshops designed to help the participants learn how to read, study, and teach God's Word.

Several years ago, as has been my custom, I retreated to one of the cabins at The Cove beforehand to prepare my heart as well as my mind for the challenge that lay ahead. The preparation did not go well, and I began to struggle through the material I would be teaching, wrestling with the outlines of the messages and feeling very inadequate to teach the leadership-level people who would be attending. The fear of failure was oppressive. It was *at that time* that God spoke to me *relevantly*, during the week prior to the seminar; and *personally*, as He came to me during my morning devotions; and *clearly*, from Isaiah 25:6: "On this mountain the LORD Almighty will prepare a feast of rich food for all peoples."

As I claimed His promise to me, I was strengthened and encouraged and had the absolute joy of watching Him turn my feeble preparation and presentations into a "rich feast" for everyone who came.

One of the most amazing, mind-blowing, thrilling aspects of hearing the voice of the Lord speak to me through His Word is that when He does, He reveals that He not only knows what's going on in my life but He also understands what's going on inside of me. He understands my fears. As King David prayerfully articulated, "You perceive my thoughts from afar.... Before a word is on my tongue you know it completely, O LORD."[14]

God Understands You

God understood how Abraham was feeling. He knew what was going on inside Abraham's heart and mind without being told.

He Understands Your Secret Fearfulness

I doubt that anyone would have known that Abraham was secretly terrified on the inside. I'm sure when he walked through the tents or checked in with his herdsmen or discussed business with his managers, his shoulders were squared, his back was straight, his head was held high, his expression was noble, and his entire demeanor was one of calm dignity. Not even Sarah could have remotely guessed that deep down inside, her husband must have been terrified of retaliation from the eastern kings.

The four kings from the East had slaughtered, pillaged, ransacked, burned, and looted everything in their path as a brutal response to the rebelliousness of the five provinces. In light of their devastating raid over tax evasion, what would they do to an unknown Bedouin chieftain who had attacked them? By now they must have realized they had been routed, not by a general and his army, but by a nomad, his servants, and his three neighbors.

The icy fingers of fear must have gotten a stranglehold on Abraham as he surely realized he was exposed and vulnerable, a sitting duck for the enraged kings.

With each passing hour the knee-knocking, hand-sweating, heart-palpitating, eye-glazing, mind-numbing, feet-paralyzing *fear* must have caused him to seriously second-guess what he had done.

He must have been plagued by what-ifs: *What if* he had done something on impulse for his ungrateful nephew that would thwart God's purpose for his life? *What if* the kings returned, killed him, raped Sarah, took all that he had? He would never have an heir, never receive all that God had intended to give him. *What if* he had just done something very foolish, very rash, very dangerous ... and for what? *What if* he had just risked everything for nothing?

Like Abraham, have you ever been plagued by the what-ifs? What has given you panic attacks? Why does your stomach turn over and your face drain of color and your heart race at just the thought of whatever it is? Are you secretly afraid you've done something that will prevent God from fully blessing you? That you will never be able to fulfill your potential? What secret fears are lurking in the deep recesses of your heart? Abraham's experience teaches us that God knows ... and God understands.

When God's Word came to Abraham, He brought peace: "Do not be afraid, Abram" (15:1). The peace God gave to Abraham was not a dream or a "hope so"; it was as real as the peace He gave to the shepherds on another starry night two thousand years later. He sent angels to announce that the *Word of God* had come relevantly, personally, and clearly ... and could be found in a manger in Bethlehem: "Do not be afraid. I bring you good news of great joy that will be for all the people.... Glory to God in the highest and on earth peace."[15]

How often I've found that my lack of peace is directly related to my lack of Bible reading. If *you* lack peace, if you are afraid, could it be that you are neglecting to read your Bible or diminishing its importance? The psalmist testified, "Great peace have they who love your law."[16]

God will give you and me promises that bring peace in the midst of our panic, but we must tune our hearts to listen to His voice.

I have always been a fearful worrier. My mother said it's in my genes. Probably like your life, mine has been filled with many circumstances I could worry about, from the health of my husband, son, and father to the future of my grandchildren and the scope of my ministry. When worries loom, I recall one of the first passages of Scripture I put to memory, a promise of peace: "Do not be anxious about anything, but in everything, by prayer and petition, with thanksgiving, present your requests to God. And the peace of God, which transcends all understanding, will guard your hearts and your minds in Christ Jesus."[17] Prayerful focus on God and His promises has brought me peace when I've been afraid.

He Understands Your Secret Loneliness

Besides being fearful, Abraham must have felt intensely alone. He had refused the wealth, plunder, possessions, prestige, and fame that should have been his after such an overwhelming victory. But his brilliant rescue hadn't made any long-term difference in Lot's life; his nephew had gone right back to living in Sodom. The captives and the kings and the kingly priest had returned to their homes, and Abraham found himself once again getting walked all over as he lived in a tent under a tree in Hebron, with nothing really to show for all he had done.

Have you ever been isolated by others because you did the right thing? Or maybe it's just your obedience to God's call in your life that dictates the hours you spend alone on the road or in a hotel room. Or maybe because of your decision to embrace the magnificent obsession, your extended family members have cut you off and turned their backs on you. Or church members have shunned you because they say, with raised eyebrows, that you're taking your "religion" a little too seriously.

In what way are you experiencing the loneliness of emotional or intellectual or spiritual or even physical exile? I wonder if Abraham's loneliness intensified his feelings of fear. I know at times it has intensified mine.

I have found that as I have made it my life's goal to pursue knowing God as Abraham did, and as I have embraced the magnificent obsession, there have been chilling times of ostracism from those whom I have loved.

On occasion my loneliness has been intensified because sometimes, even within the organized church today, knowing God has been trivialized to a holy hobby, making Him known has been formulized into a program, faith has been institutionalized as a religion, receiving the fullness of His blessing has been exchanged for health, wealth, prosperity, and a problem-free life.

The journey of obedient faith has for me at times been a long walk in the same direction with nobody. And it can be very lonely. But once again, God understands how I feel, just as He understood how Abraham felt.

I would love to know how Abraham heard the Word of the Lord. Did he hear a soft whisper? Was it just a quiet knowing in his heart and mind? Or did he look up and discover that he wasn't alone after all? There was Another seated with him in his tent, seated near enough that Abraham could see an expression of compassionate tenderness on His face, a look of full knowledge in His penetrating eyes. Did He speak in a voice like that of rushing waters,[18] reverberating throughout all time, flooding Abraham with the warmth of God's love, penetrating deep into the lonely recesses of his heart and mind, "I am ..." (15:1)?

Years later, there was another man who was filled with fear and an overwhelming sense of inadequacy and loneliness in leadership. He stood trembling before a bush that burned but was not consumed, a bush from which God spoke, commanding him to return to Egypt and demand that Pharaoh let His people go. The man, Moses, knew Pharaoh would refuse his demand. He needed something to tell Pharaoh and others so they would listen to him and heed what he said. When he boldly asked the Lord for some identification, "God said to Moses, 'I AM WHO I AM. This is what you are to say: "I AM has sent me to you."'"[19]

The name God gave for Himself to Abraham, to Moses, to you and me, is ... I AM ... from age to age the same.

> The One who never changes.[20] His mercies are new every morning, fresh every evening.[21]
>
> The One who is the same yesterday, today, and forever.[22] As He was to Abraham and Moses, He will be to you.[23]
>
> The One who is fully present everywhere all the time.[24] Nothing can or will ever separate you from His love.[25]
>
> The One who will never leave you nor forsake you.[26] You may feel lonely, but you are never alone.[27]

Praise God! He understands me! He draws near to me! And in the midst of my secret loneliness, His Word gives me an awareness of His presence in my life, just as He did for Abraham.

He Understands Your Secret Weakness

Abraham must have been overwhelmed by what he imagined was facing him: kings with a world-class army hell-bent on revenge. He wasn't a general. He had never even been in the military. And with his flocks and herds spread out all over

Hebron the way they surely were, there was no way to defend them. There were no natural defenses or fortifications to hide behind. He must have felt very vulnerable, knowing he was responsible for the well-being of his family and dependents. As a man, he wanted to be the protector. In reality, he was nothing. Except ... God was in his life, and He promised, "I am your shield" (15:1).

In what way do you feel vulnerable to attack?

> Have you recently divorced and discovered you are vulnerable to the self-righteous criticism of others?
>
> Have you recently decided to give up your full-time job to be at home with your children when they come in from school, only to find yourself vulnerable to attack from a career-oriented culture?
>
> Have you decided to go back to work full-time, opening yourself to attack from friends who feel your place is at home?
>
> Have you decided to break off a relationship because it was hindering your journey of faith, setting yourself up to be attacked by those who just don't understand?
>
> Have you taken a bold stand for the truth of God's Word, knowing you will be accused and dismissed as narrow-minded?
>
> Have you presented the gospel without compromise, only to be labeled "intolerant," "exclusive," "divisive," and "unloving"?

Are you overwhelmed, not only by what you imagine to be facing you but also by what you know *is* facing you? Then be still and know that God is right there beside you.[28] Open the ears of your heart to hear Him whisper, I AM WHO I AM.... I am your shield[29]... your hiding place[30]... your fortress[31]... your deliverer[32]... your stronghold.[33]

He understands, firsthand, in the flesh, how it feels to be alone, facing attack.[34]

Once I was invited to appear on a national television talk show and describe what I thought heaven would be like. I was told that there would be four segments, each aired on succeeding days. One would be the Islamic view of heaven, one the Jewish perception, one the secularist ... and I was asked to give the Christian perspective.

On the morning designated for the videotaping, I prayed. Then I walked onto the recording site and faced a producer who described himself as an agnostic, a cameraman who was a cynic, and a soundman who didn't say much at all.

There is no loneliness quite like the loneliness I feel when I'm in front of a television camera, knowing my image and words will be transmitted to millions of people around the world, but having no inkling as to the content of the questions I will be asked. So I took a deep breath and hid behind my "Shield." The conversation went something like this:

"Mrs. Lotz, what do you think heaven is like?"

"*The Bible says* that no eye has seen, nor ear has heard, what God is preparing for those who love Him — and Jesus said it's big enough for everyone who wants to go."[35]

"Mrs. Lotz, how good do I have to be to go to heaven?"

"You have to be perfect. *The Bible says* therefore, no one goes because of any works that he or she has done, but only according to God's mercy. It says that all of our righteousness is as filthy rags, that there is no one good enough to go to heaven on his or her own merits because no one is perfect."[36]

"Mrs. Lotz, will Jews and Muslims go to heaven?"

"*The Bible says* God is not willing that any should perish but all should come to repentance, so He invites anyone and everyone to live with Him forever."[37]

"But Mrs. Lotz, do you believe a person has to believe in Jesus to go to heaven?"

"*The Bible says* Jesus said He is the only way to heaven, and that no one will come to the Father unless they come through Him."[38]

While I've just given you a summary of the highlights in that sixty-minute interview, you get the picture. I was hiding behind God's Word. The people who watched in the editing suite, or those who watched the actual filming, or those who only saw the finished thirty seconds that actually aired, were certainly free to strongly disagree with and reject what I had to say, but they couldn't disagree with the fact that what I said came from the Bible. My answers weren't my idea; they were God's Word. And in proportion to how closely I hide behind the shield of His Word, I know I have His protection.

Abraham was assured of God's protection too. But as God plumbed the depths of Abraham's heart, He uncovered one other secret that needed to be addressed. He pinpointed the source of much of Abraham's frustration and depression.

He Understands Your Secret Emptiness

Think about it. Abraham had given up everything: Ur, Haran, the right to the best pastureland in the Jordan River Valley, the spoils of Sodom, and for what? What did he have to show for all of his effort and sacrifice? He must have felt empty and hollow inside, and God understood.

What have you given up in order to follow God in a life of obedient faith? Have you given up the idea of marriage? Children? A soaring career? A graduate degree? A larger salary? Lifelong dreams? Have you just given up what you want, period? Is the cost of discipleship getting greater than you want to pay?

It's worth keeping in mind that Lot, who *seemed* to have everything, actually had nothing of real value. Within a relatively short time, everything he had — his home, pastures, flocks, servants, family, position, reputation, possessions, neighborhood, clubs, beloved city, friends, business, and business associates — would be burned up. It would turn to ashes in his hand. It was all temporary, at best.

Lot would lose everything while Abraham still had God's peace and His presence and His protection and His provision. God gently pointed out to Abraham that "I am ... your very great reward" (15:1). In other words, "Abraham, you still have Me."

In what way has God revealed that He knows your inmost thoughts and feelings — thoughts and feelings you haven't revealed to a living soul?

When He reveals to me He knows and understands my hidden, intimate thoughts that I have never even formed into words, much less a prayer, I am left humbled and amazed at His personal involvement in my life.

Sometimes I publicly share my struggle with a sense of inadequacy so that I might encourage others. But I rarely go into detail, even as a prayer request, because the most well-meaning of my precious friends don't believe me. Or they argue with me, or they just think I'm being humble. But the feelings of being inadequate can be painful and very terrifying, adding enormous stress and pressure to some of the opportunities for service God has graciously given me.

After thirty-two years of serving the Lord outside of my home in public ministry, my inadequacy is no longer a feeling. It's now a fact that I know by experience. I know what I can't do. At the same time, I also know by experience something of what God can do in and through me if I will just make myself available. But I have to get my eyes off of myself and keep my focus riveted on Him.

Recently, I lost my focus. I became sick to my stomach and was almost paralyzed by the overwhelming fear of taking on a commitment facing me. I knew I was unprepared due to the busyness of my schedule. My thoughts were stuck in the dullness of my mind, and my physical strength was sapped by a lingering illness. I couldn't tell anyone because I knew no one would understand. Then I opened my Bible and read this story in Mark 8:14 – 21:

The disciples had previously fed five thousand people with five loaves and two fish, and had just participated in another miraculous feeding of four thousand people with seven loaves of bread. When they left the four thousand people and got into the boat to go with Jesus to the other side of the lake, they realized they had not taken any food for themselves. All they had was one loaf of bread.

As they discussed what in the world they were going to do for lunch, Jesus interrupted, surely with a pained yet patient expression on His tired face: "Why are you talking about having no bread? Do you still not see or understand? Are your hearts hardened? Do you have eyes but fail to see, and ears but fail to hear? And don't you remember? When I broke the five loaves for the five thousand, how many basketfuls of pieces did you pick up?"

"Twelve," they replied.

"And when I broke the seven loaves for the four thousand, how many basketfuls of pieces did you pick up?"

"Seven."

"Do you still not understand?"

His words gently but unmistakably pricked my spirit, because I knew He had read my heart and understood my fear of inadequacy, and now He was rebuking me for my lost focus and lack of faith.

Anne, haven't I been faithful to you every time you have stood on a platform? Every time you have sat in front of a camera? Every time you have typed at your computer? Don't you remember I have met your every need as you have ministered in the past? Do you still not understand I will continue to be faithful to you? Do you not know by now that I know you are inadequate, but I am sufficient? That you are weak, but I am strong? That you can't do anything, but if you will refocus on Me and place your faith in Me, you can do all things? Do you still not understand?

With bent knees and wet eyes, I refocused my faith in Him alone. Then I walked through the open door of responsibility that had so overwhelmed me, confident that He would be faithful to pour out His blessing and power. And He was.

In a similar way, Abraham must have been incredibly comforted by the Word of the Lord. He was learning he could trust God because God knew and understood personally, completely, and lovingly his inmost thoughts and fears. The gentle, tender way the Lord gave Abraham His full attention as He addressed the issues of his heart must have broken through the strong outer shell of Abraham's natural defenses. Abraham had learned to trust God with his fears. Now, in a torrent of emotion, Abraham began to pour out his questions and, in the process, discovered he also could trust God with his tears …

Trust God with Your Tears

Abraham had heard God's promise to make him into "a great nation" (12:2), and he had left everything behind in order to claim it. He eagerly looked forward to having at least one child, since he believed God when He said, "To your offspring I will give this land" (12:7). He had let everything go, including the plain of the Jordan and the spoils of Sodom. But it had been ten years since he left Haran. He was ten years older, and every day it was getting less likely that he would ever have even one son, much less offspring who would become a great nation and inherit the land.

Tears of Disappointment

The ten years of waiting for the fulfillment of God's promise must have stretched Abraham's faith to the breaking point. Then, in an emotional outburst that I think had to have been accompanied by tears streaming down his weathered cheeks and running down his long gray beard, Abraham blurted out his disappointment in God: "O, Sovereign Lord, what can you give me since I remain childless and the one who will inherit my estate is Eliezer of Damascus?" (15:2).

Abraham, in essence, asked God a very tough question: "God, I want to believe You know my inmost thoughts and secrets. I want to believe Your promises of peace, protection, presence, and provision. But how can I believe You when the last time You spoke You promised me a son, and I still don't have one? You promised me a reward, but where is it? Do You mean what You say? If You do, why haven't

You fulfilled Your promises to me? Lot is living it up. He's shallow and selfish but very successful. I have left everything to pursue knowing You. Am I making a fool of myself?"

What tough question are you afraid to ask the Lord? As you embrace the magnificent obsession, leaving everything behind and letting everything go when no one else in your family or your church is embarking on such a journey, do you wonder if you're making a fool of yourself? Are you starting to wonder whether knowing God is worth all you're giving up? *Are you disappointed in Him?*

Abraham was trusting God with everything, even his fear of asking tough questions, because he persisted: "You have given me no children; so a servant in my household will be my heir" (15:3). Was Abraham choking back a sob as all his inner frustration poured out? Was he saying, "What You are giving me is less than I thought. You say You are able to do abundantly more than I could think to ask,[39] but I guess You meant my servant would be my heir. To be honest, God, I *could* have thought to ask for *that*! I thought You meant I would have a son from my own body. Can I take Your Word literally? Are Your nouns, nouns and Your verbs, verbs? Or are You speaking in symbols? Allegories? Parables? Do You mean what You say? Do You say what You mean? Did I misunderstand? Did I not claim Your promise the right way? Were You speaking spiritually? Or legally? Or mystically?"

As you have studied God's Word, what nagging, troubling questions do you have? When have you poured out your heart to Him about . . .

your spouse who is so ill and just doesn't seem to get better?

a spouse you don't have but thought God had promised you?

a Christian who behaved in a godless way and got by with it?

a business partner who cheated you and profited?

siblings who stole your inheritance?

your monthly budget that won't stretch one more day?

your career?

your children?

a child you don't have?

your own health?

your home?

Have you taken God at His Word, but He just hasn't come through for you? Is what you have less than what you thought He would give? Are you thinking that what you want for yourself is more than what He wants for you?

What tears of disappointment do you have? Deep in your heart is there a nagging, troubling question? Amazingly, God welcomes your questions when they're asked of Him directly, personally, and respectfully. The answer He will give you is one He has given Abraham. It's a simple answer. We just have to trust everything completely to Him, even when we don't understand.

We are like the father who brought his troubled son to Jesus. When the man was challenged to trust Jesus completely for the healing, he exclaimed, "I do believe; help me overcome my unbelief!"[40]

Sometimes we need help to trust God completely. Abraham did.

And God understood. God encouraged Abraham by giving him another, more specific promise that he could wrap his tiny, fragile tendril of faith around: "This man will not be your heir, but a son coming from your own body will be your heir" (15:4). In other words, "Abraham, you got it right the first time. Your offspring will come from your own body. Your heir will not be your servant Eliezer, but your biological son. You have My Word on it."

If you are still waiting for God to fulfill His promise to you, if you are beginning to doubt that He will really answer, if you question whether He means what He says and says what He means, ask Him to give you another promise from His Word to confirm the original one.

After God had given Abraham another promise, He confirmed it in a beautiful, meaningful way Abraham would never forget. God gave Abraham a visual sign. He "took him outside and said, 'Look up at the heavens and count the stars — if indeed you can count them.' Then he said to him, 'So shall your offspring be'" (15:5).

In the Middle Eastern night, with no city lights to dim the gloriously extravagant display overhead, the sky must have looked like black velvet paved with diamonds, every single one twinkling as though to beckon Abraham to take the Creator at His Word. If He could put the stars in place,[41] if He knew them all by name,[42] if He could keep them in their courses above,[43] He could do anything! ... including give Abraham an heir in his old age and make his offspring more numerous than the stars in the universe.

Surely, every night following that remarkable one, when Abraham looked up and saw the star-studded sky, he heard God whisper, "Abraham, My blessing is never less than you think. What I want to give you makes what you want for yourself look miserly in comparison. I am going to pour out My blessing on you and through you for generations to come. In fact, four thousand years from now, people will still be talking about you. And writing about you. And reading about you. You are going to be a channel of My blessing to the entire world in ways you could never dream."

Abraham's response to God's Word was stunning to me in its childlike simplicity. "Abram believed the LORD" (15:6). He put the full weight of his faith down in the "wheelbarrow" of God's Word. He believed the Lord for no other reason than God had said it. There was nothing practical or circumstantial to rest his faith on, just the spoken promise and the starry confirmation. Separated from all props of human reason and clinging to God alone, Abraham's faith reached out and touched the very fountainhead of miracles!

The New Testament reveals that Abraham "did not waver through unbelief regarding the promise of God, but was strengthened in his faith and gave glory to God, being fully persuaded that God had power to do what he had promised."[44] Abraham did not look at his own body in discouragement but kept his focus on the God who is abundantly, infinitely able to do whatever He says. At that moment in time, God "credited it to him as righteousness" (15:6).[45]

The apostle Paul explained to the Galatians that when Abraham believed God's Word regarding his offspring, in some supernatural way he knew God was speaking of the Messiah,[46] the Seed of the woman promised to Adam and Eve who would take away the sin of the world and bring people back into a right relationship with their Creator.[47]

Jesus enraged the Jewish leaders of His day when He referred to the very moment when the Word of the Lord had led Abraham out of his tent. Jesus revealed that God had lifted the veil from Abraham's spiritual eyes and enabled him to look down through the centuries so that Abraham believed in Him. Abraham *saw* Him "and was glad."[48] In other words, Abraham was counted righteous when he believed God's Word as it pointed to Jesus.

The religious authorities were infuriated, rejecting outright what Jesus had said: " 'You are not yet fifty years old,' the Jews said to him, 'and you have seen

Abraham!'"[49] When Jesus responded, "I tell you the truth, ... before Abraham was born, I am!" they picked up stones to stone Him.[50]

Such a statement made in our politically correct, pluralistic society would elicit outrage today also. Yet I can't help but wonder, was this, from a New Testament perspective, Abraham's conversion? Is this the moment he actually became a child of God? Everything seems to imply that it was. If so, there is a powerful meaning for religious people today. Think about it for a moment:

God had called Abraham to follow Him in a life of faith. And Abraham had left everything behind: the familiar territory in Ur, the compromise in Haran, the failure in Egypt. He had let everything go ... the shallowness, the selfishness, the sinfulness ... in order to embrace the magnificent obsession.

Abraham had made the choice to know God. Abraham was committed to knowing God. But what Abraham had lacked was faith in Jesus as He is revealed in God's Word. Neither you, nor I, nor Abraham can know God unless we come to Him through faith in Jesus alone.[51]

> It's that plain.
> It's that simple.
> It's that humbling.
> It's that revolutionary.
> It's that radically life-changing.
> It's that *offensive*.

If it's possible that Abraham had made an initial choice to pursue and know God, had followed through with a firm commitment to live a life of obedient faith yet had never been truly "born again," could the same be true for you? Is it possible that you have been praying, reading your Bible, living out your life in obedience for ten years? For twenty or thirty years? When have you ever deliberately placed your faith in God's Word as it points to Jesus as your Messiah, Savior, and Lord?

Can you remember a moment in time when you confessed and repented of your sin, asking God to forgive and cleanse you in Jesus' name, and then invited Him to come into your life and take control? If you can't remember a time when you have done that, how do you know that you have? Please don't assume, just because you go to church and do all the "right" things (including attending Sunday school or a Bible study and reading this book), that you are right with God. The criterion is faith that trusts Him completely — genuine, authentic, saving faith is faith that is *not* placed in Jesus *plus* good works, in Jesus *plus* morality, in Jesus *plus* church membership, in Jesus *plus* religious activity, in Jesus *plus* self-sacrifice, in Jesus *plus* philanthropy, in Jesus *plus* rituals or traditions or ceremonies, in Jesus *plus* *anything*. Genuine, authentic, saving faith is faith that is placed in Jesus *alone*. Put your entire mind, heart, soul, and life into the "wheelbarrow"!

If at this moment you're not sure that God counts you righteous from His perspective . . . if you're not sure you are His child but you want to make sure you are, then right now, use the words of this prayer as your own:

> Dear God of Abraham,
> I want to know You in a relationship You acknowledge.
> I want to be right with You from Your perspective.
> I want to belong to You as Your child . . . to be a member of Your
>   family.
> I confess to You that I am a sinner.
> I choose to repent of my sin . . . to stop it . . . to turn away from it.
> I believe Your Word as it points to Jesus as my Savior.
> I believe that Jesus is Your Son who died on the cross for me.
> Would You forgive me and cleanse me of all of my sin with His blood?
> I believe that Jesus rose up from the dead to give me life, so . . .
> Right now, would You give to me eternal life in His name?
> I invite Jesus to come live inside of me.
> I open up my heart and every area of my life,
> surrendering control to Him as my Lord.
> From this day forward, I choose to live my life for Him.
> My chief aim is to know Him as Abraham did,
> to make Him known,
> and to enjoy Him on my journey of faith.
>   Amen.

Are you saying, "But Anne, I've prayed similar prayers before. And I still am not sure I'm truly right with God. If I'm honest, I would say I have some doubts even now"?

Tears of Doubt

It may encourage you to know that God knew Abraham was harboring some honest doubts. So He addressed the uncertainty He understood was in Abraham's heart by affirming, "I am the LORD, who brought you out of Ur of the Chaldeans to give you this land to take possession of it" (15:7).

Do you have a nagging uncertainty about leaving everything behind, letting everything go, then placing all of your faith in Jesus alone for your right standing before God? Are you a little uneasy, thinking that perhaps you're making a fool of yourself by embracing the magnificent obsession? After all, how could you ever really know God?

If those are your unspoken thoughts, then the God of Abraham, who knows the doubts in your heart every bit as much as He knew them in Abraham's, has a word for you. "You wonder if you've made a fool of yourself by leaving everything in order to pursue knowing Me," He says. "You have not. I am the Lord who . . .

brought you out of darkness into the light,[52]

brought you out of emptiness into the fullness of my blessing,[53]

brought you out of meaninglessness into an eternal purpose,[54]

brought you out of nothingness into a life of significance.[55]

I am the Lord who . . .

forgives you all of your sin when you confess it,[56]

assures you of eternal life when you ask for it,[57]

indwells you by the Spirit when you invite Me in,[58]

one day will welcome you into heaven.[59]

I've discovered the best way to overcome doubt is to put my focus on the Lord . . . on who He is. Then I place my faith in His Word, in what He says. Abraham wanted to make sure God would keep His Word; he wanted to make sure that if he truly left everything behind, let everything go, and trusted everything completely to Him, he wouldn't look back on his life one day and discover he had lost out over the long term.

So, to give Abraham the absolute assurance that all God had promised was so, that all He had said He would do, "the LORD said to him, 'Bring me a heifer, a goat and a ram, each three years old, along with a dove and a young pigeon.' Abram brought all these to him, cut them in two and arranged the halves opposite each other" (15:9 – 10).

To be perfectly honest, to my Western mind, what God told Abraham to do, and what Abraham did, was incredibly weird. But in Abraham's day it wasn't unusual or strange at all. This was actually the way two parties entered into a covenant with each other. "By killing and dividing the animals the parties to the treaty made it clear that the penalty for breaking the agreement was death."[60] God was inviting Abraham to enter into a binding covenant with Him.

Abraham placed the sacrifice before the Lord, and then he waited. And waited. And *waited* ... all through the hot afternoon. The flies must have been buzzing; then the "birds of prey came down on the carcasses, but Abram drove them away" (15:11). He had to protect the sacrifice until God gave him the assurance that it was accepted — signed and sealed. This covenant would be Abraham's guarantee that God would come through for him, just as He had promised. But God was silent and still. So Abraham waited.

Having done all you know to do to establish a right relationship with God, having prayed to confess and repent of your sin, having claimed Jesus as your personal Savior and Lord, asked Him to forgive you and to give you eternal life in His name, and invited Him to come live within you in the person of His Holy Spirit ...

Are you still waiting for confirmation that He has accepted you? Do you still lack assurance that you are truly saved from perishing, born again into His family, indwelt by His Spirit, with a heavenly home to look forward to when you die?

Are the vultures of doubt even now circling in your head, picking at your sacrifice of faith?

It's up to you to drive away the doubts and place your faith in God's Word if for no other reason than it is God's Word. Then just wait. He may be delaying giving you any "feeling" of deep, blessed assurance in order to test and strengthen your faith in Him alone. But the assurance will come. It did for Abraham ...

TRUST GOD WITH YOUR YEARS

At the end of what was truly a very remarkable day, as the sun went down, melting into the horizon like a liquid pot of gold, "Abram fell into a deep sleep, and a thick and dreadful darkness came over him" (15:12). As Abraham plunged deeper into the horror of that depressing darkness, God gave him a glimpse into the future.[61]

He received the assurance of his right relationship with God. But first, Abraham was challenged to trust Him with the years ahead.

God Is in Charge

Once again, the Lord spoke to Abraham, this time revealing not only that he would have many descendants but also that they would suffer. Although Abraham was not given the details, the Bible records the fulfillment of this prophecy when Abraham's grandson Jacob was exiled from the land God had given Abraham. When he returned twenty years later, he had four wives and twelve sons. Ten of the sons, in a fit of jealousy, sold their father's favorite son, Joseph, into slavery. He wound up in shackles and was sold on the auction block in Egypt, a betrayal that began thirteen years of slavery and imprisonment.

He Is in Charge of Your Descendants

What Joseph's brothers had meant for evil, God meant for good.[62] Through divine intervention, within one day's time, Joseph went straight from prison to being elevated to prime minister of Egypt. When famine struck the neighboring countries, including Canaan, Joseph's father and brothers had to come to Joseph for food. Their need and Joseph's beautiful grace and forgiveness resulted in reconciliation. The entire family moved down to live in Egypt and ended up staying long after the famine was over.[63]

After Joseph died, a pharaoh took the throne who did not know what Joseph had done. All he knew was that there were so many descendants of Abraham, Isaac, and Jacob living in Egypt, they were like a sleeping nation within his nation. He became afraid they might rise up in revolt, so he enslaved them. Once again Abraham's descendants suffered, but once again God was in charge, promising, "I will punish the nation they serve as slaves, and afterward they will come out with great possessions" (15:14). The exodus of Abraham's descendants from Egypt and their deliverance from brutal oppression is one of the greatest displays of God's glory and power in all of Scripture. When there *was no way*, God *made a way* for them to leave Egypt and reclaim the land of promise.

When I read my morning newspaper or watch the evening news on television, then look at my three beautiful granddaughters, sometimes fear stabs my heart. What will the world be like when they are teenagers? When they are young women?

Will they be safe? Like Abraham, I almost get depressed just thinking about it, yet my comfort is in knowing that God is in charge of my descendants. For me, the critical necessity is that each of them establish a personal relationship with God so they are fully His responsibility. Then I just trust Him with my children and my grandchildren. I don't know what their future holds, but I do know the One who holds it, and He will bring them through. When their world looks like it's falling apart, it really is just falling into place ... right at the nail-pierced feet of Jesus. I know. I've read the end of God's Story.

He Is in Charge of Your Death

I sometimes wonder, How will I die? Will my death be sudden and violent? Or slow and painful? Or gentle and easy? Will I be alone or surrounded by loved ones? Will it be sooner ... or later? Those are questions that have no answers. I just have to trust God with my own death and that of my loved ones.

As I watched my mother age, I knew the moment was drawing near when her faith would become sight and she would step into our Father's house. Several months preceding her move to heaven, I could see signs she was preparing to go. Because I live about a four-hour drive away from my parents' home and because my life is full of responsibility, I didn't see her as often as I would have liked. I felt very torn, wanting desperately on many days to be in two places at once. Yet God released my burden by reminding me He was in charge of the moment of her death.

Although her death wasn't easy, it came when she was surrounded by those she loved most — her husband and her children. God took care of her and received her to Himself when He determined.

God reassured Abraham, "You ... will go to your fathers in peace and be buried at a good old age" (15:15). You can't buy that kind of peace. It doesn't come in a pill, or a bottle, or on a therapist's couch. It comes from a personal relationship with the living God and knowing you are right with Him. It floods your heart as you embrace the magnificent obsession because knowing God is your heart's desire and your life's goal, remember? Death doesn't interrupt that knowledge or hinder that goal. Death is just a step over from *trusting* Him completely to *seeing* Him clearly! It's something my mother looked forward to!

God Is Committed to You

Abraham woke up from his vision. The sun had set, and darkness surrounded him. Then, in a dramatic climax to all that he had heard and experienced, God came to him.

Abraham must have held his breath. He certainly didn't move a muscle. He just watched with eyes wide open to take in everything he was seeing: "A smoking firepot with a blazing torch appeared and passed between the pieces [of the sacrificed animals]. On that day the LORD made a covenant with Abram and said, 'To your descendants I give this land'" (15:17 – 18).

When did it hit Abraham, *Something's missing! Wait a minute! A covenant needs to be an agreement between two people. God, You walked between the pieces, but I didn't. That means . . . that means . . . what does that mean?*

God had, indeed, walked through the pieces of the sacrifice alone! By Himself! God the Father had been represented by the fire,[64] God the Son had been represented by the blazing torch,[65] and God the Spirit was represented by the oath God had sworn to Abraham.[66] How astounding! What *did* it mean?

The writer to the Hebrews explains, "When God made his promise to Abraham, since there was no one greater for him to swear by, he swore by himself."[67] The incredible fact that Abraham did not enter into the contract meant that there was nothing he would ever do, nothing he would ever fail to do, nothing he could ever do, nothing he could ever fail to do . . . There was *nothing* that could or would ever, *ever* break the covenant! The validity and fulfillment of it depended upon God, and God alone. All that was required of Abraham was that he receive it.

So, in answer to Abraham's earlier question, "How can I know that I will gain possession of it?" (15:8), it was as though God said, "Abraham, this is how you will know I will keep My Word and fulfill My promises to you. Because I swear by Myself and all that I am to uphold My Word. You can trust Me because I say so. I'm committed to you."

Could it really be that simple? Could it be that I don't have to *do* anything . . . because He has done it all?

> Can I know for sure God has accepted my obedient faith?
> Can I know for sure He has forgiven me of my sin?
> Can I know He has placed His Holy Spirit within me?

Can I know He has given me eternal life?

Can I know He is even now preparing a heavenly home for me?

Yes! Yes! Yes! Yes! I can know for sure … and so can you!

Because Abraham's God is our God. And He says so.

Your hope is secure because God has made a new covenant with you. The sacrifice was not made with pieces of birds and animals but with the broken body and the shed blood of His own dear Son.

At the cross, God swore by Himself that He's committed to you. There is nothing you will ever do, nothing you will ever fail to do, nothing you could ever do, nothing you could ever fail to do … There is nothing that can or will ever, *ever*, *Ever* break the covenant. You didn't do anything to earn it, and you can't do anything to lose it. All you have to do is receive it by trusting everything completely to Him.

And if He has not withheld His only Son from you, will He not also freely give you all things?[68] Just trust Him … *Trust Him* … *Trust everything completely to Him!*

Enter into the covenant with Him by just receiving it.

     Trust Him!

He has signed the covenant with His own blood!

     Trust Him!

Climb into the wheelbarrow!

     Trust Him!

Put down the full weight of your faith on His Word!

     Trust Him!

Trust Him completely … *because He says so!*

                    And who *is He*? He is the God of Abraham!

∽ FOUR ∾

Pursue Everything Patiently

Genesis 16 – 17

Emperor moths have fascinated me ever since I first read about them in one of my favorite childhood storybooks.[1] The male has a wingspan of almost two and a half inches, while the female's is three and a half inches across. They are brown but edged in white, with orange inner, or hind, wings that are stamped with bold black-and-orange eyespots.[2] They are well named eye-catchers because they are unrivaled for their magnificence.

In my devotional reading one morning, I came across the story of a man who had found a flask-shaped cocoon still inhabited by the pupa of an emperor moth. It was hanging delicately in the heather of the moor surrounding his home. He picked it up and brought it inside his house to study it more carefully. He was intrigued by the cocoon's peculiar fibrous construction that had an exceedingly narrow opening at the neck of the flask ... much too narrow, he surmised, for the large insect to exit through.

As he examined it, he was startled to see the cocoon move, and he realized that the imprisoned moth had begun its very first efforts to escape. His attention was riveted from early morning to midday as he watched the insect's intense struggle to get out of its confinement. He noted that as desperately as the moth seemed to wrestle with its cottonlike binding, it never could get beyond a certain point.

As the man considered what could be wrong, it occurred to him that the dryness of the air in his house had probably robbed the cocoon of any elasticity, making the confining threads of fiber stronger and therefore resistant to the moth's valiant efforts. With compassionate, meticulous care, he picked up his scissors and carefully snipped the remaining threads of the cocoon to allow the moth to crawl out easily. It quickly did. In great anticipation of witnessing the miraculous transformation that should have come next, the man strained to see the glorious expansion of the wings, the explosion of color, and the development of the dramatic markings. What he actually saw was a huge swollen body with small shriveled wings that had markings in stunted miniature. Instead of flying through the air as one of the most beautiful insects in the world, the deformed creature crawled painfully around in a very abbreviated span of aborted life.

Although the man did not know it at the time, the laborious effort that an emperor moth exerts as it exits its cocoon is the very means of forcing the life-giving and life-strengthening fluids into the wings, enabling them to expand and the moth to fly. Making the exit easier had not been a favor to the insect ... it had proved to be its ruin.[3]

Like the man waiting for the emperor moth, sometimes it can be very hard for us to wait on God to do things in His time and in His way. It doesn't occur to us that He has intentionally delayed answering our prayer or fulfilling His promise because He has a higher, greater purpose in mind than just giving us what we want, when we want it, the way we want it. Delay doesn't necessarily mean denial. It's just that God often uses the delay to develop our faith in Him as we struggle to patiently pursue everything He has for us.

God sometimes seems to be *soooooo* slow! And we can become so impatient that we run ahead of Him, thinking we can either help Him answer our prayer or force Him to act on our timetable. If we don't learn to walk alongside Him at His pace, we end up making a mess. This life lesson is reinforced as we watch Abraham make the mother of all messes!

Running Ahead

Abraham ran ahead of God's timetable, and the resulting fallout is something that still impacts our world today as we try to manage the conflict between Arab and Jew, Palestinian and Israeli. Running ahead of God is very serious business.

If you and I grow impatient and run ahead of Him, we may become entangled in consequences that bind and complicate our own lives and damage the lives of others to an almost unbearable degree.

Running Ahead of God's Word

After God promised Abraham that he would have a son from his own body, expectation must have reached a fever pitch in his household. Although Abraham was eighty-five years old and Sarah was seventy-five, they were not resigned to being childless. God's promise must have reawakened old wounds as well as their intense longing for a baby until they felt they could not wait one more day.

Reading carefully and imaginatively between the lines, I detect a small tinge of bitterness in Sarah's years of barrenness: "Now Sarai, Abram's wife, had borne him no children" (Genesis 16:1). Not only did she feel the pain of an empty womb and the agonizing monthly disappointment of knowing she was not pregnant, but for years she must have watched the lines of sorrow deepen in Abraham's face. Surely she had seen how his eyes had lingered on the servants' children and how his hands had eagerly reached for their tiny ones and how his expression had revealed an unbearable ache as he released them back to their own parents. His pain would have increased hers many times over.

I could almost hear Abraham telling Sarah about the detailed confirmation of God's promise, that he would indeed have an heir, one that would be a son from his own body. I wondered if he told her one night as they were walking among the tents and he looked up into the star-studded sky. Did he stop, take Sarah in his arms, and tell her of his renewed faith? Did she see the fire of living hope in his eyes ... and become even more desperate to see his dreams come true? The Bible indicates that Sarah did not for one moment believe God's promise, at least not if it involved her in any physical way.[4] It seems she had concluded that there must be another way for God's promise to be fulfilled. Her personal, firsthand knowledge of God was too small, and therefore it seemed to limit her understanding of what He could do.

One day as she managed her household and organized the servants, did Sarah do a double take as she interacted with a young girl she had brought back from Egypt? Scrutinizing the girl carefully, Sarah must have been impressed with her strength, vitality, and beauty. Then, did something she had heard her Canaanite neighbors gossiping about come to her mind? I wonder if they had remarked that it was an acceptable practice to everyone in that day, when for some reason a woman could not conceive, to use another woman to bear a child for her.[5] Maybe they called it surrogate motherhood! However it occurred to her, Sarah suddenly knew she had the perfect solution.

What has God promised you that you desperately want — *right now*? a spouse? a job? a house? a ministry? an opportunity? an inheritance? good health? physical healing? reconciliation? respect? the return of a prodigal? the salvation of a friend or a loved one? a baby?

When you pray, have you used your imagination to tell God how to fulfill His promise and answer your desperate plea? Instead of waiting on Him, are you running ahead by manipulating what He has said to fit into your timetable or desires? Since you know what He has promised, do you feel you are justified in helping Him out?

Sarah seems so much like you and me. She must have thought God needed her help when "she said to Abram, 'The LORD has kept me from having children. Go, sleep with my maidservant; perhaps I can build a family through her'" (16:2). In other words, "Abraham, I believe God has told you that you are to have a child from your own body. But this is the same God who has made me barren. So I know He doesn't mean that I will be the mother. I've been thinking a lot about this. I think God has already provided the solution. Do you remember? When we were in Egypt, Pharaoh gave me one of his finest young servant girls. We brought her back with us. Her name is Hagar. And, Abraham, I think she would be the perfect choice as the bearer of the child God has promised you."

If Sarah had thrown cold water in his face, I'm sure Abraham couldn't have been more shocked! I know he must have looked at Sarah in utter astonishment at such a suggestion! He had been faithful to her during their entire marriage. How could she have even entertained such a thought? And Abraham surely knew God's creation principles for marriage that had been stated at the beginning of human history.[6] God's Word was clear. Marriage was an institution God had established between one man and one woman for life.[7] And God never contradicts Himself. While God had never said that Sarah would be the mother of his child, Abraham should have known she would be. God would never have given Abraham the promised child through Hagar when he was married to Sarah.

But the seed of thought had been sown in Abraham's mind. How long did it take before "Abram agreed to what Sarai said" (16:2)? I can almost hear the wheels of his thoughts turning as he began to open his mind to her suggestion, perhaps rationalizing, *Maybe I've been waiting on God for ten years while He's been waiting on me! How foolish I've been! Of course! God helps those who help themselves! And God is very practical. If He made Sarah barren, then it stands to reason He knows an heir from my own body will have to come through another woman. And Sarah has said it's okay with her if I decide to have a child in this way …*

Did Abraham think that Sarah … or anyone else … could give him permission *to sin*? Do *you*?

Recently my two daughters, their husbands, and my three little granddaughters came to my house for Sunday lunch. As I was clearing the table and preparing to serve the dessert of homemade apple pie and ice cream, the six-year-old slipped up beside me and asked, "Mimi, can we make tents in the sunroom?"

With my hands full of pie and dessert dishes, I replied, "No, not right now."

Then, as I served those still seated at the table, I heard a loud crash, then a wail. I ran into the sunroom to find my three-foot-tall Chinese vase in a hundred pieces on the floor with the four-year-old sobbing in the midst of all the brokenness.

I put my arms around little Sophia and told her not to cry, that it was just a vase and I was glad she wasn't hurt. But the wailing turned to stereo surround-sound as six-year-old Bell began to cry too as though her heart would break. With tears splashing down her cheeks, she confessed that she had told her little sister to go ahead and build the tent even though I had said no. As Sophia built the tent Bell had been told not to build, she had knocked over the vase. Bell had given her little sister permission to sin, and now the shattered pieces and the shame were the painful consequences.

As my son-in-law swept up the brokenness, he asked if I wanted to save the pieces. I just rolled my eyes and said, "That's impossible! What a mess! There's no hope of ever putting the pieces back together again."

He nodded because it was obvious I was right. Standing there, looking at those blue-and-white pieces of porcelain, I couldn't help but think not of a six-year-old's impatience and disobedience or a four-year-old's mistake as she accepted her sister's permission to disobey me, but of Abraham and the fact that human nature really hasn't changed in over four thousand years.

So let me ask you again. Whose permission to sin have you accepted? Do you think that . . .

> if your pastor says it's okay because God just wants you to be happy,
> if your doctor says it's okay because it's the only way you can relax,
> if your spouse says it's okay because you both need the extra income,
> if your friend says it's okay because everyone else is doing it,
> if your attorney says it's okay because you can get by with it,
> if your boss says it's okay because it will generate sales,

. . . then it's okay?

In what way has your impatience led you to rationalize and run ahead of God's Word? Deep down, are you a little uneasy about what you are getting ready to do — or have already done? I think Abraham was.

I can find no record that Abraham prayed about this major decision. No record that he heard from the Word of the Lord. Over his past ten years, he had cried out to the Lord many times and had heard God's Word in response. His failing to seek God in this critical situation gives the impression that he was turning away from the Lord. Maybe he didn't pray about it because he knew what God would say, and it wasn't what he wanted to hear. Or maybe he was just too impatient. Or maybe he was hoping that God would let him get by with this one sin . . . just this one time.

Have you prayed about your decision or course of action? No? *Why not?* Is it because you're afraid of what God will say to you? Do you think if you go ahead with what you want to do and it doesn't work out that you can then plead ignorance and complain, "But God, You never told me not to"? You and I need to be very careful not to run ahead of God's Word, or we will always lack the assurance that we are in God's will.

Running Ahead of God's Will

Do you sincerely want to do God's will, but you just don't know how to find it? Have you prayed and read your Bible, but you're still at a loss as to what God wants you to do? Since God expects you and me to live in obedience to His will, He will not hide it from us. But He does expect us to prayerfully seek it.

Over the years, I have used four principles that I call the "runway lights" to help me seek the will of God. Literal runway lights are used to help a pilot guide a plane to a safe landing. As the pilot attempts to land at night or in the fog when visibility is impaired, he or she knows the runway is lined with lights. If the pilot keeps the plane in line with those lights as it descends, the plane will land safely in the center of the runway.[8]

The four "runway lights," or principles,[9] I use to help guide me into the center of God's will when making a decision are (but not necessarily in this order):

- Practical circumstances
- The counsel of mature, godly people
- Inner conviction
- The confirmation of God's Word

While spiritual "formulas" can sometimes be binding and legalistic, this one has worked for me so many times, with successful results, that I have used it again and again when seeking God's will.

One of the most important ministry decisions I made came after I had participated in women's conferences for about a dozen years. I had become increasingly frustrated with the programs being offered. Many of the sessions seemed to be primarily experiential or emotional or entertaining. I became strongly convinced that women *wanted* to go deeper into real discipleship, but the programs they were being offered were being constantly "dumbed down."

My feelings became a heavy burden, and my first runway light of inner conviction was lit. While pouring out my heart in prayer, God seemed to call me to offer arena-size events for women myself, events whose sole purpose would be to focus on Jesus through messages and music and prayer and Bible study, so that each one attending would have a fresh encounter with Him. But each attempt to follow through in obedience over a two-year period ended in failure. The second runway light of practical circumstances just didn't seem to line up.

One evening while wrestling with the Lord in prayer, I asked God to either release me from the burden or open the door one more time. I specifically prayed, "Lord, if You want me to attempt this one more time, have my friend Ann call me by 6:30 this evening." Ann was the only woman I knew who had ever put on an arena event — but I hadn't spoken with her in over a year.

At 6:29 that evening, the phone rang. It was Ann! She was on a business trip, alone in a hotel room, when I had come to her mind. She was just calling to "check in" with me. I exclaimed, "Ann, you're almost late!" Then I explained that her phone call was a dramatic answer to my specific prayer, giving me one more runway light as I sought God's will.

The next morning I arose early with the decision weighing heavily on my heart. As I earnestly prayed, I referred to Peter in the boat on the Sea of Galilee during the storm. When he saw Jesus walking toward him on the water, Peter cried out, "Lord, if it's you ... tell me to come to you on the water."[10] Like Peter, I told the Lord I was willing to get out of the "boat," to leave my comfort zone of ministry and start arena events for women, but I needed Him to tell me, as He told Peter, to "Come." Walking on water is not just hard, it's impossible. I knew if I attempted to start this new phase of ministry without His express command to do so, I would not only fail, I would lose my credibility and drag a lot of people down with me.

My devotional reading always includes the *Daily Light*, and in that day's reading was a verse that led me to Matthew 14:29. As I read it, the invitation from Jesus to Peter leaped up off the page as though it had my name on it: *Anne, come.* I knew God was calling me to start what are now known as "Just Give Me Jesus" life-changing revivals for women. I knew I had the confirmation of God's Word. Once I had His Word, my beloved, godly counselors wholeheartedly supported me in stepping out in faith to begin these revivals.

This time, as I followed through in obedience, the practical circumstances fell into place, beginning with a young woman who had directed other arena events and who offered to do the same for me. Almost simultaneously, my friend Ann offered to chair the first revival and raise the money for it, and that wonderful gesture enabled me to get started.

I have now held more than thirty revivals in twelve countries, with tens of thousands of women experiencing a fresh encounter with Jesus and thousands of lives being changed forever. I know I am in the center of God's will as it involves "Just Give Me Jesus" revivals.[11]

Abraham had three out of four runway lights lined up for his decision to have a child by Hagar. His inner conviction was very strong: he *wanted* a child. The counsel of his godly wife Sarah supported the decision. Practical circumstances seemed to line up when Hagar was available. *But ...* he didn't have God's Word.

I have made decisions based on three out of the four principles, but one of them has always been God's Word. For example, I have made decisions without the counsel of my godly friends because there have been times when I felt they resisted supporting my decision out of personal concern for my well-being. Or I have made the decision without practical circumstances, believing that after I took the first step, things would open up. And sometimes my inner conviction does not surface to my conscious awareness until I have God's Word. But I have never made an important decision involving my family or my ministry without God's Word to direct me.

What decision are you struggling with right now? Who to marry? Where to live? What school to attend? What job to take? What doctor to see? What treatment to start? What house to buy? What move to make?

Seek God's will by lining up your runway lights. King David testified that God "guides the humble in what is right and teaches them his way."[12] If you seek God's guidance with an open mind, humbly willing to do whatever He says, He will teach you the right way to go and "land" you safely in the center of His will. That's His promise. On the other hand, if you seek God's will halfheartedly, as though you're just looking for a second opinion or you're curious as to what He might say, He will remain silent.

For whatever reason, Abraham did not seek God's will. It seemed to me he was willing to risk settling for less than God's best because he wanted what he wanted when he wanted it. He refused to pursue patiently everything that God wanted to give him. Maybe he rationalized his sin by thinking he would just sleep with Hagar once. If she conceived, then his course of action must be of God. If she didn't, then no harm was done since Sarah had given her permission, and he would continue to wait on God. "So after Abram had been living in Canaan ten years, Sarai his wife took her Egyptian maidservant Hagar and gave her to her husband to be his wife" (16:3).

Are you so tired of waiting for what God has promised you that you are also willing to take the risk of settling for less than His best? Are you willing to settle for ... any spouse, any job, any companion, any recognition, any promotion, any influence, any opportunity, any happiness, any relief ... just *anything* if you can have it without waiting one more day?

Running Ahead of God's Way

What are you doing to speed things up so you can have your way?

Recently, I found myself convinced that a loved one was making a wrong choice. Twice I had given my opinion, and twice it had fallen on seemingly deaf ears. Then God seemed to say, Anne, *"in quietness and trust is your strength."*[13] In other words, *Anne, be quiet and trust Me.*

But being quiet can be *so hard*! I felt if I could just say one more thing, I could convince the person. I didn't want to be disobedient to the Lord, so I told a third person to tell my loved one what I wanted to say. Thank God that I immediately felt His rebuke and revoked my appeal before the message could be delivered. My loved one eventually did make the decision I felt was right, but I've often wondered what would have happened if I had said one more thing. Would his heart have hardened, delaying the decision even longer?

Like me and many others, Abraham was impatient; he refused to wait one more day. In what I assume was a one-night encounter, "He slept with Hagar, and she conceived" (16:4). How long was it before Abraham knew the results of his decision? Was it a month? Six weeks? Three months? Was he riddled with guilt, tossing and turning at night in his bed, unable to shake that queasy feeling in the pit of his stomach as he wondered, *What if this was not what God had in mind?*

Actually, having a child by Hagar was not at all what God had promised. Abraham was trying to accomplish God's will and produce an heir through his own self-effort, not in God's way. He was running full speed ahead.

Soon Abraham's fears must have been eclipsed by his excitement in knowing that Hagar was carrying his child. News must have spread quickly, and surely there was celebration in the tents of Abraham and Sarah. They were going to have a child, at long last! The queasy feeling, the sleepless nights, the guilt-ridden conscience were things of the past! He must have thought he'd gotten by with his impatience because, obviously, God had blessed him! He was going to be a father after all!

What has made you think you've also gotten by with your impatience and disobedience? That peace of mind can be very short-lived, can't it?

For what must have been several weeks, or even months, everyone seemed to benefit in Abraham's home. As the one who carried the baby, Hagar must have been greatly elevated in her position within the household. I can see her moving into a more luxurious tent closer to Abraham and Sarah's tent. Surely she was treated with a new respect by her peers and enjoyed new acceptance among Abraham's associates.

But then … a change in her attitude? Did she begin to demand special treatment? Did she ask for servants to bring her breakfast in bed, and to fan her in the noonday heat, and to draw her bath at night? The initial happiness that may have occurred at the announcement of her pregnancy was very short-lived, because "when she knew she was pregnant, she began to despise her mistress" (16:4). In her secular, self-centered mind, she believed her ability to conceive made her somehow better than Sarah. That's when Abraham's home life began to unravel. That's when I could hear the echo of the porcelain vase hitting the brick floor, shattering into broken pieces that we're still trying to sweep up today.

Sarah responded to Hagar's arrogance with anger, and she lashed out at Abraham with totally illogical reasoning: "You are responsible for the wrong I am suffering. I put my servant in your arms, and now that she knows she is pregnant, she despises me. May the LORD judge between you and me" (16:5). Once again as I listened carefully, underneath Sarah's anger at anyone and everyone, I could hear the anguished cry of a woman who knew it was all her fault.

And Abraham — who had hunted down and defeated the world-class army of the eastern kings who had captured Lot — wilted in the face of his wife's wrath. I can see him throwing up his hands in exasperation as he abdicated his leadership responsibility in the home, replying, "Your servant is in your hands.… Do with her whatever you think best" (16:6). After all, how could he tell Sarah the right thing to do when he had been so wrong himself? So he just walked away, and "then Sarai mistreated Hagar; so she fled from her" (16:6).

Sarah, the princess, the adored wife of the man who was embracing the magnificent obsession, mistreated Hagar, a pregnant Egyptian servant girl.

Have you been mistreated? By whom? By the spouse of a church leader? By someone who called himself by God's name? Did he or she claim to be a Christian? If so, your pain is probably intensified because along with it you feel condemned and disapproved of … by God.

Recently, my husband, Danny, experienced inexcusable treatment at the hands of church leaders who called themselves Christians. After four years of meeting with a group of men to pray regularly for God's leadership and blessing, he joined them as they incorporated into a church body. We were part of the new church fellowship for several years, during which time he served in a leadership role as Sunday school teacher and elder.

During that time, he was dismayed as he witnessed what all too often takes place behind the closed doors of religious institutions — hypocrisy and piety, politics and pride, manipulation and meanness, control and cliques, self-promotion and status-seeking, truth-spinning and arm-twisting. His heart was shattered — and mine along with his.

While the people who attended the church were very dear, good people, they were prevented from knowing what was taking place behind those closed doors. What Danny saw and heard was so grievous, he exclaimed that if he didn't know God, he wouldn't want to know Him, and if the leadership in that church represented genuine believers, he would never want to be one.

Finally, he walked out with the young pastor the elders had humiliated and sought to drive away.[14] For one year as a result of his experience, he and I did not attend any church.

I was heartbroken. I wrote a letter to each of the other elders at the church explaining our position and asking for reconciliation. I never received a response. And so we simply separated ourselves from the congregation. We became believers in exile.[15]

The separation was more painful on my husband than on me because he had invested so much more valuable time and heartfelt energy and focused prayer in the formation of the church than I had. But the interesting discovery that I made during that time was that rather than hinder the magnificent obsession in my life, the experience actually intensified it. More than ever before, I wanted to embrace a genuine God-filled life. And I wanted to know Him for Himself, not for the tarnished reflection that can sometimes be seen in those who call themselves by His name.

RUNNING AWAY

When Hagar fled from Sarah, she also ran away from God's people. She was an unwilling victim, a servant who had to do what Abraham and Sarah told her to do. When suddenly her world turned upside down, she must have thought, *I'm not going to stay around and take this. The pagans back in Egypt treated me better than these so-called godly people. I'll just go back to Egypt.* So Hagar, carrying

Abraham's unborn child, ran away — away from God's people and God's presence and God's promises and back to pagan gods and spiritual darkness.

Who are you running away from? a parent or a partner? a lawyer or a lover? a priest or a professor? a spouse or a sibling? a doctor or a dealer? an employee or an employer? a roommate or a relative? a neighbor or an investor? a banker or a broker?

Whoever you're running from, don't blame God for others' behavior. I understand the desperate desire to run from *them*, but not from *Him*.

Maybe it's not a *who* you're running from, but a *what*: a memory or a marriage, a demand or a divorce, a problem or a pressure, a diagnosis or a death, a responsibility or an opportunity, a friend or a failure, a church or a career, a business or a _____. You fill in the blank.

Running away never really solves anything. It just delays dealing with whatever or whomever you are running from.

But no matter where you are, no matter how far you've run, remember this: God is so good! From the very beginning of human history, He has revealed Himself to be the One who seeks us until He finds us. At the dawn of time, when Adam and Eve disobeyed Him, then ran away to hide in the bushes, He patiently and persistently sought them out. In His loving-kindness, He refused to leave them forever cowering in their fig leaves and sin.[16]

God Seeks You

The story of Hagar's flight is riveting. As her sandaled feet moved swiftly over the rough, rocky terrain that emptied into an endless desert, she must have felt lonely and confused and terrified and angry. Her heart must have been beating out of her chest when "the angel of the LORD found Hagar near a spring in the desert" (16:7). Scholars agree that when the "angel of the LORD" appeared in the Old Testament, it was a "theophany," an appearance of the pre-incarnate Son of God — Jesus before Bethlehem.[17]

This is the first time we encounter Him in Scripture, right here, at "the spring that is beside the road to Shur" (16:7), revealing Himself to a woman, not a man; to an Egyptian, not a descendant of Abraham; to a sinner, not a saint; to a slave, not a king. What an undeserved, gracious intervention of the Creator in Hagar's wretched, pitiful, sin-soaked life. He sought her … and He found her.

Why did God intervene? Why didn't He just let Hagar run away and keep on running until she was totally removed from Abraham's life? Or let her die in the desert, or have an untimely miscarriage, or return to Egypt where she would never have been heard from again? If He had done so, it would have seemed to solve a lot of practical problems in Abraham's household. But God did intervene because, while He had chosen Abraham as the one through whom He would bless the world, Hagar represented the world that He wanted to bless. *God loved Hagar as much as He loved Abraham!*

God loves you, and God loves me, and God so loves the whole world that He sent the Angel of the Lord — Jesus Christ — to seek those who are separated from Him and on the run. Today the Angel of the Lord is no longer pre-incarnate, but post-incarnate. He is Abraham's ultimate promised Seed, the unique Son of God, who left His throne in heaven and came down into the world "to seek and to save what was lost."[18] He finds us on the desert road ... the place of emptiness and spiritual dryness, running away from our hurt and pain and grief and anger into the nothingness and helplessness and hopelessness of a world in rebellion and separated from Him by sin.

Are you someone who is on the desert road of despair, running away to anything or anywhere as long as it's not where you've been? My prayer is that the Spirit of the same Angel of the Lord, who sought and found Hagar, will use this book to open your eyes to His presence and open your ears to His voice.

God Speaks to You

As Hagar knelt to get a refreshing drink from the spring, did she hear a sound that was more beautiful than the sound of the gurgling water, clearer than the sound of a singing bird, softer than the sound of the desert wind, gentler than the sound of her own mother's voice? I wonder if Hagar's eyes were so blinded by the dust mingled with her tears that it took a moment for her to focus. When she did, she must have seen a rather shadowy, mysterious figure gazing at her with a compassion that reached back from before the foundations of the world were laid, and reached ahead all the way to the cross, and reached up all the way to heaven, and reached down to her right there on the desert road that led to Egypt.[19]

Then, as she strained to hear every word, she heard Him ask, "Hagar, servant of Sarai, where have you come from, and where are you going?" (16:8). He knew her name! He knew who she was! And He cared enough to get involved in her life, saying, in effect, "Hagar, will you talk with Me for a moment about what you're doing and where you belong? You're Sarah's servant. Don't you think you belong with her? Are you sure this is what you want to do with your life and where you want to go? Is this really wise? Will this course of action make you happy? Hagar, let's think this through carefully, together."

When have you talked to the Lord about where you've been and where you're going, about what you're doing and who you belong to, about how you're feeling?

God already knows all the answers. He just wants you to talk things over with Him. Have you? As you've prayed, have you been complaining that you're just a victim? That you're not responsible for what happens? That the mess you're in is someone else's fault? Hagar was disarmingly honest and admitted exactly what she was doing. She told the Angel, "I'm running away from my mistress Sarai" (16:8).

The Bible doesn't give us the details, but I can't help but wonder if Hagar also told Him what had happened ... how she was given by Pharaoh to Abraham and Sarah as though she were subhuman, a prize horse or cow ... how frightened and alone she had been when she left the familiar surroundings of Egyptian culture and found herself in the Canaanite wilderness ... how she had tried her best to please Sarah and fit into her new life ... how unfair it was that she would never have her own husband and her own family and her own children ... how Sarah had come to her and commanded her to sleep with Abraham ... how she had been robbed of her innocence ... how surreal it had been to discover she was carrying Abraham's baby ... how she had taken advantage of the situation knowing she was carrying the old man's treasured possession ... how she felt they owed her after all that had been done to her ... how she had despised and rebelled against Sarah's authority and superiority that had forced her into motherhood before she was a wife ... how Abraham, after sleeping with her and impregnating her, had shown such indifference to her that he just looked the other way when Sarah abused her ... how Sarah had stripped her of her privileges and slapped her and sent her back to the servants' quarters.

Did Hagar choke on her sobs, her breath coming in ragged gasps as she poured out her heart to Him? And did He put His arms around her, pull her head onto His chest, stroke her hair, and just hold her close to His heart for a few moments until her sobs grew quieter and her breathing more regular? Then did He gently whisper as He instructed, "Go back to your mistress and submit to her. ... I will so increase your descendants that they will be too numerous to count" (16:9 – 10)? In other words, "Hagar, the only way to resolve this entire mess is to repent of your sin. Turn around. Go back. If you do, I will immeasurably bless you, your son, your grandchildren, and future generations. I will give you an honored place in history, Hagar. Pursue patiently everything that I want to give you and your unborn child by doing the right thing and submitting to Sarah."

God Sends You Back

Do you really want to resolve the mess you're running away from? Do you want God's blessing to fall on you and your family? your business? your church? your school? your town and city and state and nation? The first step is to turn around in your attitude of pride and rebellion, reverse the direction of your self-will, submit to God's authority wherever He places you, and pursue with patience all that He has for you.

But turning around is so hard to do, isn't it? It's painful to turn around, to confront the past, to change your perspective, to die to your pride, to acknowledge your part, to deny your pleasure, to face the person, to take your punishment, to pay the price for your own shortcomings and confess your own sin while leaving the other person to God.

But I can almost hear the applause of heaven as those who have gone before encourage and challenge us: "Repent, then, and turn to God, so that your sins may be wiped out, that times of refreshing may come from the Lord, and that he may send the Christ, who has been appointed for you — even Jesus."[20]

The pathway to blessing,
the doorway to happiness,
the roadway to freedom,
the gateway to joy ...
is repentance!

Turn around! *Turn around!*

Hagar turned around, not petulantly or reluctantly or hesitatingly, but with the joy of knowing she herself — not just Abraham, but a little Egyptian servant girl — *she herself* had a personal relationship with the living God, the Creator of the universe! I can almost see her clasping her hands to her chest, eyes wide with wonder, as she exclaimed, "You are the God who sees me,... I have now seen the One who sees me" (16:13).

As Hagar slipped back into Abraham's household that night, ignoring the stares of the other servants and the glare of her mistress, was there a purpose to her steps and a light in her eyes and a glow on her face and a smile on her lips and a peace in her heart? Did she look past the stars in the sky that were not as numerous as her descendants would be and whisper to herself, "He sees me. He sees me! God sees me ... and I have seen Him!"?

I can only imagine the look on Sarah's face when Hagar returned! It would have been a quite different expression than the glowering, contorted rage that had disfigured it when Hagar was abused, or the gloating, smug look when told that Hagar had run away. Consternation. Anger. Guilt. Misery. But I wonder if Sarah also slowly turned around and did some soul-searching and heart-cleansing of her own. For the next twenty years or so, Sarah would be faced with the consequence of her sin every day, because a few months later, "Hagar bore Abram a son" (16:15).[21]

My children are now grown. But from time to time, I have seen the consequences of my sin and failure and mothering mistakes causing them to suffer. Whenever I see evidence of my failure in them, I bow my head and thank God that He is the One who sees me, the One who loves me, and the One who "in all things ... works for the good of those who love him."[22]

What consequences of sin from the past are you living with at present? Does your child today have an eating disorder due to your neglect ...

in the past?

Has your company declared bankruptcy because of your lies and deception ...

in the past?

Has your child recently married into a family that you treated rudely ...

in the past?

Has your spouse filed for divorce because of your unfaithfulness ...

in the past?

Are you struggling with cancer because of an unhealthy habit ...

in the past?

Would you take a moment now to thank God that He is the One who sees you, the One who loves you, and the One who "in all things ... works for the good of those who love him."[23] *All things!* Including past things, the consequences of which are your own fault!

I don't know how Abraham reacted when he discovered that not only had Sarah mistreated Hagar, but Hagar had run away, taking his unborn child with her. I've wondered if he went out under the big oak tree and cried out to God, "Have mercy on me, O God, according to your unfailing love; according to your great compassion blot out my transgressions. Wash away all my iniquity and cleanse me from my sin. For I know my transgressions, and my sin is always before me. Against you, you only, have I sinned and done what is evil in your sight."[24]

Then I wonder if he added, "Please, God, protect Hagar and my child. Don't let my sin cost the life of my child. Bring Hagar and the unborn baby safely back here." Abraham must have prayed, because the answer to his prayer is wrapped up in the name he gave to Hagar's baby boy: "Abram gave the name Ishmael to the son she had borne" (16:15). The name "Ishmael" means "God hears."[25]

God heard Hagar's cry of confession on the desert road. And God heard what must have been Sarah's angry protests and Abraham's anguished plea.

But they did not hear from God for the next thirteen years ...

RUNNING ALONE

There is no loneliness like the loneliness when God is silent. We are told that "Abram was eighty-six years old when Hagar bore him Ishmael" (16:16). Thirteen years later, "when Abram was ninety-nine years old, the LORD appeared to him" (17:1).

> Thirteen years with no awareness of God's presence in his life.
> Thirteen years that had no eternal significance.
> Thirteen years that were wasted.
> Thirteen years to reflect on his impatience.
> Thirteen years of settling for less than everything God had wanted
>   to give him.
> Thirteen years that must have seemed like a lifetime.
> Thirteen years of running alone.

I wonder what Abraham thought during those years that were a biblical blank. Did he constantly berate himself for his impatience with the if onlys?

If only Sarah hadn't suggested I have a child with Hagar.

If only her suggestion had not come right after God had promised me an heir from my own body; the timing made the temptation irresistible.

If only I hadn't become so impatient with God's timing.

If only I hadn't given in to my desire for a child.

If only Hagar had not been available.

If only we had never brought her back from Egypt.

If only I had never gone to Egypt in the first place ...

Have you ever had an attack of the if onlys? They can send you into a downward spiral of depression as they seem to extend way, way back in your life, can't they? There have been dreadful times in my life when I have curled up in a fetal position and sobbed into my pillow ... *if only*! I've had to take all of those painful regrets to the foot of the cross and leave them there, lay myself down in God's grace, and plead for His mercy to break the emotional and spiritual paralysis *if onlys* can cause.

Added to the misery of the *if onlys*, I've wondered if Abraham felt hopeless, thinking he had forfeited God's promises because he had stepped out of God's will for just one night with Hagar. Did he conclude that since he would never have the son God had promised him, he would just settle for a compromise in Ishmael? At night, did he keep his eyes focused on the ground, afraid that the very stars in the sky would remind him of what he had missed?

Did it take thirteen long years to bring Abraham to the place where he was ready to honestly and fully admit his failure? Did it take thirteen years for him to acknowledge he would never be satisfied with anything less than everything God wanted to give him? Did it take thirteen years for Abraham to once again fall in step with God and run alongside Him?

RUNNING ALONGSIDE

What would it have been like to be Abraham? A person who had failed miserably because he wasn't willing to pursue everything *patiently*? What would it have been like to live with the hollow emptiness of a life that would never be satisfied, of a goal that would never be achieved, of a potential that would never be realized, of a promise that would never be fulfilled?

Do you think because of past sins that you can never claim God's best? That you have no choice but to settle for less than everything God wants to give you? Then be encouraged! Praise God! He is the God of second chances ... and third ... and fourth. Who knows? Maybe Abraham's thirteen-year wait was part of God's process, not to punish him, but to restore him.

Offered the Chance to Begin Again

The apostle Peter was also someone who had failed miserably and needed restoring on the inside. Similar to Abraham, he had made an impulsive mistake. Jesus had warned Peter that he would deny Him, and Peter had vehemently protested that the other disciples might do such a wicked thing, but that he would die first.[26]

But as the sun came up, Peter denied Jesus three times.[27] And then, before Peter's horrified eyes, he saw Jesus tortured, tried, crucified, and buried. There was no opportunity to make it right, to say he was sorry. To Peter, the three days between Friday, when Jesus was crucified, and Sunday, when He was raised from the dead, must have seemed like Abraham's thirteen years. It must have seemed like a lifetime of silence and stillness and soul-searching struggle with the if onlys.

But the silence was dramatically shattered forever on that Sunday morning when Jesus was raised from the dead! Later that same day, Jesus appeared to Peter along with the other disciples in the upper room.[28] But I wonder if Peter hung back, his shame of denial clouding his joy.

Jesus understood. Later He met with Peter beside the Sea of Galilee to heal Peter's spirit. He gave Peter the opportunity to confess his love three times to replace the crippling memory of the three denials, then Jesus recommissioned him for service. And Peter was restored!

His joy still permeated his life years later when he testified, "Praise be to the God and Father of our Lord Jesus Christ! In his great mercy he has given us new birth into a living hope through the resurrection of Jesus Christ from the dead."[29] Peter knew the living hope of a second chance! He knew that failure does not have to be final.

If you have failed like Peter did and like Abraham did, then please, keep reading. Because God shattered the thirteen-year silence: "When Abram was ninety-nine years old, the LORD appeared to him and said, 'I am God Almighty'" (17:1). God's voice must have thundered with mind-gripping, heart-stopping volume that rumbled across the open spaces, reverberating throughout Abraham's tent and permeating his past, present, and future as He identified Himself as One who is sufficient.[30] In other words, "Abraham, I AM who I AM. I never change. I am eternally the same. And I am sufficient to meet all your needs. I don't need your help. I can answer your prayers Myself. I am totally sufficient in Myself to keep My promises to you, regardless of how impossible they may seem to you."

God refocused Abraham's faith on Himself. It was as though He gripped Abraham's face in His hands, turned it toward His own, and commanded, "Look at Me!"

Are you afraid to refocus on God's face after failure because you think you will "see" anger or disdain or condemnation or rejection or indifference? Then look again! God loves you! He wants you to know Him, and He is sufficient for your every need.[31] He understands why you failed, and He will pinpoint the reason to help you guard against failing again.

God understood that one reason Abraham failed was that he did not trust God to be sufficient to give him an heir from his own body, through Sarah. So instead of identifying Himself in some other way, He left no doubt in Abraham's mind that He was sufficient to accomplish His will, in His righteous way.

Before Abraham could catch his breath or begin to explain or rationalize or defend his behavior, God continued to speak. What God said next must have sounded to Abraham not like thunder, but like the most thrilling rendition of the "Hallelujah Chorus": "Walk before me and be blameless" (17:1).

What a symphony of grace those words must have been to Abraham's ears! God was speaking to him once again! God was breaking His silence. And even more amazingly, God was offering Abraham the chance to begin again! God was saying, in effect, "Abraham, I want you to *walk*; stop running ahead. And I want you to walk before Me; stop running alone. I want you to be blameless; it's time you grew up in your faith and behaved rightly toward others."

God deeply desired for Abraham to have everything He wanted to give him. He didn't want Abraham to miss out on a thing. After Abraham's impatient behavior, that was *grace*! Then God continued, "I will confirm my covenant between me and you and will greatly increase your numbers" (17:2).

Abraham had not permanently blown it after all! The fulfillment of God's covenant, in the end, didn't depend on Abraham's faithfulness to God, but on God's faithfulness to him! Abraham must have had a flashback to the night when he had seen the torch and the firepot pass through the pieces of sacrifice. Abraham's ears must have echoed with the sound of God swearing by Himself that He was committed to Abraham forever.

Overwhelmed with what surely was reverential fear, humility, and a heart full of gratitude, "Abram fell facedown" (17:3). Prostrate before God, Abraham was silent. There was no argument or discussion or explanation or question or defensive excuse. And Abraham was still. There was no struggle against God's timing or with God's way of doing things. Abraham was fully surrendered in his heart, mind, soul, and body as he lay listening to the voice of God speak to him after thirteen years of silence. As he listened, he heard God change his name from Abram to Abraham, signifying that not only would he have descendants as numerous as the stars of the sky but also that many nations would come from him (see 17:5).

In the silence, God reiterated His promises as though to underscore His authority and sovereignty and sufficiency: "I will make you very fruitful; I will make nations of you.... I will establish my covenant.... the whole land of Canaan ... I will give as an everlasting possession to you and your descendants after you;... I will be their God" (17:6–8). Abraham may have delayed God's will, but he had not, *he could not*, thwart it. And neither can you. And neither can I. God's will *will* be done "on earth as it is in heaven," if for no other reason than it's God's will.[32]

As God confirmed His original covenant with Abraham, He added several details, one of the most important being the outward sign of circumcision: "This is my covenant with you and your descendants after you, the covenant you are to keep: Every male among you shall be circumcised. You are to undergo circumcision, and it will be the sign of the covenant between me and you" (17:10–11).[33]

Before Abraham could fully absorb that astounding detail, God gave another one that was almost more than Abraham could take in. "God also said ..., 'As for Sarai your wife, you are no longer to call her Sarai; her name will be Sarah. I will bless her and will surely give you a son by her'" (17:15).

His reaction to the news that Sarah would bear his child was so genuinely authentic ... he was dumbfounded! Stupefied! With his face pressed against the ground, "he laughed and said to himself, 'Will a son be born to a man a hundred years old? Will Sarah bear a child at the age of ninety?'" (17:17). Or, in other words, "God, You've got to be kidding!"

What God had promised was almost beyond belief, and yet as incredulous as he felt, Abraham *must* have believed because there was no rebuke from God for his laughter, as there was later when Sarah herself laughed after God gave her the same news.[34]

It's encouraging to know that all God required from Abraham was faith the size of a mustard seed to move mountains and do the impossible.[35] Abraham's experience teaches me that the critical issue is to place all the faith I have in the Lord God Almighty. So I don't look at my circumstances, or listen to the opinions of others, or depend on my resources, or trust my feelings. I just plant my feet on His promises in His Word and stand there. What God says is so. You and I and Abraham can count on it!

Perhaps Abraham was emboldened by God's tolerance of his muttered questions to himself, or perhaps he spoke aloud before he even had time to think. Amazingly, Abraham blurted out a concern that flowed straight from his father-heart: "If only Ishmael might live under your blessing!" (17:18).

It is heart-wrenching to hear Abraham's love for Ishmael. Even though Ishmael had been conceived in sin, even though he was the fruit of Abraham's impatience and self-will, even though he was a symbol of the huge complicated mess Abraham had made, even though he was the first of many broken pieces to come, Abraham still loved him. Ishmael was still his son. And Abraham discovered that the gracious, merciful heart of God was big enough for Ishmael too.

Do you have an "Ishmael"? Who or what is the heart-wrenching consequence of your own sin and failure? Is your Ishmael a child conceived outside of marriage? a divorce? a remarriage following divorce? a partnership established in self-will? something that you impatiently seized for yourself and now know was outside of the will of God, but you are attached to it? If God blessed Abraham's Ishmael, why do you think He will not, or cannot, bless yours? Just ask.

While God promised to bless Hagar's son, He confirmed that the covenant would be established with Sarah's son: "My covenant I will establish with Isaac, whom Sarah will bear to you by this time next year" (17:21). With that final word, God placed all of His "cards" on the table and left. Now it was up to Abraham to decide what to do.

Accepting the Chance to Begin Again

A chance to begin again can involve renewed effort and energy, the retaking of responsibility, some self-denial and sacrifice, and even hardship. Sometimes we are just too tired, too lazy, too discouraged, too disheartened, too hurt, too ashamed, or too depressed to begin again. Sometimes we don't give a second chance a second thought.

Abraham was almost one hundred years old. All of those excuses could have been his. But none of them were! "On that very day Abraham took his son Ishmael and ... every male in his household, and circumcised them, as God told him. Abraham was ninety-nine years old when he was circumcised, and his son Ishmael was thirteen; Abraham and his son Ishmael were both circumcised on that same day. And every male in Abraham's household ... was circumcised with him" (17:23 – 27).

Four times Abraham's obedience was clearly stated. He unhesitatingly, immediately, thoroughly, completely, and totally did everything "as God told him." I have no doubt that his obedience was not easy or comfortable or convenient or pleasant. I'm sure it was not a popular decision in his household — at least not with the male members. But with resolute determination not seen in many men half his age, Abraham put the past behind him.

As the burden of guilt over his failure and the nagging fear of being disqualified for God's blessing rolled away, the agony of circumcision must have brought not only tears of pain but also tears of joy. God was giving him a second chance! Abraham seized the offer to begin again as once more he eagerly and passionately embraced the magnificent obsession.

What about you? Instead of pursuing patiently all that God has for you, have you been ...

running ahead?

running away?

running alone?

Isn't it time you fell in step with God and started running alongside Him?

Would you take this moment to put the past and all of its failures, mistakes, shortcomings, and sin behind you? Take the chance God offers you right now to begin again ... and embrace the magnificent obsession.

⟡ FIVE ⟡

Lift Everything Up

Genesis 18 – 19

The International Conference of Itinerant Evangelists has been held three times, in 1983, 1986, and 2000, always in Amsterdam, the Netherlands. Its purpose has been to encourage, equip, and enable men and women from more than 186 different nations to "do the work of an evangelist."[1] Many of the participants had never been out of their local or tribal area, much less to another country or continent.

Communication at the conference was a challenge of herculean proportions. Each plenary session was simultaneously translated into twenty-six languages. As the delegates entered the main hall of the Rai Center, they picked up a headset, dialed what looked like a radio attached to it, and heard what was being said from the platform in one of the twenty-six languages. But communication on a personal level — discussions involving meals, lodging, trains, and simple directions to various breakout sessions — was daunting.

Before the evangelists arrived in Amsterdam, each had been sent through the mail information regarding practical arrangements. In this packet was a sticker printed with the name of the assigned hotel. Upon arrival at the airport, each participant was met by a conference official. The luggage, with the appropriate sticker attached, was taken ahead to the designated hotel while the evangelist was taken to the conference hall to register.

One evangelist received his packet of information, including the hotel sticker, which was stamped "American" in bold blue letters. He responded respectfully to the organizers, saying that although he knew the conference was sponsored by Americans, he resented being labeled one too. At the conference's registration tables, he handed the workers the packet envelope. Inside was the hotel sticker, torn into four neat pieces. The organizers had given him the correct information — he was assigned to the American Hotel — but they had failed to communicate with him. I wonder if he ever found his luggage once he got to Amsterdam!

Another evangelist arrived at the conference, registered, and then sat down. When he was told by a steward that it was time to get on the bus to be taken to his hotel, he firmly said, "No." Another official came over and said clearly, "Sir, you must go! You have registered, and now it's time for you to leave."

The evangelist began to weep. He held tightly to his chair, shook his head, and said, "No. *No!* I will not leave."

When finally a steward was found who could communicate with the evangelist, he discovered that the evangelist thought that after traveling around the world to get to the conference, he was now being sent home!

Like the evangelists, sometimes I feel that I have all the correct information, yet somehow I'm not communicating with God. As a result I have become more determined to learn how to really pray. I'm not interested in fancy rhetoric, or eloquent oratory, or endless monologues, or mystical languages.

I don't want to engage in hyperventilating, chair-jumping, room-rocking, head-banging, or aisle-dancing theatrics.

And I don't want to adopt one of the religious mantra-chanting, bead-counting, incense-burning, rag-tying rituals.

I just want to talk to God.

I want to talk to Him . . . but not do all the talking.

I want to know that He is listening.

I want to hear what He says back to me . . . and understand what He means by what He says.

I want my prayers to be like reversed thunder.

When I pray, I want to get heaven's attention.

And I want answers to my prayers.

I want to pray like Abraham did . . .

> when he built his altars,
> > when the Lord appeared to him,
> > > when the Word of the Lord came to him.

I want to pray for the salvation of those who are facing God's judgment.

I want my prayers to be clear, completely understood two-way conversations with God, the kind of communication Abraham had with Him.

I want to pray for others like he prayed for Sodom ...

Prayer Believes

Fourteen years after Ishmael was born, and within the same year God had confirmed His covenant, Abraham "was sitting at the entrance to his tent in the heat of the day" (Genesis 18:1).

He may have been trying to catch any small desert breeze that might have drifted his way. Most activity would have ceased at that time of day as everyone rested and tried to escape the oppressiveness of the heat. In the quietness, I can almost hear the flies buzzing and the cattle lowing and, from time to time, a servant calling out. As he looked into the distance, I wonder if he could see heat waves shimmering and little dust devils dancing.

Maybe he was feeling the weariness of age and dozed off for a moment before he caught himself, "looked up and saw three men standing nearby" (18:2). Did he blink hard, look again, rub his eyes, and look again, wondering if he was seeing some sort of mirage? No one in that part of the world would be foolish enough to travel anywhere in the middle of the day. And these strangers would have had to travel a great distance just to move through all of Abraham's flocks and herds. Knowing that whoever it was would need to get out of the broiling sun, Abraham "hurried from the entrance of his tent to meet them and bowed low to the ground" (18:2).

With gracious eastern hospitality, Abraham welcomed them: "If I have found favor in your eyes, my lord, do not pass your servant by. Let a little water be brought, and then you may all wash your feet and rest under this tree. Let me get you something to eat, so you can be refreshed and then go on your way — now that you have come to your servant" (18:3 – 5).

The visitors gratefully agreed. While they refreshed themselves, Abraham "hurried into the tent to Sarah" (18:6). Was he sweating profusely and breathing in gasps as he clapped his hands to get her immediate attention and instructed her to bake fresh bread? I can imagine what she thought, even if she didn't say a word: *Abraham, you're crazy! The heat is stifling. Just moving about is uncomfortable, and you want me to start baking? And broiling over an open fire? I'm an old woman. What in the world has possessed you?* But she did as she was asked.

As Abraham supervised the calf being butchered and the meat being prepared, once again I can "hear" the wheels of his mind turning over and over as he wondered, *Who are these men?* Did he think there was something familiar about them? Something he couldn't pinpoint . . . Was it their faces? Their voices? Their demeanor? Their accent? Their expression? When did it suddenly hit him? *It's the Lord!*[2]

Gathering together everything he could think of that might be refreshing to weary travelers, his hands must have trembled as "he then brought some curds and milk and the calf that had been prepared, and set these before them" (18:8).

I wonder what would it have been like *to serve the Lord something to eat.* To do something for the One who had done so much for him. I'm sure that's why, like any good host, "while they ate, he stood near them under a tree" (18:8).

Abraham undoubtedly watched the Lord, who not only received what was offered but seemed to enjoy it. What must it have been like for Abraham to see the Lord cut a piece of steak that he had prepared, put it into His mouth and chew it, then reach for the milk to wash it down? And then to see *the hands that had created the universe* break off a piece of Sarah's freshly baked bread!

Abraham must have hovered nearby to make sure they had everything they might need and to be available to get them anything else they wanted. How could he have torn himself away from such a scene? But he also must have known God was there for a purpose. Surely God wouldn't come to visit him in the middle of the day just to eat lunch! Abraham knew He had to have something on His mind. What could it be?

He didn't have to wait long before they inquired, "Where is your wife Sarah?" (18:9).[3] When Abraham responded that she was in the tent, "the Lord said, 'I will surely return to you about this time next year, and Sarah your wife will have a son'" (18:10). Those quiet, calm words must have had the full force of a cannon blast! I wonder if Abraham's back suddenly stiffened. Had he shared this startling revelation with Sarah following his previous conversation with God (17:15 – 16)?

And, as a woman I can't help but wonder if, when he did, she had looked at him with a stupefied expression in stunned astonishment, then burst into laughter that had a ragged, bitter edge. I would imagine her unbelief had been so rooted in years of barrenness and hopelessness that she was incapable of opening herself up one more time to an unfulfilled dream she had buried long ago. If so, just the mere suggestion from her husband that she would have a baby after ninety years of childlessness must have raked raw the wound she still carried in her heart. Surely she had resigned herself to going to the grave without ever giving birth to her own child.

Abraham must have known how Sarah would react to hearing this news. Being familiar with her ways, he would have known that she was close by, in the other tent. He must have known that, like most women, she was insatiably curious and would be straining to hear what these unorthodox visitors had to say. Sure enough, Sarah's intense desire to know more got the best of her as she pressed her ear to the tent flap. I guarantee she didn't want to miss a word! Then, when she heard one of the visitors tell Abraham that she was going to have a baby, she "laughed to herself as she thought, 'After I am worn out and my master is old, will I now have this pleasure?'" (18:12).

It must have been difficult to keep her chuckle to herself, but she did. No one saw the merriment in her eyes, or the humorous expression on her face, or heard any sound come out of her upturned lips. She must have wondered how in the world Abraham was going to handle the conversation now! How could he remain gracious in the face of such foolishness and impudence? She surely listened even more intently — and with amusement — from the privacy of her hidden vantage point.

But before Abraham could say anything at all, as the thoughts still raced in his mind and the words still stuck on his tongue, the Lord asked, "Why did Sarah laugh and say, 'Will I really have a child, now that I am old?' Is anything too hard for the LORD? I will return to you at the appointed time next year and Sarah will have a son" (18:13 – 14).

The twinkle in Sarah's eye must have disappeared more quickly than she could blink. The humorous expression surely vanished, and I imagine a sickly gray pallor appeared as fear gripped her. How could anyone have heard her? She had made no sound. How could anyone have known? She was alone.

Responding on impulse, Sarah did what she had seen her husband do when he was afraid. She "lied and said, 'I did not laugh'" (18:15).[4] And the Lord, who knows all things, including our thoughts from afar and our words before they are on our tongues,[5] corrected her.

"Yes, you did laugh," He said.

Sarah's knees must have buckled. Did she clutch the tent pole to keep from collapsing on the ground? Did she shake her head back and forth, numb with the knowledge that she had been speaking with the Lord? And she had just *lied to God*! What shame! What sorrow! And what joy as she realized that even though He knew she had laughed at Him, and lied to Him, He still had promised to give her a son. At that very moment, with her ear pressed to the back of the tent flap, with her lie still scorching her lips, with the knowledge that the One who was seated under the shade of the great oak tree was God Himself ... Sarah's faith was born! Her personal relationship with God was established by faith in God's Word ... faith that had to be in place before she could supernaturally conceive a baby at ninety years of age ... faith that would literally give birth to a miracle!

As Abraham followed the exchange, he must have looked in consternation at the Lord when told that Sarah had laughed — because he surely hadn't heard anything. Did he look back and stare hard at the tent where the unmistakable sound of Sarah's voice denied the laughter — and then look back again at the Lord? What was going on? His every sense must have been on high alert.

When did the Lord's words register with Abraham? When did it hit him that God had come, not to speak with *him*, but to speak to *Sarah*? To build her faith so that, after twenty-five years of praying and seeking God and claiming His promises, finally, *finally* his prayer would be answered? *Within the year!* The stunning, dramatic revelation made Abraham's response even more remarkable to me, because "when the men got up to leave, they looked down toward Sodom, and Abraham walked along with them to see them on their way" (18:16).

I would have totally understood if Abraham had eagerly waved good-bye to his guests, run to the tent where Sarah now cowered, gathered her up in his arms, and exclaimed, "Sarah! Sarah! Did you hear that, Sarah? What do you think? What do you say now? We're going to have a baby! That's not what *I* said but what *God* says! Believe God's word, Sarah. A lifetime of waiting is over! Twenty-five years of walking by faith has paid off! You're going to be a mother! Sarah, let's go pick out a tent for the nursery."

But unbelievably, Abraham walked away with the three men! He got up, left Sarah, and walked with the Lord! He seemed to be more enthralled about being with God and getting to know Him better than he did with receiving the answer to the prayer of a lifetime.

A critical lesson for you and me on prayer has begun. Because that's where real prayer starts ...

PRAYER STARTS

Prayer doesn't necessarily start with ...

a lofty salutation,

or an organ prelude,

or wafting incense,

or a repetitive chant.

Prayer begins with our relationship to God that the Bible describes as a walk.[6]

Prayer Starts with Our Walk

Walking with God is like walking with a friend. When I'm home, I get up early in the morning and walk two and a half miles around a lake in a nearby park. I started this habit twenty-five years ago to increase my energy level. Walking briskly not only makes me feel better physically but it also seems to be refreshing therapy for my spirit. I love the soft colors of the sky at dawn, the sounds of the wildlife beginning to waken, and the feeling of fresh newness that permeates the air.

I usually walk with a friend, not only for safety reasons but also for the fellowship. Over the years, I've worn out several walking partners. But two basic rules have stayed the same. The first rule is that we must walk in the same direction. The second rule is that we must walk at the same pace. If either of those rules is not kept, then it doesn't matter how much I enjoy the other person, or how committed we are to our friendship, or how much we both need the exercise, we won't be walking together.

The same two basic rules apply to walking with God. If we want to walk with

Him, we must walk in His direction, which means we must surrender the will of our life to Him. We can't go off in our own direction, deciding our own goals and pursuing our own purposes. And we must walk at His pace, which means step-by-step obedience to His Word. And since we would have no idea what steps He is taking on a particular day, we have to read and apply His Word on a daily basis so we can walk at His pace.

One thing I have discovered is that God won't adjust His pace or direction to suit me. I have to adjust my pace and direction to His if I want to walk with Him.

How is your walk? Are you walking at His pace and in His direction? Do you even *want* to walk with God? I do. I want to walk with Him . . .

> as Adam did — so personally that I live in the paradise
> of His presence.[7]
> as Enoch did — so consistently that increasingly I live
> in heavenly places.[8]
> as Noah did — so obediently that God can use me to save
> others from His judgment.[9]
> as Abraham did — who walked with such sensitivity that
> he knew what was on God's mind and heart.

If you and I don't walk with God, how will we know what to pray for? How will we know what's on His heart and mind? We won't. We will end up praying what's on *our* minds and what's in *our* hearts, struggling to get Him to walk at our pace and in our direction. Again and again, as I've walked with God, He has imparted His burden to my heart.

Several years ago, I was teaching the life of Abraham in multiple sessions during a very intense seminar. The afternoon before giving the message on Genesis 15, I slipped away to spend some quiet time in reflection and prayer, seeking the Spirit's confirmation of what I would be saying. I became so sleepy that I went to my bedroom to lie down for a few minutes. But I just couldn't seem to relax and unwind. So I got up, drank a glass of cold water, munched on an apple, walked for a few minutes to wake myself up, then prayed. As I prayed through the message, I became very burdened that there was someone who was not saved attending the seminar which was designed for Christian leaders. As preposterous as it seemed, I couldn't shake the heaviness in my heart.

That night, when I delivered the message, I felt prompted by God's Spirit to give a strong appeal to anyone present who was not assured of a personal relationship with God. I invited those in the audience to enter into a covenant with Him, a covenant signed by the blood of His own Son and extended to us by grace at the cross of Jesus Christ. I explained that no one had to earn it or work for it or deserve it or be good enough to get it. The covenant is freely offered to anyone willing to receive it by faith in Jesus. Following the message, I led the group in prayer for anyone who wanted to accept God's offer of a covenant relationship through faith in Jesus Christ as Lord and Savior. Then I left and went back to my room for the night.

During the Bible study workshop the next morning, I took questions from the platform. One very discerning student explained that she had observed during the message the night before that I seemed to spend extra time on Genesis 15:6, after which I had presented a very strong appeal for salvation. She wanted to know why. I told her about the burden I felt God had given me during the previous afternoon's preparation for someone at the seminar who was unsaved. I explained that the burden had been on my heart during the message and that when it came to my mind specifically, I released it by presenting the gospel aimed at whoever that person might be.

Following the workshop, as we took a break for lunch, a beautiful young woman came up to speak with me. With tears glistening in her eyes, she said softly, "Anne, I'm the one."

I must have looked puzzled. But then she continued, "Anne, I was raised in a strongly religious home. I've actually been trained in Christian organizations in college, and I'm active in my church. But inside I've been restless. Some friends invited me to come to this weekend because they were sure it would be a blessing. So I came. But yesterday afternoon, I went for a run on the mountain at the very time you said you were praying in your cabin. As I was running, I told God I just didn't get it, I just didn't fit in. I told Him everyone seemed to enter into the worship through the music and they loved the messages, and I thought the weekend was okay but not that meaningful. I thought it must be that my personality isn't suited for this kind of thing. I actually thought of leaving the seminar.

"But Anne, last night, when you presented the gospel, I knew I had never established a personal relationship with God, so at the end of your message, when you prayed from the platform, I prayed with you. I confessed my sin and invited

Jesus into my life." Then, barely able to get the words out because of her emotion, she said, "I've been born again. I get it now."

As she finished her story, I felt weak in my knees, realizing I had almost taken a nap the afternoon before instead of spending time in prayer! What if I had slept instead of prayed! God would not have had the opportunity to impart His burden to my heart, and this gorgeous young woman would not have come to faith ... at least not during that weekend. God taught me an incredibly valuable lesson, that someone's eternal life may depend on my daily walk with Him! Walking is not an option; it is serious, life-and-death business! Prayer that starts with our walk is essential — not just for us, but for *them*!

My desire to walk with God was immeasurably renewed during that seminar. I committed to walk with Him consistently and daily more than ever before. Now I get up early each morning before meeting my friend for our exercise routine, making time to read my Bible and pray. It means I have to separate myself from my nice cozy bed, quietly slipping away from my sleeping husband to meet the Lord and intentionally adjusting my direction and pace for the day to God's.

Prayer Starts with God's Word

Abraham had to leave the shady comfort of the big tree of Mamre, slip away from Sarah, and make the time to walk with God. What will you have to leave, from whom will you have to slip away, where will you have to go in order to make time each day to adjust your pace and direction to God's?

Knowing the Mind of God

The effort was more than worth it for Abraham, because it was while he was walking with God that God began to reveal His thoughts: "Then the LORD said ..."

When was *then*? It was while they were walking!

"Shall I hide from Abraham what I am about to do?" (18:17). That's pretty amazing, isn't it? *While* they were walking together, it was as though Abraham could hear what was on God's mind. And he made the incredible discovery that God was up to something! God was about to "do" something and wanted to reveal His plans to Abraham.

God is as active today as He was in Abraham's lifetime. Do you know what He's "up to"? God is doing something in our neighborhood, our city, our state, our nation, and our world, but we will never know what it is, much less how we can participate with Him in it, unless we walk with Him.

When I walk with my friend around the lake, we talk about anything and everything: recipes, grandchildren, sales, ball games, politics — whatever happens to be on our minds.

Wouldn't you love to have that kind of free-flowing discussion with the Lord and find out what's on His mind? Is God thinking about stars or planets, black holes or sinkholes, governments or nations, the culture or the church, sin or suffering, demons or angels, hell or heaven, all those big things that He's so good at managing? With so many important things on His mind, it's almost beyond human imagination to even dream that He would have one thought to spare on someone like me. Or you. Or Abraham. Yet God reveals what's on His mind to those who make the time to walk with Him as a friend.

Jesus encouraged His disciples to walk with Him when He revealed that He no longer called them "servants, because a servant does not know his master's business. Instead, I have called you friends, for everything that I learned from my Father I have made known to you."[10] One of the primary things Jesus has made known to us is the very nature and character of God![11] Jesus has made His Father known to us so we can know Him as Abraham did ... and make Him known to others.

God affirmed that He would reveal His thoughts to Abraham because "I have chosen him, so that he will direct his children and his household after him to keep the way of the Lord by doing what is right and just" (18:19). God knew that for Abraham, the magnificent obsession was not a passing fancy, an impulsive whim, an emotional feeling, a superficial pastime, a momentary desire.

It was his life's goal backed up with a daily commitment hammered out by faith on the anvil of his experience. God knew that the magnificent obsession was so woven into the fabric of Abraham's mind, heart, soul, and body that his children and his children's children would embrace it too.

And they did! Through Abraham's family, God unveils Himself in the law, which reveals His perfect standards that we all fall short of — in the sacrifices that teach us His requirements for approaching Him, in the ceremonies that show us how He wants to be pleased, in the written revelation we call the Old Testament Scriptures that give us a progressive glimpse of His love and purpose for the human race, and in Abraham's descendants themselves who provided a human lineage for His Son, Jesus Christ, in whose face we see God clearly and fully.

I wonder what God thinks about me. Does He know He can depend on me to give godly direction to my children and my grandchildren — direction that comes not just from what I say but from who I am and what I do? *Has He chosen me* as one to whom He can reveal His heart and mind because He knows *I have chosen Him* to walk with? To live for? To serve? To pursue in a personal relationship that is my magnificent obsession?

Who sees God in my life to the extent that they are blessed? And what am I doing to rear my children and grandchildren with the high goal of being a blessing to others? It's obvious that God's purpose for Abraham included using not only him but his entire family as a channel of blessing to the world. What goals have you set as a parent for your family? Could you have set them too low because you are not walking with God?

Knowing the Heart of God

As Abraham *continued* to walk with God, God revealed not only the thoughts on His mind but also the burdens on His heart.

Some insights and understanding I will only receive as I keep walking with God . . . every day. "*Then* the Lord said, 'The outcry against Sodom and Gomorrah is so great and their sin so grievous that I will go down and see if what they have done is as bad as the outcry that has reached me. If not, I will know'" (18:20 – 21). Who had been crying out against Sodom and Gomorrah? The angels? The rocks?[12] An unknown priest such as Melchizedek? The Spirit of God? One or two righteous people living in the area? No one knows. The Bible tells us that "the eyes of the Lord are on the righteous and his ears are attentive to their cry; . . . The righteous cry out, and the Lord hears them."[13] But we do know that someone's cry had become God's burden.

What have you been crying out to God about? When I have read the morning newspaper or watched the evening news on television, I have cried out about . . .

- *the resignation of a pastor because of his affair with a gay prostitute,*
- *the abuse of innocent children by those in ministry,*
- *the worship of other gods hidden under the cloak of multiculturalism,*
- *the rejection of truth hidden under the cloak of moral pluralism,*

- profanity, obscenity, and pornography called freedom of expression,
- the secularization of America called separation of church and state,
- the redefinition of marriage and the family unit,
- the killing of the unborn legalized as a woman's right,
- the neglect of discipline defended as necessary to protect our children's self-esteem,
- immorality not only accepted but applauded and glorified,
- reliable standards of right and wrong rejected in the name of tolerance,
- perverted sex, sadistic violence, and the evil occult promoted as games ... for our children,
- and a church that is more concerned about ...

> programs than prayer ...
> traditions than truth ...
> a new sanctuary than sinners ...
> political change than heart change ...
> its reputation than repentance ...
> while all around us the world is unraveling!

How can any righteous person today not cry out?

The glaring truth is that only the righteous today know how abominable in God's eyes these things are! And even the righteous wouldn't know, except for God's Word. Because God's Word is like our schoolmaster, teaching us God's perspective and God's principles, God's wisdom and God's way, God's standards and God's truth, God's viewpoint and God's values.[14]

Without God's Word, we're just guessing.

Have you ever hung wallpaper and just guessed if you were hanging it straight? In my younger days, I wallpapered a room in my house that way. It was just a small bathroom, and the job looked easy to do since the walls had tile halfway up, diminishing the area that needed papering. I began the project with great enthusiasm and was quite proud of myself for saving time by not bothering with a plumb line. I started carefully in the corner behind the door, measured the angle of the paper with my eye, and was sure I had positioned it straight. I worked my way around the bathroom, strip by strip, until I finally ended up where I had begun ... behind the bathroom door. Except that the patterns on the beginning and ending strips didn't match at all. I was off by at least two inches. I learned the hard way that I should have used a plumb line, because wallpaper can look straight yet be very crooked.

As you and I "eye" the way we live our lives, or the way others live theirs, things can seem fairly "straight." We compare ourselves with each other and constantly adjust our values to fit the cultural norm. But before we realize it, our society is in a crooked, mismatched mess — and so are we. Which is why the Bible says we need the plumb line of God's Word.[15]

God's Word tells us . . .

> what is right and what is wrong,
> what is pleasing to God and what is not,
> what is good for us and what is destructive,
> what is wise and what is foolish,
> what will work and what will not,
> what will bring God's blessing, and
> what will provoke God's judgment.

Without God's Word, we're *just stumbling* . . . from one generation to the next!

As God spoke to Abraham, He became almost "transparent" when He revealed that His heart was broken over the sin of Sodom and Gomorrah. He described their sin as grievous — and *grief* is a love word. A person only grieves over the brokenness or the lostness or the deadness of a loved one. Through God's Word, Abraham discovered God was grieving.

I want to have a strong heart, but I don't want to be hard-hearted, so I have asked the Lord to break my heart with the things that break His. And the only way I can know the things that break His heart is to ask Him in prayer, then listen as He tells me through His Word. That's how I know those things that have made me cry out to Him have made Him cry first. Because God sees everything everywhere as it happens.

God told Abraham He was going to "go down and see" (18:21). If He cared enough about Sodom and Gomorrah to give those cities His undivided attention, how could I ever think He cares about our world any less? And remember, He had just told Abraham the son He had promised would be born within the year. This son would be Isaac, who represented the nation of Israel in embryo form. And the nation of Israel would be His vehicle for imparting the revelation of Himself to the world through the law and the sacrifices and the ceremonies and the prophets and, ultimately, through His own Son.

If it's amazing Abraham chose that moment to leave Sarah and walk with God, it's even more amazing God chose that moment to walk with Abraham! The celebration in heaven over the initial founding of Israel must have reverberated throughout the universe! And yet God set it all aside as though He had nothing else to do and there was nothing else going on except what was taking place in Sodom and Gomorrah.

Don't misunderstand God's little side trip. He knew exactly what was going on in Sodom and Gomorrah. He just wanted Abraham and Lot and you and me to look over His shoulder and see too. Otherwise we might question the severity of His judgment. Instead, His personal involvement compels me to worship, because...

Two thousand years later, He came down again to see. He actually lived for a while among us.[16] What He found was that "all have sinned"; there was "none righteous, no, not one"; and "the wages of sin is death" — separation from God.[17] So the Angel of the Lord incarnate, God Almighty, Abraham's Lord "made himself nothing, taking the very nature of a servant, being made in human likeness. And being found in appearance as a man, he humbled himself and became obedient to death — even death on a cross!"[18] Because *my sin* — and yours — was so grievous in God's eyes that it demanded nothing less than the blood of the incarnate God, blood that was infinite in worth, its value beyond all thought. The shedding of His blood reveals that evil and guilt were infinite, thus demanding such a price.[19]

And surely, with tears in His eyes, He still comes down today to see, not for His own information, but for ours. In the light of His holiness, the wretchedness of sin, the sinfulness of sin, is revealed. I can't help but cry out for His mercy on me and on our nation. And when I do so, I'm aware that real intercessory prayer for those in danger of God's judgment has begun...

PRAYER STAYS

I know Abraham must have been aware of what God was going to find in Sodom. In the somewhat limited civilization of his day, surely he knew something of the extreme wickedness for which the city was known. So as the three men he was walking with turned toward Sodom with the intention of exposing its wickedness, "Abraham remained standing before the LORD" (18:22). This may seem confusing because, up until this point, the three men have acted almost as one. However, we know from Genesis 19:1 that two of the "men" were angels, while it's obvious from this chapter that one was the Lord Himself in human form. And the burden on the Lord's heart was beginning to weigh heavily on Abraham's heart. So he detained the Lord for a few more minutes as the other two men turned away.

Prayer Stays in God's Presence

Abraham's staying in the Lord's presence reminded me of the way the disciples on the road to Emmaus also lingered in Jesus' presence thousands of years later. They had been walking along on the Sunday following the crucifixion, sharing together their agonizing despair at the sudden turn of events. Exactly one week prior to their walk, Jesus had been welcomed into Jerusalem as the Messiah, riding on a donkey, with people spreading palm branches before Him and shouting, "Hosanna!" "Blessed is he who comes in the name of the Lord!" "Blessed is the King of Israel!"[20] They had thought He was going to redeem Israel. Instead, the religious leaders arrested Him, convicted Him of blasphemy, then turned Him over to the Roman authorities, who pronounced Him innocent of all charges, yet who crucified Him as though He were a criminal.

As they discussed these things, "Jesus himself came up and walked along with them; but they were kept from recognizing him."[21] When He asked them to explain what they were talking about, they poured out their confused hopelessness to Him. They even related that women were spreading a rumor that they had seen Jesus risen from the dead, but no one really believed them.

Jesus rebuked them for their lack of faith and then began to explain "what was said in all the Scriptures concerning himself."[22] As they reached their destination, Jesus acted as though He was going to continue walking, but the two disciples strongly urged Him to stay with them.

Later they told others that as He opened up the Scriptures to them, their hearts had burned within them. His teaching must have resonated deep within. They knew He spoke the truth, and His words were challenging, convicting, encouraging, comforting, and filled with confident hope. They couldn't bear for the conversation to end, so they begged Him to join them for dinner. They just wanted to linger ... to stay in His presence. So Jesus turned aside and broke bread with them. When He did, their eyes were opened to see Him as the risen, living Lord!

So often when I've rushed through my prayer time, jumped up off my knees, quickly shut my Bible, closed my notebook, and hurried to take on my day, I've thought of Abraham and of the disciples on the Emmaus Road who lingered in God's presence. I wonder ... what blessings have I missed because I haven't made the time to stay in His presence? Has God wanted to reveal Himself to me in a way I've never seen before, but I've been in such a hurry I didn't have time to linger? Do you rush through your time with God too? Let's slow down ... let's keep our eyes closed and our heads bowed for just a few minutes longer. Let's reflect on the day's Scripture reading for just one more moment. Will we hear God whisper to our hearts? Will we sense God drawing near to us?

As Abraham stayed in God's presence, God stayed in his. God allowed Himself to be detained. What a wonderful truth that when you and I draw near to God, He draws near to us too.[23]

Prayer Approaches God's Person

Did Abraham's knees grow weak and his heart palpitate and his hands tremble as he was consciously aware that the Lord was a living Person? He "approached him" (18:23). One vitally important aspect that I try to nail down in my own prayer life is this basic, fundamental yet mind-blowing truth: I am speaking to a living Person! One who has ears to hear me and eyes to see me and a heart to love me and hands to guide me and a will to direct me.

God is not a ghost, or an icon in a stained-glass window, or a marble statue in a sacred hall, or the figment of someone's imagination, or empty space, or the First Cause, or the Force.

He is a living Person who loves you and me and invites us to draw near "in full assurance of faith" ... that "if we ask anything according to his will, he hears us." But don't overlook the condition to effective prayer: "anyone who comes to him must believe that he exists and that he rewards those who earnestly seek him."[24]

Do you believe that God actually exists exactly as He is revealed in Scripture? When you pray, are you confident that you are speaking to a living, invisible Person?

After twenty-five years of following the Lord in a life of step-by-step obedient faith, Abraham was fully convinced that God was a living, loving, listening Person. As Abraham began to really communicate with God in prayer, he had my undivided attention ... because that's what I want to be able to do too.

PRAYER SPEAKS

Abraham felt burdened for the spiritual condition of the world around him, for the city closest to him, for his own family members who he knew were in danger of coming under God's judgment. Like my burden during the seminar I told you about earlier, Abraham had become burdened as he walked with God, and his burden came straight from God's heart. And God's heart was burdened because He had shared His concern with Abraham, then stayed to speak with him about it.

A *burden* is usually understood as something negative — a heavy load of thoughts or worries that weighs us down. Sometimes we immediately know the source of the burden; other times it is simply an unidentified sense of heaviness or concern.

One night around 2:00 a.m. my husband woke up with a heavy burden on his heart for the coaches and professors at the University of North Carolina at Chapel Hill. He woke up a friend, told him what was on his heart, and prayed with him. The result is a weekly Bible study planted on the campus. A year after its inception, it is attended by dozens of men. The burden on my husband's heart came from the heart of God.

A couple of years ago, my ministry was made aware of a seventy-eight-year-old woman who kept ordering boxes of the small devotional *Daily Light*. As she prayed for American troops fighting in Afghanistan and Iraq, she felt God had led her to do what she could to get a copy of the *Daily Light* into the hands of the chaplains to give to the troops. As of this date, Ann Vanderford has raised the resources to order almost two thousand copies of *Daily Light*, which she has personally purchased, packaged, and shipped out.[25] Her burden came from the heart of God.

If you are like I am, you are constantly telling God about the burdens you bear. I never cease to be amazed that God cares about every single one of them. But do you and I care about His burdens as much as we care about our own? Do I even know what His burdens are? What burdens are you aware of that are on the heart of God? Like my husband and Ann Vanderford, Abraham knew of one burden on the heart of God, and he was willing to share it.

Prayer Speaks Honestly

Abraham asked some hard questions, but in a very respectful manner. His questions were not accusatory. He was honestly looking for answers.

Has anyone ever told you a true believer doesn't question God? Or that if you were really a person of faith, you would never ask why? People who say such things may not question God, but *I* do. I've heard it said that while skeptics argue with each other, believers argue with God. Certainly the Old Testament prophets and leaders, as well as the New Testament disciples, felt very free to question God. It's the only way I know to get answers. God welcomes our questions. So go ahead. Ask. Just be respectfully honest when you do.

Several years ago, I questioned God when my son went through a divorce.[26] I just couldn't understand why God had allowed such a living death to happen to someone I not only love but also have prayed for every day of his life. Like Abraham, I poured out my heart to God, including my questions. In response, God graciously focused my attention on the story of Mary, Martha, and Lazarus in John 11. Three times in the opening verses of this chapter, it clearly states Jesus loved Lazarus, Mary, and Martha. And I knew God was telling me that He loved me — and my beloved son.

Yet God allowed Lazarus to become seriously ill. When he did, Mary and Martha sent word to Jesus, asking Him to intervene. To do something. To make Lazarus better. Or at least to keep him from getting any worse. When Jesus received their message, He did not come immediately, but stayed where he was for two more days. From Mary and Martha's point of view, He remained silent and still, and Lazarus died. As I studied this story, God again seemed to speak to me and tell me that sometimes He allows bad things to happen to those He loves. To those I love. He taught me that sometimes, even after I have sent Him a message through prayer, the very situation I prayed about can get dramatically worse.

Amazingly, Jesus told His disciples *He was glad* Lazarus had died and He was going to Bethany to see Mary and Martha. That one phrase wrenched a very emotional question from my heart: "Lord, how could You be glad that someone You loved had died? And that his sisters were now in the agony of grief? How could that possibly make You happy? Does that mean, Lord, You are happy I'm struggling? Happy my loved one is suffering?" Rather than rushing on through my list of questions and requests, this time I lingered to catch His answer. I just couldn't believe He would be *glad*.

In the numbing silence that followed, His voice seemed to whisper into my heart, *Anne, I'm glad because there is something more important ... a grander purpose ... than just your health, wealth, prosperity, and problem-free life ... or that of your son. There is a much higher purpose than giving you what you want, when you want it, the way you want it, and how you want it.*

I was desperate to know what that grander purpose was! Then He answered me from that same verse: "I am glad I was not there, so that you may believe."[27]

Then it hit me! It was my faith that was more important to Him than my feelings or the well-being of my loved one! His purpose was to develop my faith for an even greater goal of displaying His glory in and through my life.

I am learning to be at peace, content with whatever transpires, because I know I can take it from His hand.

I am learning to die to what *I* want, when *I* want it, and I choose to trust God to accomplish what *He* wants.

I am learning to stay focused on Him, fulfilling my obligations.

I am learning to love others and care for their needs when my own heart is broken.

I am learning to live truth before others even when I can't see results.

I am learning to be faithful when my flesh wants to run away.

And as I am learning, I am also hoping that God's glory peeps through the cracks in this clay pot.[28]

If I had not been honest enough with God as I asked my questions, I would not have received His answers. I was like Martha when Jesus arrived in Bethany. She immediately hit Him with her honest questions: *Why didn't You come earlier? Why didn't You answer our prayer the way we asked You to? Why did You let this bad thing happen to our brother?*

Jesus' answer to her questions, as well as His answer to her sister's questions and mine, was basically, "Trust Me. Martha, Mary, and Anne, when you don't understand, just trust Me. There is much more at stake here than what you can see or touch or feel or hear. Trust Me! I have a greater purpose in mind than you could ever know. Trust Me!"

Such a simple answer. Such a profound truth. Such a rock-solid command around which to wrap my trembling shards of faith. As a result of the faith developed and strengthened in Martha, Jesus performed His greatest miracle. He raised Lazarus from the dead! Oh, for a faith like that ...

> Faith that can raise the dead to life.
>
> Faith that can heal the sin-sick soul.
>
> Faith that can bring the prodigal home.
>
> Faith that can reconcile a broken relationship.
>
> Faith that can find and save the lost.
>
> Faith that can cast out demons.
>
> Faith that can move mountains.
>
> Faith that receives miracles in answer to prayer.
>
> Faith that rests in God and God alone.
>
> Faith that is worked out through questions and answers
> and simple trust and obedience.

If you and I never ask God our honest questions, how will we ever get answers? How will our faith develop to the point that God can use us effectively for anything, much less as a channel of His blessing and His glory?

The legitimacy of my honest inquiries was confirmed when Abraham asked his questions:

> "Will you sweep away the righteous with the wicked?"
>
> "What if there are fifty righteous people in the city?"
>
> "Will you really sweep it away and not spare the place
> for the sake of the fifty righteous people in it?"
>
> "Will not the Judge of all the earth do right?" (18:23 – 25).

In other words, "God, You are righteous. But this just doesn't seem right to me. I've walked with You for twenty-five years. Destroying the righteous along with the wicked doesn't seem to match what I know about You."

What is the Lord doing that doesn't seem right to you? Are you harboring your doubts? Repressing your confusion? Would you instead respectfully ask God about it?

Keep in mind that you get your sense of rightness from God. Your sense of fairness and justice is only a shadow of His. So undergirding your honesty should be the knowledge that He is the Judge of all the earth and He always, *always*, *Always* does everything exactly, perfectly right! Because He is *right*eous.

When the Lord responded positively to Abraham's concerns, saying He would "spare the whole place" if He found "fifty righteous people in the city of Sodom," Abraham was encouraged to continue. He did so with great humility, almost fearful of his own boldness as he qualified his next question: "Now that I have been so bold as to speak to the Lord, though I am nothing but dust and ashes, what if the number of the righteous is five less than fifty? Will you destroy the whole city because of five people?" (18:26 – 28).

Mindful that he was just a little dust person, Abraham appealed to the very character of God as he had come to know Him. He was appealing to God from a position of respectful worship. From a position as God's friend. Others who knew God less intimately might have been afraid to ask such a question. But Abraham knew Him as few others did. There was nothing casual or flippant or familiar in his tone. He knew God is God! And he knew that God is righteous and just but also gracious, and that in wrath, He remembers mercy.[29]

When I pray, I want to keep in mind that I am me, and God is God. My appeal is not based on my own merits or position; I'm just a little dust person. It's based on the relationship I have with His dear Son, who has extended to me the gracious privilege of asking His Father anything in His name.[30] So go ahead and ask. Ask Him your tough questions and your troubled questions. Just be respectful. And be honest.

Prayer Speaks Responsively

Once again, God's positive answer encouraged Abraham to continue to pray — and in a way so responsive he seemed to be almost haggling with the Lord:

> "What if only forty are found there?"

The Lord said,

> "For the sake of forty, I will not do it."

Abraham said,

> "What if only thirty can be found there?"

The Lord said,

> "I will not do it if I find thirty there."

Abraham said,

> "What if only twenty can be found there?"

The Lord said,

> "For the sake of twenty, I will not destroy it."

Then Abraham said,

> "What if only ten can be found there?"

And the Lord said,

> "For the sake of ten, I will not destroy it" (18:29 – 32).

This passage emphatically underscores to me that one of the key components of communicating effectively with God is that my prayer should be responsive. It is not a monologue, it is a dialogue.

Recently my daughter and her husband went out to dinner with several friends. My daughter was so excited to get out of her house, away from her toddlers for an evening of adult conversation. To her dismay, one of the women at dinner talked incessantly. She never seemed to take a breath or even to come up for air, so a two-way conversation was impossible. My daughter chuckled as she related the evening to me because the talkative woman was also a mother with small children who very probably felt like my daughter had, needing desperately to have someone other than a two-year-old to talk to. Yet she had been insensitive to the needs of the other young parents at dinner.

How many times must the Lord feel the same way as I conclude my prayer time? I wonder if He wants me to know, *Anne, I wanted to say something too. Why did you do all the talking? Learn to come up for air once in a while and let Me speak to you! I want to engage in dialogue, not listen to your monologue.*

But then, how do you and I dialogue *with God*?

By his example Abraham teaches us that it's actually quite simple. We say something, then God says something. We say something, then God says something. We speak or pray responsively. When this kind of dialogue takes place, God can lead us in prayer.

This responsive format of prayer was very precious to me recently. While I was in the process of writing this book, my husband's health deteriorated. After two 911 calls on his behalf in two days and then an additional physical collapse, my nerves were frayed. I needed a word from the Lord, so I went to talk with Him about it. I opened my Bible to the place where I had been reading the day before. It was Exodus 15, the glorious Song of Moses that the children of Israel sang after they had walked through the Red Sea on dry ground, escaping from their enemies.

I said,

> Lord, I feel besieged by invisible enemies. My parents' health is fragile, my ministry responsibilities are coming at me like a freight train while I'm tied down on the tracks, one of the chapters of this book I have just spent a week writing has disappeared from my computer, this rough draft is due to the publisher in four weeks, all of which now seems like nothing compared to Danny's health. Please help me!

He said,

> Anne, first and foremost, I love you. My love for you never fails. I am the One who redeemed you from your bondage to sin and have set you free to serve Me.[31]

I said,

> How can I serve You here? Under all this stress? I'm afraid I won't make the right decisions and Danny will suffer because of it. I'm afraid I won't know how to handle the next crisis, or that I won't be here when it happens. I want to serve You by serving Danny in such a way that he feels loved and comforted and cared for wisely. And I want to do all of this while maintaining my ministry responsibilities, including writing this book! I'm overwhelmed!

He said,

> Anne, take My hand. I will lead you. I will be with you every moment.[32] I will never leave you nor forsake you.[33]

I said,

> But God, I am so weak. I'm having a hard time controlling my emotions. I'm not sure I can discuss this with anyone right now, not even a doctor

or a nurse. And I'm so inadequate to handle these major health issues and the decisions required.

He said,

Anne, I know you are weak. You have always been weak. But I am strong. I have always been strong. And at this very moment I am totally sufficient for your needs and Danny's. Let Me be your burden-bearer.

I said,

But I don't know what to do next. I don't know which doctor to call. And not only the *quality* of Danny's life, but his life itself is depending on our making the right decisions. What do I do?

He said,

I will guide you. You start making the phone calls, and I will open doors for you to get in to see the right people. I will make sure you end up in the place I want you to be. You can count on Me.

And I said,

I will count on You. I will trust in You and not be afraid. Thank You … with a humble heart filled with gratitude and love.

That prayer worked! I knew I had actually communicated with the living God because He saw us through! Even before Danny's health turned around, God gave us incredible peace and joy in the midst of all the stress. He led us to the right doctors, each of whom took enormous personal interest in Danny's condition. And He put us on the hearts of His people everywhere (or so it seemed), many of whom called, came by, prayed with us on the phone, or just dropped us a note to tell us they cared. The chapter of my book that disappeared from the computer was never recovered, but it was rewritten. And my parents' situation actually improved, at least temporarily, while I was unable to be with them.

When was the last time you had a conversation with God?[34] Next time you pray, take your Bible into your time alone with Him. Open it to where you've been reading, or just open it to your favorite passage. Read it carefully, then think for a few minutes about what it means. Let God lead you in prayer. Meditate on His Word. Is there a lesson or principle God wants you to learn and apply to your life? Or a command to obey? Or a warning to heed? Or an example to follow? Just talk to Him about it. But don't do all the talking.

Prayer Speaks Persistently

Abraham asked God again and again what he wanted God to do. When Abraham began his prayer, I'm not sure he knew himself exactly what he wanted. I think he just hoped to do something to save Sodom from judgment. But as he prayed, God led him, and his request became more and more focused until it was very specific. Eventually he prayed for ten righteous people, the number of family members he had living in Sodom.[35] In essence, Abraham's prayer was, "God, please save my loved ones from Your judgment . . . and use them to save others."

Sometimes, when we don't know what to pray, it helps to just start praying. God can direct us more specifically as we pray.

The prophet Daniel demonstrated this truth. He was an old man who had been a captive in Babylon for approximately sixty-seven years; he had read in the book of Jeremiah that God had promised the captivity of Israel would last only seventy years.[36] So Daniel poured out his heart in prayer for his people. He wrote, "While I was speaking and praying, confessing my sin and the sin of my people Israel and making my request to the LORD my God . . . while I was still in prayer, Gabriel, the man I had seen in the earlier vision, came to me in swift flight. . . . He instructed me and said to me, 'Daniel, I have now come to give you insight and understanding.'"[37] While Daniel was praying, God sent the angel to give him insight and understanding.

What an encouragement! You and I don't have to know exactly what to pray or how to pray in order to start praying. Just pray! God will guide you and me into what He wants us to ask Him for as we persist in prayer. But there does come a point when we need to stop praying and start trusting . . .

PRAYER STOPS

While I should pray without ceasing,[38] how do I know when to stop the dialogue and to start trusting? I'm sure you know people who continue talking long after they should quit. They are boring and irritating and embarrassing to be around. Whatever they were saying would have been so much more effective if they had just known when to stop.

Prayer Stops with the Assurance God Has Heard

Abraham knew when to quit. He stopped praying "when the LORD had finished speaking" (18:33). Up until that moment, God's step-by-step responses to Abraham's requests had seemed to encourage Abraham's persistence. Abraham's prayer had been based on God's promises that were given to him as he prayed. Then God stopped promising. He was silent, "and Abraham returned home" (18:33). If Abraham had continued, he would have been talking to empty space, just wasting his breath.

Abraham's real prayer had started with a burden God had imparted to his heart through His Word as they walked together. The prayer continued when Abraham asked questions and received answers from God that were promises on which he could base his faith. His prayer was not based on what he hoped or wanted or wished or thought. In the end, his final prayer for Sodom was based on what God had said to him: "For the sake of ten, I will not destroy it." And that's where Abraham planted his faith. He had God's Word, and he would hold God to it. God did not give Abraham faith to pray for fewer than ten, because God did not give Abraham a promise He would spare Sodom for fewer than ten.

Sometimes I pray past my faith. When my prayers are based on my own dreams or fantasies or hopes or wants, whether for a child's future, or a ministry opportunity, or the physical healing of a loved one, they are out there in spiritual cyberspace, accomplishing nothing. They feel flimsy, even to me. I don't really have the assurance God has heard me or will answer me. But when God gives me a promise to wrap my faith around, I am confident of being directly connected to His will, and I know He has heard and will answer in His own time and in His own way.

So, who or what is *your* Sodom? For whom are you desperately praying? Is it someone you sense is provoking God's judgment? Is it someone whose lifestyle is so out of tune with God's will and God's way and God's Word that it's just a matter of time before the person self-destructs? Are you scared for him or her? Then start praying. Ask God to give you a promise on which you can base your faith. Feel free to ask Him for another promise to confirm the first one, and keep your prayer fresh. Maybe God will give you another promise or a further word that will lead you in how to pray specifically. Claim His promises, remind Him of what He has said from time to time. Then wait until He answers.

Prayer Stops with the Anticipation God Will Answer

When Abraham stopped talking to God, it didn't mean he stopped thinking about Lot and the impending destruction of Sodom. His subsequent action revealed he was very anxious to discover how God would answer his prayer.

Habakkuk was an Old Testament prophet who also poured out his heart in prayer for his Sodom, which was his own nation of Judah. Judah had declined until it was on the verge of moral and spiritual bankruptcy. Habakkuk knew God would not tolerate Judah's wickedness. But when he prayed, God's answer indicated the judgment was going to be even more severe than he had imagined, which increased the desperate urgency of his prayer. After a long list of questions, as he wrestled with God's revealed will for Judah, Habakkuk knew God had heard his cry, and he was so filled with anticipation as to how God would answer he said, "I will stand at my watch and station myself on the ramparts; I will look to see what he will say to me."[39]

Abraham also climbed up on the "ramparts" to see how the Lord would answer. The very next day after he had prayed, "Abraham got up and returned to the place where he had stood before the LORD. He looked down toward Sodom and Gomorrah, toward all the land of the plain, and he saw dense smoke rising from the land, like smoke from a furnace" (19:27 – 28).

How devastating that would have been! How utterly defeated he must have felt! I wonder if in his shock at what he saw his stomach turned over and he retched in horror, thinking, *God, You promised You would spare Sodom for ten righteous! That's what You said! You promised me You would spare Sodom for … Oh God! Oh no! Do You mean to tell me there weren't even ten righteous people in the entire city? But God, my family was there! Does that mean … ?*

The smoke that rose up from the plain was the unmistakable answer to his unspoken question. In Sodom there were not even ten members of his own family who were righteous. He must have slumped away with leaden feet and bowed head, believing all had been lost, including Lot.

I wonder … have you ever been like Abraham … or me? After prayer, have you "seen" what you thought was God's answer? Has it been much less, or even contrary, to what you have prayed? Like Abraham, have you also thought that all was lost? Are you so defeated in prayer that you're tempted to quit? Are you reasoning that since prayer doesn't seem to make any difference anyway, why bother? Could it be that your view has only touched the surface and that the God who loves you and listens to you is moving in ways that you cannot "see"? Sometimes outward, circumstantial evidence can give a false reading on what God is doing.

What Abraham couldn't see, and at the time didn't know, was that "when God destroyed the cities of the plain, he remembered Abraham, and he brought Lot out of the catastrophe that overthrew the cities where Lot had lived" (19:29). In answer to Abraham's prayer, all of Sodom was not saved, but God remembered Abraham! And the one Abraham cared about most was saved. Twice Lot had chosen to live in Sodom. He had not heeded the warning God had given him when he had been taken captive by the eastern kings. He didn't deserve to be saved. He had been superficial, selfish, and sinful. But the angels had dragged Lot out of the city for no other reason than God remembered Abraham. And God is gracious.

Praise God! He did not save Sodom for the sake of ten righteous because they were not there, but He did save Lot for the sake of one righteous man who cared enough to pray![40]

Abraham was just one person who was willing to stand in the gap for his family.[41] And because he did, Lot was saved.

⌒⌒

Are you unable to stand in the gap for anyone because your prayers are just . . .

wishing?
or hoping?
or fantasizing?
or imagining?
or daydreaming?

I want to be a person who stands in the gap for my family, my friend, my neighbor, my city, my state, our nation, and our world. I wonder, who would be saved today from God's judgment if I would really communicate with God about them? This thought is haunting to me. And I'll never know until I do! So, I think I'll start now.

Would you do the same? Learn by Abraham's example to communicate with God by lifting up everything and everyone in prayer.

~⟆ SIX ⟅~

Cast Everything Out

Genesis 20 – 21

Some of the world's most beautifully scenic, charming countryside is found in England. With rolling hills and misty valleys, stone wall fences enclosing sheep in green pastures, fragrant roses climbing over thatched-roof cottages, and winding village lanes, the view from almost every angle can be a feast for the eyes. But the landscape that has inspired artistic masterpieces throughout the centuries also holds drama.

One of the dramas occurs every spring in the postcard-picturesque countryside as all the birds busily build their nests. All the species of birds, that is, except one. The cuckoo bird flies throughout the forest until it finds a sparrow's nest, then it deposits its oversized egg there.[1] While it flies off to live a relatively carefree life, the little English sparrow returns to the nest and finds her own three dainty little eggs, plus one big brown ugly cuckoo egg. But the sparrow doesn't notice the difference and nestles down over all four eggs.

When the eggs hatch, three dainty little sparrow chicks emerge, plus one big clumsy cuckoo. The mother bird still does not notice anything out of the ordinary, so she leaves the nest to search for food. When she comes back to the nest, she dangles a worm over the four baby chicks. Three dainty little sparrow mouths open wide, cheeping with hunger, while one big ugly cuckoo mouth squawks loudly. The cuckoo gets the worm. Again and again, the cuckoo, with its larger and louder mouth, gets fed the most. The result is either the cuckoo grows so large it shoves the sparrow chicks out of the nest before they can survive on their own or it actually starves the smaller chicks to death by eating all the food.

An observer can always tell when a cuckoo is in an English sparrow's nest because the ground underneath is littered with dead little sparrow chicks. It's impossible for all to survive in the same nest. The only way a mother sparrow could save her own chicks would be to push the cuckoo out of the nest before it could grow and harm the others. But this never happens because the sparrow is oblivious to the problem.

To me, the parallel between the sparrow's nest and Abraham's home seems strikingly similar. Abraham's son Ishmael was similar to the destructive cuckoo. However, unlike the mother sparrow, Abraham was made aware of the problem and he had to make a hard choice. He had to either cast his son Ishmael out of the home or watch as Ishmael destroyed Isaac. The drama that took place in this family is one that the New Testament uses to illustrate another drama that takes place in our own hearts. We too have an Ishmael, or a cuckoo, within us that must be cast out if our life of faith is to grow and thrive.

The drama in Abraham's home was preceded by repeated failure in his life. After twenty-five years of following God step-by-step in a life of obedient faith, after twenty-five years of pursuing God and all the blessings He had for him, after twenty-five years of embracing the magnificent obsession, Abraham failed ... again ...

Break the Cycle of Sin

Have you ever failed ... again? Have you ever done something you didn't want to do, then asked yourself, *Why did I do that*? Have you guiltily suspected that there must be something uniquely wrong with you? I know I have. And so, to me, Abraham's failure is actually not only a story rich in life lessons, it is also an encouragement.

One of the first lessons is that Abraham seems to have been set up for repeated failure by his fragile emotional state. After twenty-five years of living a life of faith, Abraham had been told he and Sarah were going to have the child God had promised, the child through whom God would bless the world. The thrill of knowing that lifelong dream was going to be realized within twelve months must have been an emotional Himalayan peak, which made the plummet to the emotional pit even more devastating when he saw the smoke billowing from the plains of Sodom. He knew the city had come under God's judgment because not even ten righteous people had been found there. When he saw the smoke, he must have assumed everyone had been destroyed, including his nephew Lot.

Abraham must have grieved deeply over his perceived loss of Lot. The pain must have been excruciating. Did he hold himself responsible for bringing Lot out of Ur in the first place? Did he wrestle with the guilt of exposing Lot to temptation by taking him down to Egypt? Did he struggle with having given Lot the choice to live in Sodom? Was he spiritually discouraged to the point of despair over the fact that after twenty-five years of living a life of faith, his prayers had not been enough to save Lot from the disaster of God's fiery judgment?

What is your emotional state? What guilt or discouragement or grief or struggle has perhaps set you up for failure? *Watch out . . .*

Abraham's emotional state must have been similar to that of someone who has attended the funeral of an unsaved loved one and has rehashed all the misguided choices and missed opportunities he or she had for leading that person to faith. Death is so final. Defeat seems so personal. Failure seems so total.

The Cycle of Repeated Failure

Abraham must have been trying to put the painful memories behind him. He pulled up stakes and "moved on from there into the region of the Negev and lived between Kadesh and Shur. For a while he stayed in Gerar" (Genesis 20:1). Moving would have been no small feat. He would have had thousands of dependents and tens of thousands of flocks and herds to organize. For a man one hundred years of age, just the mental effort of planning such a transition would have been exhausting in itself, much less the actual physical journey.

So when he arrived in Gerar, he must have been physically worn out from the journey, spiritually defeated by his perceived failure in prayer, and emotionally depressed over the loss of Lot. He was at an extremely low point in almost every area of his life. And it was then that, *once again*, he was beset by overwhelming fear for his own personal safety. *Once again*, Abraham "said of his wife Sarah, 'She is my sister'" (20:2). *Once again*, Abraham lied. *Once again*, Abraham failed.

What sin or failure have you repeated *once again*? Why did you do it?

One reason Abraham may have failed again is that he never set straight with Sarah his previous sin of lying to Pharaoh. When he had returned from Egypt, he had gone back *to Bethel*, but there is no record that he also went back *to Sarah* and apologized, no indication he ever said, "I'm sorry. I was wrong to lie about you. I promise never to do that again." He seemed to have left the door open to lying again. And he did.

The fear of personal harm seems to have been something of a phobia in Abraham's life, a "besetting sin."[2] Abraham sinned because he was afraid.[3] But Abraham also sinned for the simple reason that Abraham was a sinner.

Our contemporary culture . . .

mocks sin,

denies sin,

excuses sin,

defends sin,

ignores sin,

rationalizes sin,

enjoys sin,

flaunts sin,

promotes sin,

glorifies sin,

applauds sin,

redefines sin,

relabels sin . . .

but God *hates* sin.[4] Ultimately, it cost Him the life of His own beloved Son.

Abraham's lies again exposed Sarah to irreparable harm, not only to herself personally but also to God's plan for the promised child to come. Because "then Abimelech king of Gerar sent for Sarah and took her" (20:2).[5]

God had just promised that within the year Sarah would have a baby. What if Sarah, who had been taken into Abimelech's harem, was forced into an intimate relationship with him? What if she bore a child by him? Or what if she gave birth to Abraham's child, but under a cloud of suspicion as to who the father truly was? The complications were endless. Just the damage to Abraham's relationship with Sarah, who once again in her old age found herself betrayed by her own husband, must have been enormous! Yet Abraham did not seem to give the consequences, or the feelings of his wife, a second thought. He just didn't seem to me to take his lying seriously.

While our culture doesn't seem to take lying seriously, the greater shame is that many Christians don't seem to take sin very seriously either. We seem to think . . .

> we can sin and get by with it,
>
> we can sin and leave the consequences to a good counselor,
>
> we can sin and survive,
>
> we can sin and rationalize that it's okay because everyone does it,
>
> we can sin and claim to be under God's grace, not His law,
>
> we can sin and say it was just a small one,

but sin is serious in God's eyes. Why do you and I tolerate and toy with sin that cost the Son of God His life? Why don't we take it seriously . . . *for Jesus' sake*?

God takes our sin very seriously. He dealt with Abraham's sin by exposing it so that Abraham would be shamed and Sarah would be protected: "God came to Abimelech in a dream one night and said to him, 'You are as good as dead because of the woman you have taken; she is a married woman'" (20:3). God's severe reaction to Abimelech's involvement with a married woman should be posted in every office and every bar and every club in this country! Our pop culture that flouts God's principles of purity, fidelity, and morality needs to hear God say once again, *"You're as good as dead!"*

Abimelech, a man I would characterize as an unbeliever, immediately saw the seriousness of what he had done. When Abimelech defended himself before God and explained how he had been deceived, God replied, "Yes, I know you did this with a clear conscience, and so I have kept you from sinning against me. That is why I did not let you touch her. Now return the man's wife, for he is a prophet, and he will pray for you and you will live. But if you do not return her, you may be sure that you and all yours will die" (20:6 – 7).[6] Abimelech immediately summoned his officials, told them what had happened, then "called Abraham in and said, 'What have you done to us? How have I wronged you that you have brought such great guilt upon me and my kingdom? You have done things to me that should not be done'" (20:9).

We can feel Abraham's shame as one more time he found himself in the humiliating position of being rebuked by a pagan king. After returning to Bethel from Egypt, Abraham not only *should* have known better, he *did* know better. Yet he had lied again. He had mistakenly thought there was "no fear of God in this place" (20:11), when actually there was a lot of fear of God in Gerar.

I could almost see Abraham's face flush deep red. Did his heart pound and his stomach painfully knot? Did tears well up in his eyes? Was his voice husky with emotion as he confessed exactly what he had done and why he had done it? Did he straighten his shoulders, lift his noble head, and look Abimelech in the eye as he publicly admitted before the king and his cabinet officials, "I said to myself, 'There is surely no fear of God in this place, and they will kill me because of my wife.' Besides, she really is my sister, the daughter of my father though not of my mother; and she became my wife. And when God had me wander from my father's household, I said to her, 'This is how you can show your love to me: Everywhere we go, say of me, "He is my brother"'" (20:11 – 13)? That was a very honest confession!

What is surprising is that Abimelech did not throw Abraham out of Gerar. Instead he accepted Abraham's confession, gave him the choice of wherever he wanted to live, returned Sarah to him, and showered them both with gifts!

I wonder... because of Abraham's emotional, physical, and spiritual frailty, was he so humiliated that he was on the verge of quitting? Was he broken in his spirit? Had he expected more of himself than repeated failure after twenty-five years of getting to know God and living a life of faith? Was he one step away from giving up the magnificent obsession and going back to Ur — or at least to Haran?

What about you? Are you ready to quit too? Are you so disappointed in yourself, so shocked by your failure and sin, that you too want to give up on the magnificent obsession? Are you convinced that while it may be a lofty ideal, it's just not attainable? Are you on the verge of *going back*?

God is so gracious to sinners, even those of us who are repeat offenders. There have been times when I knew I deserved God's punishment for my attitude or my actions or my words. Several years ago, I found myself wrestling with a sin which has been a source of struggle and frustration for most of my life. Faced with my repeated failure, I crawled back in humiliation to the foot of the cross, where I expected to hear God tick off, one by one, the dire consequences of my sin or, at the very least, to hear Him sternly rebuke me. Instead, God affirmed His love for me and His promise of blessing and His call upon my life. My heart melted! I got up off my knees and, instead of quitting, I passionately recommitted myself to Him. I learned once again, from firsthand experience, that "a bruised reed he will not break, and a smoldering wick he will not snuff out."[7]

Tears well up in my eyes as I realize how gentle God was with Abraham. Not only was Abraham showered with gifts of land, silver, servants, sheep, and cattle, but Abimelech was healed when Abraham prayed for him. And Abraham, who had poured out his heart for Sodom, was tenderly encouraged by God that his prayers were indeed effective for those in danger of judgment.

The Cycle of Repeated Failure ... Again and Again

While I may have a hard time admitting it, Abraham's struggle with repeated failure is a familiar struggle in my own life. Because I am a sinner too. And so are you. All of us ... from the greatest to the least, from the most knowledgeable to the most ignorant, from the most religious to the atheist, from the richest to the poorest, from the oldest to the youngest, from the most mature saint to the newest believer, from those who walk by faith to those who won't believe anything until they see it ... all of us are sinners.[8] And for those of us who have embraced the magnificent obsession, the sin in our lives produces a struggle with repeated failure.

What have you done *once again*? What excuse do you have for your repeated failure?

Are you spiritually weak because your prayers seem to be unanswered and you are tempted to doubt God has heard and will answer you? Have you taken your eyes off the Lord and placed them on your circumstances?

Are you physically exhausted? Has it been weeks since you've had a good night's rest and months since you've had a real break? Are you tempted in your weariness to let your guard down?

Are you emotionally drained from the loss of a loved one through divorce or death or just a disagreement? Are your grief and stress blinding you to the need to be alert to the danger of failing — again?

We make ourselves vulnerable to repeated failure when, although we confess our sin to God, we never correct it with the other person. When we don't correct it, we leave the door slightly ajar and the sin will come back to repeat itself in our lives ...

Acknowledge the Conflict with Sin

As I have grown in my knowledge of God's Word and matured in my faith and walked more closely with the Lord, I have been faced with a very unpleasant surprise: my conflict with sin has not lessened; it has intensified! In response I have had only two real options: I could decide I can't get past this conflict, quit, and just be grateful I'm going to heaven when I die, *or*, by God's grace and in His power, I could break the cycle of sin!

I've opted to break the cycle, first of all, by acknowledging the conflict. The conflict going on in my life — and, I expect, in yours — is illustrated by the conflict that took place within Abraham's home.

The Conflict within Abraham's Home

Following Abraham's repeated failure in Gerar, his confession of sin to Abimelech, and the evidence of God's direct intervention to extract him from a dangerous situation, "the LORD was gracious to Sarah as he had said, and the LORD did for Sarah what he had promised. Sarah became pregnant and bore a son to Abraham in his old age, at the very time God had promised him" (21:1 – 2). How thrilling! How astounding! What a ...

mind-boggling,

barrier-breaking,

promise-keeping,

prayer-answering,

miracle-working

God is our God! Who could imagine that a ninety-year-old woman would conceive and carry a baby? My mind is not creative enough to even imagine Sarah with an enlarged waistline and then a protruding belly that confirmed even before delivery that what God says is so!

Did she go on bed rest for her last trimester? Or even the last two trimesters? Or did the supernatural quickening of her body that enabled her to conceive also give her the strength and energy of a much younger woman? Surely, after a lifetime of longing and barrenness, the joy of feeling the flutter of life within revitalized her. Did she get up every morning and look at herself in the mirror to make sure her pregnancy wasn't a dream? Did she walk away from the mirror praising

God for His faithfulness and goodness and graciousness not only to her husband, Abraham, but also to herself? Was she apprehensive about the delivery? And how did she know it was time? Did her back begin to ache strangely? Did her water break suddenly? Did she double over with a sudden hard contraction? How did she ever deliver a baby at her age? That alone was surely as much of a miracle as the conception!

My mind's eye can almost see the expression on her sweat-streaked face as she saw her infant son for the first time. All the ridicule she had faced from other women, all the agonizing monthly disappointments she had endured, all the sorrow she had felt and had seen reflected in Abraham's eyes were swept away as though they had never been! Unspeakable joy must have welled up in her heart, spilling out in tears from her wrinkled eyes and laughter from her aged lips! At long last, Sarah was a mother!

How long did it take Sarah to tear her eyes away from her baby and look at her husband, who surely had rushed into the tent at the sound of the first healthy cry? What overwhelming, glorious pleasure it must have brought her to see Abraham sweep the baby into his arms and give "the name Isaac to the son Sarah bore him" (21:3). With delirious delight, "Sarah said, 'God has brought me laughter, and everyone who hears about this will laugh with me.... Who would have said to Abraham that Sarah would nurse children? Yet I have borne him a son in his old age'" (21:6 – 7).[9] If her staff had known the "Hallelujah Chorus," they would have sung it!

Abraham immediately claimed God's covenant promises for Isaac, and "when his son Isaac was eight days old, Abraham circumcised him, as God commanded him" (21:4). The child of promise was now also the child of the covenant.

As Abraham sat by the crib, gazing on his miracle child, the child of promise, I wonder if Ishmael shyly came in to see his new half brother. And did Abraham wrap his arms around Ishmael and reassure his firstborn son of his love and of the special place Ishmael would always hold in his heart? Abraham must have known that the entrance of baby Isaac into the home would demand a lot of adjustment for Ishmael, who at fourteen was a teenager with needs of his own.

For fourteen years Ishmael had been an only child enjoying his father's undivided attention and affection. Abraham must have lavished a lot of time on Ishmael, teaching him about caring for and multiplying flocks and herds; about managing a household so large it was almost a small nation; about determining direction and time from the sun, moon, and stars; and most important, about the God whom Abraham was so obsessed with knowing, following, trusting, and obeying.

As Isaac grew, Ishmael must have been fascinated by the little toddler. I expect he was proud to be the big brother and found secret pleasure in taking the baby by the hand and feeling Isaac's chubby little fingers wrap around his as he took him for walks, showed him the animals, and taught him about what he was seeing. Isaac must have adored his older sibling, looked up to him and absorbed everything he did and said like a little sponge. Surely the blended family was more wonderful than Abraham had even dreamed it would be!

Abraham's home must have been a very happy place! A place filled with peace and joy and love and a deep sense of satisfaction and fulfillment and completion — for about three years. And then, did Ishmael find that, increasingly, Abraham was distracted? That he no longer seemed to have as much time to spend with him as before? Did Ishmael notice how Abraham's eyes sparkled when he saw Isaac or talked about him? When did he become aware that although he was the firstborn, he was second-class? Was it a thoughtless remark one of the servants made about Isaac being the son of the princess and Ishmael being the son of a slave that sowed a seed of resentment in Ishmael's heart? Or was it simply that the two boys developed radically different personalities? When did the natural sibling rivalry Ishmael must have felt turn into real hatred toward and jealousy of his little brother? Whatever the reason, Abraham's home was changed into a place of tension and conflict.

Conflict may have been simmering underneath the surface, but the day the conflict became obvious and could no longer be ignored was noted: "On the day Isaac was weaned Abraham held a great feast. But Sarah saw that the son whom Hagar the Egyptian had borne to Abraham was mocking" (21:8 – 9).

As the music was playing and people were eating and friends were talking and children were cavorting and the festivities were in full swing, Sarah must have looked around and noticed that Isaac was nowhere to be seen. Did she quietly slip away from the guests to search for him, going through the tents until she heard voices? Did she stop and listen more carefully until she could distinguish who was speaking and what was being said?

There was no doubt. She recognized one of the voices as that of the teenage Ishmael.[10] I wonder if she recoiled in horror as she realized he was mocking her son.[11] The mocking had turned ugly as Ishmael must have ridiculed Isaac's faith and his covenant relationship with God and the promises to be fulfilled in his life. I would imagine at that moment the princess became the dragon! It then must have been Ishmael's turn to recoil in horror as he took one look at Sarah's face contorted in fury and instantly knew he had crossed the line of permissible behavior.

The Conflict within Our Hearts

Peace and harmony had reigned in Abraham's home while Ishmael was an only child. But when Isaac arrived, it was just a matter of time before things got tense and the peaceful atmosphere shattered. While Isaac was very young, as long as Ishmael could dominate him, put him in his place, and generally have authority over him, things were quiet. But as Isaac grew in size and understanding, with a will of his own, the conflict erupted.

The New Testament uses explosive tension in Abraham's home as an illustration of the conflict within our own hearts. It's a conflict that takes place within every believer. Those who are unsaved can experience relative peace and harmony in their lives, unaware of the high standards of God's Word and uncaring as to whether or not they measure up. So although they are still sinners, the sin in their lives doesn't really bother them. They are therefore spared the conflict believers experience.

I'm reminded of our nature and our tendency to sin by an incident that took place when my younger daughter was small. One day she came running to me, complaining that something had bitten her on her tummy. When I lifted her shirt, sure enough, I saw a small red dot. I looked all over her chest and back but didn't see the insect responsible, so I told her that whatever it had been was gone.

She skipped off to play but in a few moments came back saying he had bitten her again. I lifted her shirt again and saw two red spots. So I took off her shirt, examined her carefully for a small spider or ant or mosquito or even a flea, saw nothing, then put a clean shirt on her and told her she was fine. A few moments later, she threw herself into my arms, tears streaming down her cheeks, and wailed that she had been bitten all over. This time, when I lifted up her shirt, I saw that her stomach and chest were covered in red spots! She hadn't been bitten by an insect; she had the chicken pox! The first spot had indicated she had the disease, even though I was unable to diagnose it until she broke out all over.

If you and I have even one "spot" of sin ... if we have ever sinned once in all of our lives ... that one sin indicates that we are riddled with the disease.[12] Some of us have more "spots" of obvious sin than others, but the Bible is clear that all of us are moral failures.[13] In the Bible this original, sin-infested nature is called our "old self,"[14] our "flesh,"[15] our "sinful nature,"[16] our "Adam,"[17] or our "Ishmael."[18] This old nature will never please God, and it will never see God.[19] You can learn to manage it, educate it, and drug it, but you can never transform it. Nothing but a brand-new nature will solve the human moral dilemma. Our old natures will never be "cured" of sin, which is why Jesus said, "You must be born again."[20]

Once you and I are spiritually reborn, we are given a totally new perfect, sinless nature, indwelt and empowered by the Holy Spirit. Being born again does not mean that you turn over a new leaf or that you just try harder to be good. It doesn't mean that you start going to church or singing in the choir. It doesn't mean you begin giving to charity or volunteering to work in the church nursery. It is actually a supernatural miracle that occurs in response to your decision to receive Jesus Christ by faith as your personal Savior and Lord when God places the life of Christ within you. He gives you new emotions to love God and love people you previously didn't even like, a new will to choose to do what is right and pleasing to God, and a new intellect to understand the truth and spiritual things. However, you and I will always have our old natures to contend with.

What takes place spiritually at your rebirth is very similar to what took place physically within the Virgin Mary. When the angel came to her and told her, "You have found favor with God. You will be with child and give birth to a son, and you are to give him the name Jesus," Mary was astounded! What he said was a practical impossibility! So she asked the angel, "How will this be ... since I am a virgin?" And the angel answered her by explaining, "The Holy Spirit will come upon you, and the power of the Most High will overshadow you. So the holy one to be born will be called the Son of God.... For nothing is impossible with God." Mary, in simple, childlike faith, took God at His Word and responded, "I am the Lord's servant.... May it be to me as you have said."[21]

In response to her faith, God supernaturally implanted her with the physical life of Jesus. Likewise, when you and I take God at His Word and place our faith in Him for our salvation and eternal life, He implants us with the spiritual life of Jesus.[22] Just as Mary carried within her the physical life of Jesus, you and I carry within us the spiritual life of Jesus. The Bible calls our new nature our "new creation,"[23] our "new self,"[24] or our "Isaac."[25] It is Jesus living inside of us.

And when Jesus comes to live within us, there is such joy! We experience the thrill of having our sins forgiven, being reconciled to God, looking forward with hope to our heavenly home, knowing the "blessed assurance [that] Jesus is mine."[26]

Then our hearts are flooded with peace, our days are filled with purpose, our eyes are focused upward, our spirits bask in His unconditional love, our souls rest in His grace. And our life in Christ is more than wonderful — *for a while.*

Following your salvation, how long did peace and joy and love fill your life? Was it for a week? Or a month? Or a full year? When did you first become aware that something was terribly wrong? Did you begin to struggle with things that previously you hadn't even paid much attention to? Did old weaknesses or temptations or habits or values suddenly flaunt themselves in your face, dragging you away from what you knew God wanted for you? Are you still struggling?

What you are experiencing is the classic struggle between your old and new nature ... your Ishmael and your Isaac. The two natures are like oil and water; they will never mix. The apostle Paul warned the Galatians about this same struggle when he wrote, "The sinful nature desires what is contrary to the Spirit, and the Spirit what is contrary to the sinful nature. They are in conflict with each other, so that you do not do what you want."[27]

The new nature is empowered by the Holy Spirit, so in the fresh beginning of your Christian life you experience a measure of victory over the old nature. But in time, the new nature seems weaker because you are not accustomed to living in it; it's "new." And the old nature that has been in your life longer seems to dominate through force of habit; it's "old." You are used to acting, reacting, thinking, talking, and feeling the way your old nature determines. And make no mistake about it. The old nature is in rebellion against God and wants the place of authority in your life. So the conflict intensifies.

If you do nothing because it seems easier and more natural to succumb to the old nature, your new nature will never develop into the fullness of Christ within you, and you will live a miserable, defeated, frustrated life of failure after failure after failure.

I know this kind of frustration by experience, and so did the apostle Paul. His words encourage all of us who have lived with this inner conflict: "We know that the law is spiritual; but I am unspiritual, sold as a slave to sin. I do not understand what I do. For what I want to do I do not do, but what I hate I do. And if I do what I do not want to do, I agree that the law is good. As it is, it is no longer I myself who do it, but it is sin living in me. I know that nothing good lives in me, that is, in my sinful nature. For I have the desire to do what is good, but I cannot carry it out. For what I do is not the good I want to do; no, the evil I do not want to do — this I keep on doing."[28]

What an incredible testimony! I feel like I could have written that myself! In fact, if I were to personalize this passage for myself, it might look something like this:

> I know that Bible reading and Bible study are good for me, but I am unspiritual, dominated by old, sinful habits that I seem to have no power to overcome. I do not understand what I do. I keep wishing I could relive my failures and somehow take them back. And if I do what I do not want to do, I agree that the law is good because it awakens my conscience. The root of the problem seems to be much deeper than just wanting to be good and not wanting to be bad. I know that nothing good lives in me, that is, in my sinful nature. For I have the desire to do what is good, but I cannot carry it out. I just fail and fail and fail and fail.

It's so hard to acknowledge that, on my own, I have no power to be good in God's sight. But then I'm reminded that all of my righteousness is so permeated with sin that even the best things I could come up with are tainted.[29] For instance, if I publicly pray an eloquent prayer that sounds polished, personal, and powerful, as soon as someone comments on how inspiring it was, I'm thinking to myself, *It was, wasn't it?* Or, in my busyness, I go out of my way to do something for a friend who gratefully thanks me and remarks that she can't believe I would be so thoughtful when I have so many things pressing me, and I think to myself, *I was very thoughtful, wasn't I?* Or I can humbly take a backseat at a dinner and think to myself, *Anne, you are so humble.* Just the sin of pride alone is enough to contaminate any good works I may do.

Is that the missing piece to your puzzle? Are you striving to solve the problem of sin in your life because you think that the power to be good is in *you*? Are you one who says, "Well, there's a little bit of good in everyone," when actually, from God's point of view, there is no good in anyone.

Like Brer Rabbit hitting the tar baby, the harder I try to be good or to please God, the more I seem to get stuck in my cycle of failure and frustration until I can honestly confess that there is not one good thing in my old nature. The apostle Paul's candid exposé climaxes in an emotional outburst that has echoed in my heart many times: "What a wretched man I am!"[30] The word he uses for *wretched* is the same word that would be used to describe a soldier exhausted from battle. And what could be more wretched, more spiritually exhausting, than ...

> trying to please God and never pleasing Him,
> trying to be right and always making mistakes,
> trying to be a godly witness and constantly causing others to stumble,
> trying to maintain daily prayer and Bible reading and
>   constantly being inconsistent,
> trying to be patient, or kind, or gentle, then after two days of
>   constant interruptions and headaches, being right back where I was!

Those are just a *few* of my past frustrations![31]

Paul too lived with frustrations. Exclaiming how wretched he was, he uttered this desperate plea: "Who will rescue me from this body of death?"[32] He described his frustration of living with his old nature as a "body of death," a phrase graphically drawn from his own culture. In Tarsus, where Paul was from, when someone murdered another person in cold blood, the dead body of the victim was strapped to the killer, leg to leg, arm to arm, chest to chest, until the victim rotted. The killer had to "wear" the body of death as a gruesome punishment that reminded him of his crime every second of every minute of every hour of every day for weeks on end until the decaying infection spread to the killer and executed him. Paul was desperate to be rescued from his "body of death" ... and so am I!

At this stage in the Christian life, as I see it, we have two options. The first is a much more prevalent choice than the second, and it is to begin to wear a mask. You can become so paranoid about the conflict within your heart that you think somehow you're unique, that something drastically weird is wrong with you. So you start pretending to be more spiritual than you are. You live in your old nature but put on an act of living in your new nature. You become a little plastic

Christianette. Churches today are filled with those who have made this choice. Like the churches of Sardis and Laodicea,[33] they have turned perception into reality and deeply resent an authentic Christian whose life reveals their pretense and phoniness.

The second option is the one that Paul chose and, by God's grace, I have chosen as well. It's the option to break the cycle of sin and failure. There are no shortcuts. There is no quick fix. But there is victory ...

Experience the Conquest of Sin

Victory began for me when I recognized I was in a battle. This battle would never be won if I refused to acknowledge my failure to overcome sin. Have you been afraid to confess the strong grip sin has on your life because it makes you feel you're a failure as a Christian? And if you're a failure as a Christian, are you assuming God will not love you or use you? You may even spiral downward and begin to doubt your salvation and the security of your eternal life. Would you honestly admit to the presence of sin in your life and then choose to abhor the utter sinfulness of it? If so, you're now ready for conquest!

Choose to Obey God's Command

Abraham teaches us how to solve the conflict in our hearts by the way he solved the conflict in his own home. His action seems harsh, almost cold and cruel, but it was taken in obedience to God's command. His victory began when he no longer ignored the conflict, no longer pretended the conflict wasn't there, no longer covered up the conflict, no longer rationalized the conflict, even in his own mind. He dealt with it.

Sarah was the one who brought it squarely to his attention when she delivered the ultimatum: "Get rid of that slave woman and her son, for that slave woman's son will never share in the inheritance with my son Isaac" (21:10). Like the sparrows and the cuckoos, Ishmael and Isaac could no longer coexist if Isaac was to develop and have any kind of promising life. Ishmael had to go.

Abraham's face must have turned several shades of pale as Sarah's words pierced the depths of his very soul. Nausea must have choked him and the tent must have swirled around him as he stared hard at his wife. Yet even while his heart must have shouted, *No! No! No! A thousand times, no!* his head surely told him he had known this day was coming. He had seen the conflict and could ignore it no longer.

As right as it was, the decision was not easy. "The matter distressed Abraham greatly because it concerned his son" (21:11). As heart-wrenching as I know it must have been, Abraham immediately knew the wisdom of such an action, if for no other reason than God immediately confirmed Sarah's point of view, telling Abraham, "Do not be so distressed about the boy and your maidservant. Listen to whatever Sarah tells you, because it is through Isaac that your offspring will be reckoned. I will make the son of the maidservant into a nation also, because he is your offspring" (21:12 – 13).

Such a hard message to hear. Yet so wise. Later, as Isaac's personality developed, Abraham would see that Isaac tended to be a follower. He was a sweet, submissive, and gentle child. He would have so adored and emulated his older brother that Ishmael could have turned his heart away from the Lord. As for Ishmael, by now he was almost twenty years of age. It was time for him to be on his own. He too needed to develop into the man God intended him to be.

So, with Sarah's angry words ringing in his ears and with God's Word encouraging his heart — and with tears streaming down his age-lined face and running down his long gray beard — "Early the next morning Abraham took some food and a skin of water and gave them to Hagar. He set them on her shoulders and then sent her off with the boy" (21:14). And God, who loved Hagar as much as He loved Abraham, and who loved Ishmael as much as He loved Isaac, "was with the boy as he grew up" (21:20).

Choose to Put Off Your Old Nature

When Abraham acknowledged the conflict in his home, God's Word came to him, giving him specific encouragement and instruction on how to solve it. When I have acknowledged the conflict within my own heart, God has encouraged and instructed me also through His Word, reminding me that I too have some hard choices to make: "You were taught, with regard to your former way of life, to put off your old self, which is being corrupted by its deceitful desires; to be made new in the attitude of your minds; and to put on the new self, created to be like God in true righteousness and holiness."[34]

"Put to death, therefore, whatever belongs to your earthly nature: sexual immorality, impurity, lust, evil desires and greed, which is idolatry.... You must rid yourselves of all such things as these: anger, rage, malice, slander, and filthy language from your lips. Do not lie.... put on the new self, which is being renewed in knowledge in the image of its Creator."[35]

God is obviously instructing you and me to cast out our Ishmael,[36] but how in the world do we do that? How can we possibly put to death our old nature inside us? There are no ...

> pills to take,
> tonics to drink,
> formulas to follow,
> guns to aim,
> incantations to chant,

just choices to make! Unlike Ishmael, who left quietly and decisively one morning, I can testify from personal experience your old nature will die slowly and over time. But you *can* conquer it ... one choice at a time, dozens of times a day, every day for the rest of your life.

Choose to Exercise the New Nature

The choices we make are like a spiritual workout routine. Because I travel so much, I have never joined a gym, but several years ago I hired a personal trainer to teach me how to use simple elastic bands. I take the bands with me wherever I go, and three times a week I try to faithfully exercise certain muscle groups to build up my body strength. If I merely pulled on the bands one or two times, once in a while, I would remain as I have been, weak and flabby. But as I have pulled on the bands in repetitious cycles consistently, my muscles have become stronger until I can actually see and feel the difference.

The choices we make every day exercise our will like the bands exercise my muscles. They determine whether we will grow spiritually strong or remain spiritually weak and dominated by our old nature. For example ...

If I hurriedly run to the grocery store to pick up a forgotten item because I have company coming any minute and find there are five people in the only line open and the checkout clerk is gossiping with a friend on her cell phone, making everyone wait, I have a choice to make. If I rudely tell her off when it's my turn, I've just exercised my old nature.

If I go to visit my father, taking along a home-baked apple pie, and then my brothers walk in wanting some pie too, I have a choice to make. If I cut myself a bigger piece and give them smaller pieces, I've just exercised my old nature.

If I go to the church picnic and see that there is a shortage of my favorite casserole, I have a choice to make. If I choose to quickly grab a serving for myself before someone else gets it, I've exercised my old nature.

If I'm stuck in traffic and someone is trying to merge from my right, I have a choice to make. If I pull up to the bumper of the car in front of me and edge that merging car out of my lane, I've exercised my old nature.

If my grandchild repeatedly interrupts me when I'm trying to answer my emails before the family gathers for dinner, I have a choice to make. If I command her sternly to stop bothering me and leave the room, I've exercised my old nature.

If my husband, who is getting increasingly hard of hearing, asks me for the third time to repeat something I've said, I have a choice to make. If I yell at him and tell him he needs a hearing aid, I've exercised my old nature.

Let's think of some examples of *you* exercising your old nature ...

If you decide to fix a special meal for your spouse on Valentine's Day, setting the table with candles and fresh flowers, then your spouse walks through the door nonchalantly two hours late, you have a choice to make. If you sulk or throw the cold food, wilted flowers, and burned-down candles in the face of the offender, you've exercised your old nature.

If you're running late for work, don't have a clean shirt to wear, then find the unwashed laundry stacked up in a basket, you have a choice to make. If you yell at your stay-at-home spouse and demand to know what he or she did all day yesterday, you exercise your old nature.

If you get to the office, find the computer server is down, your assistant is late, the key to your file drawer has been misplaced, and your most important client is due in five minutes, you have a choice to make. If you kick the computer and demand your assistant work through lunch and late into the night, you exercise your old nature.

If you leave your job an hour early but fill out your time card as though you've worked a full day, you have exercised your old nature.

The growth and strength of our old natures are determined choice after choice after choice — choices about spending money and spending time, about who our friends are, and about the places we go, the pastimes we indulge in, the responses we make to stressful situations. Choice after choice, large and small, public and private, personal and professional, each one exercises our spiritual muscles. We can live in our old natures by making the easy feel-good-for-a-moment, pleasure-for-a-season choices, then wear a mask, pretending we're for real, or we can make choices that will strengthen our new natures.

Paul bluntly reinforced the need to cast out our old natures when he wrote to the Galatians, "Now you, ... like Isaac, are children of promise. At that time the son born in the ordinary way persecuted the son born by the power of the Spirit. It is the same now. But what does the Scripture say? 'Get rid of the slave woman and her son, for the slave woman's son will never share in the inheritance with the free woman's son.' Therefore, brothers, we are not children of the slave woman, but of the free woman."[37]

Get rid of your old nature! Deny your natural responses and choose to exercise your new nature ...

When delayed at the grocery store, if I choose to patiently wait my turn, helping the clerk bag another customer's items as well as my own, commenting that I know it must be tough to be the only checkout clerk on duty, I've exercised my new nature.

If I'm serving the apple pie to my father and brothers and I cut them the most generous slices, I exercise my new nature.

If at the church picnic I see that there's not enough of my favorite casserole to go around and choose to wait until everyone else helps themselves before I do, I've exercised my new nature.

If while I'm stuck in traffic someone tries to merge from the right and I slow down, signaling the other driver to slip in front of me, I've exercised my new nature.

If my grandchild interrupts me repeatedly when I'm trying to answer my emails and I choose to gently explain to her that I'm trying to get some work done, then give her a tablet of paper and a pen suggesting that she "work" quietly while I do, I've exercised my new nature.

If my husband asks me to repeat something I've already said three times and I choose to go up to him, gently take his face in my hands, and repeat for the fourth time what I said, I've exercised my new nature. (Then, if I glare at him over my shoulder, mumble that he still needs to get a hearing aid, and, when he asks me to repeat what I've mumbled, I say, "Oh, nothing" … I've just exercised my old nature again.)

If your spouse is two hours late for your special dinner on Valentine's Day and you choose to greet him or her warmly, serve the plates of food you've kept warm in the oven, and ask nicely what the delay was, then add reasonably, "Please, next time give me a call to let me know you're running late," you've exercised your new nature.

If you're late for work, can't find a clean shirt, and you choose to tell your stay-at-home spouse, "You must have had a tough day yesterday. I'll just wear yesterday's shirt under a jacket and no one will know the difference," you've just exercised your new nature.

If you get to the office, find things are unraveling, take a moment to pray for help, explain to the client that it's simply one of those days, and do the best you can, you've just exercised your new nature.

If you need to leave your job an hour early and get approval from your supervisor first, making sure you duly note it on your time card, you have just exercised your new nature.

Choices. I told you they weren't easy. Sometimes the small, irritating ones are the hardest of all to make. But actually, if we make the choice, the indwelling Holy Spirit of God supernaturally gives us the power to carry it out.

After Paul poured out his heart in Romans 7, describing the wrestling match with his old nature, he came to a thrilling conclusion. When he cried out in agony, "Who will rescue me from this body of death?" he answered his own cry: "Thanks be to God — *Jesus will*!" He summed it up by stating, "Therefore, there is now no condemnation" to live a life of defeat and failure "for those who are in Christ Jesus, because through Christ Jesus the law of the Spirit of life set me free from the law of sin and death."[38]

Free! Free from the power of sin in my life! Free! Free, at long last!

Next time you're tempted to tell a white lie by exaggerating the truth, next time you lose your temper or steal someone's reputation through gossip, remember, each temptation is also a test that determines the strength or weakness of your will to make right or wrong choices. And the choices add up. God has given you His Spirit so that you have the power to make the right choices. As you do, and as your new nature grows, you will instinctively react and respond in the Spirit.

Our choices have very serious consequences. Right choices lead to freedom. Not only do they determine whether we conquer the sin in our lives and experience victory over failure, but they also determine the validity of our personal witness. Wrong choices keep you defeated in a cycle of failure.

On the one hand, if you live in your old nature, you may be born again and go to heaven when you die, but no one will ever see Jesus in you. You will be so dominated by the old nature that the new nature will be buried and virtually invisible to an observer. People won't even know you are a Christian. You will never fulfill the potential God has for your life. You will never be a channel of blessing to others. You will never really know God as Abraham did and make God known to others. Even if you tell other people about Him, you won't have any credibility because all they see is the old nature. To them, you don't look much different than they do. And you will never be pleasing to God.[39]

On the other hand, if you live in your new nature, over time you will become so Christlike that even casual acquaintances will recognize the difference in your life. After Abraham cast Ishmael out of his home, "at that time Abimelech and Phicol the commander of his forces said to Abraham, 'God is with you in everything you do'" (21:22). *At that time*, at the very time Abraham had cast Ishmael out, his neighbor who had formerly rebuked him for his sinful behavior could now see God in his life. To me, that makes all the large and small, hard and easy choices worth the difficulty many times over.

There is another, even more serious consequence to the choices you and I make. When we get to heaven, our old natures will drop off, and only our new natures will remain for eternity.[40] The new nature in some believers will be larger and stronger than the new nature in others. No one knows how this difference will play out ...

Maybe the one with the undeveloped new nature will have very little responsibility, while the one whose new nature is fully developed will have great responsibility and leadership.

Maybe the one with the undeveloped new nature will have no reward for the life lived on earth, while the one with a fully developed new nature will have many crowns.

Maybe the one with the undeveloped new nature will be clothed in a skimpy garment of white, while the one with a fully developed new nature will have a glorious garment that rivals the most magnificent wedding gown.

Whatever the difference will be, Paul challenges you and me to take very seriously the choices we make on a daily, moment-by-moment basis. He solemnly warns us that while we will never be judged for the guilt of our sin, since Jesus took the judgment for us on the cross, we will be held accountable for the way we have lived our Christian lives.[41]

If we live our earthly lives in our old natures, making choice after choice according to what we want instead of according to His will (which we don't seek in prayer), our own way instead of His (which we don't like because we believe the end justifies the means), what we think is right or what everyone else is doing instead of in obedience to His Word (which we never make time to read), then our lives are like wood, hay, and stubble when we pass through the fire of God's holiness. Our lives will be burned up. We will have nothing to show for our time spent here on earth. We will still be saved but as though by fire. We will still be welcomed into heaven, but we will barely have squeaked through the door.

On the other hand, if we live in our new natures, making choice after choice according to His will that we diligently seek in prayer, His way that considers the process as important as the end result, His Word that we make the time to read, study, apply, and obey, then our lives are like gold, silver, and precious stones. When they pass through the fire of God's holiness, they survive, and we are rewarded with heavenly crowns for our earthly lives that have been lived to His glory.

Years ago, I heard a great Bible teacher issue a challenge that not only haunts me with fear of failure but motivates me to be very disciplined and intentional about living in my new nature. He asked this question: When you get to heaven, and ...

> *for the first time* you see Jesus face-to-face,
> > *for the first time* you fully comprehend what it cost Him
> > > to open heaven's gates for you,

> *for the first time* you understand the height and depth
> and breadth and length of His love,
> *for the first time* you possess your eternal treasures,

don't you think you will want to have something to give Him in return for all He has given you? On that day, will you have the ashes of a wasted life to press into His nail-scarred palm? Or will you have a crown to lay at His nail-scarred feet? Nothing I could ever give Him would be adequate to express my heartfelt appreciation for all He has done for me, but a crown would be *something* to give ...

What happens at the judgment seat of Christ *then* is determined by our choices *now*. Praise God! We're not there yet. There is still time!

> There is still life to be lived!
> There are still choices to be made!
> There is still time to strengthen your new nature!
> There is still time to have something to show for your life lived down here!
> There is still time to have something to lay at His feet!

Which will it be? Are you going to be stuck in your cycle of sin forever, just succumbing to the conflict and living in defeat and failure while pretending you are something else? Or will you break the cycle? Acknowledge the conflict. Live in the freedom and experience the victory that comes as you conquer the sinful old nature in your life, choice by choice by choice.

Choose now to cast everything out in order to embrace the magnificent obsession ... while there is still time. And *enjoy* being free at last!

～ SEVEN ～

Lay Everything Down

Genesis 22

Ten thousand feet up in the mountains of Afghanistan, behind enemy lines, the air was cold and thin. On June 28, 2005, four elite Navy SEALs carefully picked their way through the rocky terrain. Their mission was to scout out a young terrorist named Ahmad Shah who led a vicious band of killers known as the Mountain Tigers.

Suddenly, with no advance warning, the air around the SEALs erupted in a three-sided firestorm. They had been betrayed by locals, their presence and location given to the enemy, who outnumbered them fifty to four. Trying to escape the assault, the four men, each wounded, began bounding down the steep face of the mountain, leaping twenty to thirty feet at a time. Forty-five minutes into the fight, the enemy had the advantage, not only of numbers, but also in terrain. The SEALs were relentlessly pursued and pinned down in a ravine.

One of the four, Lt. Michael Murphy, was determined to get help for his fellow SEALs. Because the terrain would not allow a clear radio signal to headquarters, he "did not love [his life] so much as to shrink from death."[1]

Instead, fully comprehending the danger to himself, the gravity of their position, and the necessity of getting outside support, Lieutenant Murphy stepped out of the protective covering of the rocks. Clearly exposing himself to enemy fire, he coolly made contact with his base and requested assistance. While calmly giving the specifics of his unit's location, the size of the enemy force that had pinned them down, and the request for immediate help, he was shot in the back. The bullet's impact caused him to drop his transmitter.

Still under fire, he picked up his radio, finished his call, and continued to fire on the advancing enemy. He returned to cover with his comrades, and the battle raged for another one hour and fifteen minutes, exploding through hills and over cliffs until the SEALs ran out of ammunition.

In the end, Gunner's Mate Second Class Danny Dietz, Sonar Technician Second Class Matthew Axelson, and Lieutenant Murphy were dead, along with thirty-five Taliban fighters. The fourth SEAL, Hospital Corpsman Second Class Marcus Luttrell, was blasted by a grenade and knocked unconscious. When he regained consciousness, he was dehydrated, with a bullet in one leg, shrapnel in both legs, and his back broken in three places. Yet he crawled seven miles, evading the enemy.

On July 2, 2005, his rescue was bittersweet. It had been made possible by the heroic act of Lieutenant Murphy, who had willingly laid down his life to save him.[2] As a result, Lieutenant Murphy posthumously received our nation's highest award, the Medal of Honor.

Jesus summed up such selfless sacrifice as the ultimate expression of devotion when He explained, "Greater love has no one than this, that one lay down his life for his friends."[3]

In Abraham's pursuit to know God as his friend, he came to the supreme test of his devotion: whether or not he was willing to lay down not his own life but his most precious possession.

What is your most precious possession? Whatever it may be, to embrace the magnificent obsession, to know God as Abraham did, to be God's friend, to receive all that He has for you, to experience the God-filled life, you must lay it down ...[4]

IT'S A COMMAND

Abraham's most precious possession was Isaac. When Abraham sent Ishmael away, Isaac was, for all intents and purposes, his only son. He must have given Isaac even more time and attention in an effort to erase the agonizing pain he had experienced as he watched Ishmael and Hagar trudging down the road toward the wilderness.

The scene of their dismissal, the wounded look in Hagar's eyes when he told her she had to take Ishmael and leave, the damp feel of the water skin as he draped it on her shoulder, the expression of guilty resentment on Ishmael's face, the fleeting glimpses of incredulous servants peeking out of tents to see what was going on — all of that must have been branded on Abraham's mind to replay itself hundreds of times over.

Abraham must have thought he had laid down everything when he gave up Ishmael. But then, about ten years after that critical decision and decisive action to cast everything out, "God tested Abraham" (Genesis 22:1).

God tests His children. How I need to be reminded of this over and over. Do you need to be reminded too? What hard place are you in now that could be a test? Maybe it has come to you in the form of a temptation or an attack from the enemy, but God has allowed it to test you.

Satan tempts you and me to weaken us and draw out the sin in our lives, but God's purpose in testing us is to strengthen our faith and draw out the good.

Sometimes I'm aware I'm being tested. Other times, it's only in retrospect that I understand what was going on. God has tested . . .

- my commitment to get up early for prayer and Bible reading by allowing me to be so sleepy when my alarm sounds in the morning that I have felt drugged,
- my availability to serve Him by allowing family opportunities to arise *after* I have confirmed a ministry opportunity,
- my faith in His promise by allowing circumstances in my life to contradict it,
- my dependence upon Him by giving me a forty-five-minute message that program organizers have said I have fifteen minutes to deliver,
- my obedience to His call in my life by allowing extremely attractive, lucrative offers to distract me,
- my resolve to prevail in prayer by giving me no evidence that He is answering, and
- my life's goal of knowing Him — the magnificent obsession — by shrouding Himself in the darkened cloud of unexplainable circumstances and heartache.

Be prepared, because God will test you too.

If you have decided to leave everything behind, He may allow your past to suddenly be so attractive that you can't bear to think of never going back or your failure to be so painful you can't bring yourself to forgive yourself, much less receive His forgiveness.

If you have decided to let everything go, He may allow one thing in your life to become so desirable you feel you just have to have it.

If you have decided to trust Him completely with everything, He may allow one unfulfilled promise to loom so large in your mind you doubt His Word, or He may allow your commitment to tithe to be challenged by an unexpected bill.

If you have decided to lift everything up, He may allow circumstances to indicate He is unresponsive to your prayer, and the person you're praying for may appear to harden his heart.

If you have decided to cast everything out, He may allow so many irritations to disrupt your day that your angry old nature is ready to boil over.

If you have decided to lay everything down, He may allow your life to be so blessed that you don't think it's really necessary after all.

God tests us, but He always measures the test in proportion to our faith. Twenty years earlier or ten years earlier or even five years earlier, Abraham would not have been capable of passing the supreme test God gave him at this stage of his life. The Bible says the test was given "some time later," when God knew Abraham's faith could handle it.

I've discovered that God knows exactly when and how to test me. But He has reassured me He will never give me a test or temptation greater than I can bear, although He does give me tests that I *think* are greater than I can bear — which is what makes them a test.[5]

A Personal Command

There is no doubt that this was a test for Abraham, because God called him by name: "He said to him, 'Abraham!'" (22:1). For me, one of the most thrilling blessings of knowing God is that He calls me by my name. *He knows me.* And He speaks to me personally through His Word.

While in the process of writing this book, I have had more than the usual number of crises, problems, challenges, demands, hurts, and confusion, which I realize in retrospect have been tests. One morning, when I opened my Bible, I turned to the "wrong" page. I had been studying Exodus 16 in my devotional time, but I opened "by mistake" to Exodus 20. Before I realized it and could turn to the right passage, verse 21 caught my eye. God had instructed Moses that He would come in a "dense cloud" on Mount Sinai, then verse 21 says, "The people remained at a distance, while Moses approached the thick darkness where God was."

As I read it, then reread it, I heard God speaking to me: *Anne, most people remain at a distance from Me when they think drawing near will involve crises, problems, challenges, demands, hurts, and confusion — tests — all the things you've been going through. They are afraid of the "cloud" of suffering or pressure or pain, the darkness of confusion and lack of vision for the next step. But I want you to be like Moses and embrace the cloud and the thick darkness — because that's where I am.*

When I turned back to Exodus 16, He confirmed His Word to me when I read, "They looked toward the desert, and there was the glory of the LORD appearing in the cloud."[6] The passage assured me I would glimpse His glory in the midst of all that I was doing and going through — and I did! Reflecting on my experiences, I was aware of specific evidence of His goodness and faithfulness, His kindness and gentleness, His power and His presence, His provision and His protection.

I've looked toward the desert of what seemed like emptiness and dryness and weakness, and I've glimpsed His glory in the cloud!

Praise God! He speaks to me ... and you ... and Abraham ... personally, in the language of our lives at any given moment in time. But we have to be available and willing to hear what He has to say. When God called Abraham by name, Abraham replied, "Here I am" (22:1).

If I had not gotten up for my early morning time of prayer and Bible reading, if I had not been studying Exodus paragraph by paragraph, if I had not been willing to take a moment to read what was on the "wrong" page before turning back to the passage I had intended to read, I would not have heard God speak to me that morning. God speaks, but I have to be available to listen.

I wonder, how available are you to hear God's voice? What does God want to say to you that you have yet to hear because you haven't made the time to listen? I've wondered that about myself when, for whatever reason, I've gone through the day without opening my Bible. What promise would He have given me to turn my doubt into confident hope? What encouragement would He have given that would have carried me through my day with joy? What warning would have alerted me to impending danger or attack? What command would He have issued that would have kept me in the center of His will?

What have I missed because I was too busy, or too worried, or too sleepy, or too distracted to make myself available to Him?

A Painful Command

Abraham was listening when God spoke to him. And what God said must have been very hard to hear. I too have discovered that God is not always easy to listen to. Sometimes He convicts me of sin. Sometimes He forbids me to indulge in a favorite pastime. Sometimes He calls me to step out of my comfort zone and onto the surface of the stormy sea. Sometimes He commands me to do something I don't really want to do, something that's painful. In times past, God has commanded me . . .

to love someone who has rejected me,

to forgive someone who has wronged me,

to serve someone who resents me,

to help someone who has not helped me,

to remain silent and absorb unjust abuse.

What has He said to you that was hard to hear? What has He commanded you to do that you didn't want to do? God told Abraham, "Take your son, your only son, Isaac, whom you love, and go to the region of Moriah. Sacrifice him there as a burnt offering on one of the mountains I will tell you about" (22:2).

Abraham must have been incredulous. God was telling him to take his most precious possession — "his only son, the son whom he loved" — and lay him down, sacrifice him on the altar. That was a pulse-stopping, heart-shattering, mind-boggling, stunningly unbelievable command!

Isaac was more than Abraham's only son; he was the son of promise. The son he had prayed for and longed for and waited a lifetime for and for whom he had left everything twenty-five years earlier in order to claim God's promise. All of Abraham's hopes and dreams were wrapped up in Isaac. The fullness of God's blessings and future purpose for Abraham were so entwined with the life of Abraham's son that to sacrifice Isaac would be like sacrificing himself.

What is your most precious and valued possession? Is it your spouse? your children? your career? your desire for a child? your desire for a spouse? your desire for a career? your plans for the future? your financial portfolio? your time? your reputation? your business? your talent? your body? your sex life? your ability? your health? your ministry? your freedom? your friends?

I've identified my Isaac by asking myself what would I cling to while I laid down everything else? What would you cling to? Whatever that is, that's your Isaac. It may seem small and insignificant to others, but it's extremely precious to you.[7]

Would you be willing to lay it down?

Would you lay down …

your pride, being the first to say you are sorry?

your spouse, releasing him or her for full-time Christian service?

your child, allowing him the freedom to find God in his own way?

your reputation, taking a public stand for your faith in Christ?

your future, giving up your own goals and dreams to Him?

Or, instead, do you carefully calculate what you will — and you won't — give to Him? Do you deliberately determine how much time or effort or money you can give to Him without having to give up time or effort or money you want for yourself? Do you give to Him painlessly because you don't give until it hurts or until it costs you any real sacrifice? Actually, a sacrifice isn't a sacrifice *until* it's a sacrifice, is it? And real sacrifice is a commitment to follow through — with no limits, boundaries, or reservations — in obedience to God's command …

It's a Commitment

Not only was Abraham commanded to sacrifice his only beloved son, but he was told to do it on one of the mountains in the region of Moriah. He was to perform his sacrifice on a mountain just a stone's throw from Calvary, where two thousand years later another Father would sacrifice His most precious possession — His only, beloved Son.

This was a command that required total commitment to obey.

When my life has been wrapped around my Isaac and I've had to lay him down, it has been a sacrifice, not just of him but of me too. Is your life so entwined with your most precious possession that sacrificing it would demand a sacrifice of yourself? A sacrifice of your heart and your will and your mind and your strength? Is God commanding you to lay *yourself* down on Calvary's mountain, at the foot of the cross? Is it time for you to surrender not 50 percent or 75 percent or 90 percent of your life to Him, but time for you to surrender *all*? If you want to embrace the magnificent obsession, then the time has come for you to make a total commitment. But the choice is still yours. As the choice has been mine.

The Commitment Begins with a Choice

It is natural for me to assume Abraham's reaction was one of total disbelief: *Lord, that doesn't sound like You. You promised to make of Isaac a great nation, and he's not even married. I don't yet have even one grandchild, much less descendants like the stars of the sky. If I sacrifice Isaac, what will become of Your promises? I think I'll go discuss this with Sarah ...*

Can you imagine what would have happened if Abraham had discussed God's command with anyone, much less Sarah? Without doubt, his resolve to obey God's command would have been weakened. Maybe he could have used her reaction as a reason for disobedience: *Well, God, You know Isaac is Sarah's son too, and she said absolutely that I could not take him away and sacrifice him to anyone or anything! So, You understand, if it was just up to me, I'd do it. But I can't go against my wife.*

The Choice Made Privately

Abraham didn't discuss God's command with anyone; instead, he made his choice to obey privately. His example gave me encouragement when I began the "Just Give Me Jesus" revival ministry.

I had shared my decision to start a revival ministry with a few trusted friends and family members, most of whom were supportive. Several, however, lovingly counseled me that the work would be too hard, that women would not respond to such a simple program, that it would never work to offer it free of charge, that I would bankrupt my ministry and destroy my own credibility. Abraham's example taught me to make the decision privately, based strictly on what I believed to be God's command. If I hadn't, their counsel would have given me such pause and weighed so heavily that I might have disobeyed what I believed to be God's Word to me.

What are you discussing with others that you should be deciding in private?

Has God commanded you to share the gospel with your neighbor? Have you discussed this with your spouse? Did your spouse warn you that the gospel might be offensive and could turn a congenial neighbor into a hostile one?

Has God commanded you to start a Bible study in your home? Have you discussed it with your neighbor? Did she warn you that it might also offend those of other faiths, and you would sow division on your street?

Has God commanded you to separate from certain bars and clubs? Have you discussed it with your coworker? Did he warn you that you risked losing the business contacts necessary for your job?

Has God commanded you to tithe? Did you discuss it with your financial adviser? Did he warn you that tithing would seriously interfere with your cash flow and suggest that maybe you could consider it next year?

Has God commanded you to confront injustice? Did you discuss it with the other person who was also treated wrongly? Did that person say not to get involved because the penalty could be the loss of a job or a position in the community?

I've discovered that so often our friends or family members want to protect us. They don't want us to get hurt or to lose out or to come up short. And therefore, sometimes they don't give us wise counsel. If we're not fully committed to obeying whatever God says, their counsel can be just the excuse for disobedience we're looking for. So I've found, like Abraham, some choices need to be made in private. I have also found that once I make the decision to obey God's command, whatever it is, peace floods my heart.

The Choice Made Peacefully

The hardest part of a decision, to me, is often just discerning the will of God. But once I know for sure what His will is, and once I make the decision to be obedient, the rest is almost easy. I have peace.

Abraham rose up "early the next morning" (22:3). God must initially have spoken to him either in the afternoon or the evening. Does that mean Abraham then went to sleep?[8] How could he have possibly slept after such a command? He must have understood God's command and made the firm choice to obey, therefore he had peace in his heart.

What decision are you still wrestling with God about? Aren't you tired of the struggle? Isn't it time you just gave up, gave in, and laid it all down? God wants to fill your heart with His peace.

The Choice Made Promptly

I wonder if Abraham rose up early before he could have any second thoughts. There was no apparent doubt, hesitation, questioning, delays, or procrastination. He obeyed promptly.

A couple of years ago I received a phone call from two dear friends, inviting me to speak at an evangelistic luncheon they wanted to host in their city. My schedule was already full, and I was sure I would have to decline, but I promised to pray about it. When I prayed, I felt God speaking to me from His Word, telling me not to decline but to accept their invitation. I thanked Him for such clear, immediate direction. In my heart, I was already looking forward to going to my friends' city for what I knew would be an adventure of faith.

I was caught up in many pressing issues at the time and did not immediately return their phone call. I knew I would accept, but for reasons I can't remember now, I procrastinated in telling them. Before long, I was on the road again, and I *forgot* to call them back! About four months later, I remembered! When I tried frantically to reach them, I couldn't because they were then on the road traveling. About six months after the initial invitation, I finally connected with them. As a result, I spoke at the luncheon, but it was held about eight months later than they had originally planned. While many lives were changed, I am haunted to this day by what would have been had I been prompt in my obedience. I had missed God's timing, and I believe I missed the fullness of what He wanted to do.

The Choice Made Practically

From the maps I have studied, the region of Moriah seems to have been about thirty miles from where Abraham was living. And he was well over a hundred years of age. He must have known it would not be an easy trip, and if he was going to get there at all, he would have to make practical arrangements. So he "saddled his donkey. He took with him two of his servants and his son Isaac. When he had cut enough wood for the burnt offering, he set out for the place God had told him about" (22:3).

By his thorough preparation, he was making sure that he left no way of escape for himself. He knew he would need the donkey to help carry the wood and, from time to time, carry Isaac and him on such a long journey. He made sure he cut the wood in case there were no trees where he was going. And he took the fire and a knife to complete the sacrifice as God required. It would have been tempting to have taken Isaac for the offering, the donkey for transportation, the wood and the fire for the sacrifice, and then, when he arrived, to discover he had not brought a knife to slay his son. He could have shrugged and said, "God, you know I made the choice to obey. But I guess I just can't. I forgot the knife. You understand."

I've actually used that excuse regarding my early morning prayer time. I know God has commanded me to get up early and spend time with Him. I have made the choice to obey, but how many times have I overslept because I forgot to set the alarm? Even as I apologize and say, "You understand," I can almost hear Him sighing and saying, "Anne, I understand, all right. What I understand is that you weren't thorough in your practical preparation because you never fully intended to follow through in obedience."

It's foolish for me to even try to give Him an excuse. He sees right through it.

The Choice Made Patiently

As I watched Abraham making this hard journey, he was not only practical, he was persistent. "He set out for the place God had told him about. On the third day Abraham looked up and saw the place in the distance" (22:3 – 4). Those must have been the three longest days of Abraham's life. They must have felt like the equivalent of the twenty-five years Abraham had waited for Isaac's birth. His feet must have felt like lead as he put one foot in front of the other for thirty miles. Just because he had peace in his heart didn't mean it was an easy commitment. It must have taken every ounce of his willpower for him to persist day after day after day.

I can hardly imagine how patient Abraham must have been when, at the end of that long first day, he still hadn't arrived where God wanted him to be. There was no further word from the Lord, no blessing, no encouragement … just a dusty road still stretching out before him, a hard ground to sleep on, and a trusting boy whose company Abraham must have treasured. The second day was more of the same. Still there was no outward sign or feeling or confirmation that he had made the right decision. All he had to go on, and to keep on going on, was the Word of God.

Obedience requires persistence — and patience.

God has commanded me to get up early to spend time with Him in prayer and also to read His Word, listening for Him to speak to me, but many, many mornings when I have gotten up early and read my Bible, I have had no special word from God. After several mornings of silence, the temptation is to roll over and go back to sleep when the alarm goes off, since God doesn't seem to be speaking to me anyway.

But I've learned by hard experience to patiently persist, knowing the very morning I sleep in could very well be the morning when God does speak into my life. Or it could be that the very afternoon following the morning I sleep in, someone calls needing a word of wisdom or counsel, and I'm spiritually dry with nothing to offer.

How many blessings, how many words of encouragement, how many answers to my questions, how many insights into His Word, how much wisdom have I *missed* because I just haven't patiently persisted in my pursuit of His voice?

I doubt that Abraham ever tossed in his sleep at night, wondering what he might have missed; instead he made a clear, firm choice to obey God's command, then he confidently committed to follow through.

The Commitment Is Carried Out with Confidence

When at long last Abraham reached his destination, "He said to his servants, 'Stay here with the donkey while I and the boy go over there. We will worship'" (22:5). For three days, I'm sure Abraham must have thought of nothing other than what God had commanded him to do. He had had time to reflect on the details, the nuances, the implications, the consequences of what God had said.

If he was going to be bitterly resentful, he had had time for it to build in his heart. He could have said, "God, I've been following You for forty years or more, and I can't believe You would 'reward' me like this. I've been good. Why would You do this to me? You told me Yourself that You would bless me.

"Well, this is about as far from being blessed as I can imagine. I gave You one son. Why would You take this one too? I know I have to be obedient, but I don't like it. In fact, I don't think I will ever get over it. My relationship with You will never be the same. You no longer seem good or loving or right to me. And did You ever stop to think how this will affect Isaac and his opinion of You? I sure hope You know what You're doing, because I think You're making a mess of things."

What is your honest opinion of God? What has He either allowed in your life or actually led you into that has been hard — and hurtful? Do you think He is like your legalistic pastor? Or your abusive father? Or your overbearing spouse? Are you secretly resentful? Do you doubt His goodness? His righteousness? His loving-kindness *toward you*? Do you lack confidence in His character?

One of the primary tactics of the enemy is to tempt you and me to doubt God's Word and to doubt God's character. Since the garden of Eden, Satan has tried to cast God in such a negative light that we lose confidence in who He is and what He has said, and therefore we draw away from Him and disobey Him.[9]

Confidence in God's Person

If Abraham was tempted to lose confidence in God, I could see no evidence that he fell for it. He had no deep-down doubts or resentments or anger. After all, he had been walking with God for forty years! By personal experience, he knew ...

God's sufficiency to supply all of his needs,

God's mercy to bail him out of failure again ... and again,

God's blessing upon blessing in spite of his failure,

God's grace to save Lot from judgment in answer to prayer,

God's love as his shield and his reward,

God's goodness to give him the desire of his heart in Isaac,

God's greatness to give Isaac to him through Sarah!

What do you know of God from your experience? Make your own list. Use the experiences as stepping-stones in your walk of obedient faith.

After forty years of walking by obedient faith, Abraham knew God! Without question, he was so totally confident in God and in what God had said that his obedience was his personal tribute. It was an act of worship!

Worship is not necessarily ...

arm-raising,

hand-clapping,

feet-dancing,

body-swaying,

tear-jerking

outward motions while we sing praise songs or listen to fiery sermons. Worship is the way we attribute worth to God. In my life, I've found that . . .

the tougher the assignment He gives me,

the more painful the experience He allows me,

the greater the sacrifice He demands of me,

the more unknown the way He leads me,

the more thorough the conviction of sin He reveals to me,

the more difficult the obedience He commands of me,

the more supreme is my worship experience.

The reason it's a worship experience is because I would only . . .

complete the assignment,

trust the experience,

make the sacrifice,

walk into the unknown,

confess and crucify the sin,

obey the command

because He says so. I wouldn't do it for anyone or anything else. But I do it willingly, gladly, obediently, and confidently . . . *for Him*! It's my act of worship.

I also have an only beloved son. He has been through cancer, a divorce, and some other very hard things. Several years ago, from this very passage of Scripture, God commanded me to lay him down on the altar of sacrifice. Unlike Abraham, I wrestled mightily with the painful command. Finally, God seemed to whisper in my heart, *Anne, are you trying to protect your son from Me? What do you think you can do better for him than I can?*

The Lord seemed to reassure me with the fact that Abraham walked up the mountain with Isaac. They went together. In fact, he never left Isaac throughout the entire journey or sacrifice. And God seemed to promise me, *Anne, if you lay your son down, give him completely, totally, fully to Me, as his heavenly Father, I will never leave him for a moment. I will watch over him, protect him, direct him, 24/7. Anne, I love him more than you do. Just lay him down.*

So I have, while keeping my focus on the One who is in the shadows of my son's life, the One whose eyes never leave him and whose hands never let go. And that is worship.

Confidence in God's Promises

Abraham then told his servants a truly incredible and very revealing thing. He told them to stay with the donkey while he and Isaac went up the mountain to worship, adding, "Then we will come back to you" (22:5). This astounding statement indicated he was truly at the pinnacle of his faith.

We will come back? Didn't he understand that he would be sacrificing Isaac on the mountain and *only he* would be coming back? I wanted to take him to the side and confront him, "Abraham, what in the world are you thinking?"

I found the answer to my prying question in the New Testament. The book of Hebrews tells us Abraham was so confident in God's promises, the fulfillment of which rested on Isaac and the descendants who would come through him, that he believed he would indeed sacrifice his son, but that God would raise him from the dead![10] Now that's confidence! Confidence in God's promises and also confidence in God's ...

> death-defying,
> grave-robbing,
> devil-smashing,
> earth-shaking,
> mountain-moving,
> history-splitting,
> *resurrection power!*

Confidence in God's Power

Abraham was fully expecting to experience God's power in a way he never had before! He was confident that God's power would bring glory from his grief, triumph from his tragedy, blessing from his brokenness, praise from his pain, and life from Isaac's death!

Are you so focused on what you must lay down you have lost focus on God's person and God's promises and God's power? Are you so focused on the cross and the tomb you are blinded to the resurrection and the crown? Would you take a moment to refocus? God is good. His promises are true. And His power is limitless. Place your confidence in Him. Unless you do, you will never reach the point where you can truly lay everything down before Him. You will always have some hesitation or reservation or question. It's when you lay everything down that you no longer just embrace the magnificent obsession. You begin to experience it!

The Commitment Is Brought to Completion

God had been testing Abraham's resolve to complete the sacrifice by the three-day delay the journey required. During that journey, Abraham had had ample opportunity to have second thoughts and turn around. He could have decided that all he truly wanted at that stage in his very old life was to have Isaac. Period. He could have decided, after all, that he really loved Isaac more than he wanted to keep pursuing God. He could have decided he was satisfied with knowing God to the extent he did, which was more than most people ever would. He could have fallen short of God's purpose for his life and missed the full potential of all that God had for him and just settled for less.

But Abraham wanted everything God wanted to give him. *Everything!* So "Abraham took the wood for the burnt offering and placed it on his son Isaac, and he himself carried the fire and the knife" (22:6).

As Abraham and Isaac begin their hike up the mountain, leaving behind the dusty road and the wilderness heat, there was no indication that Abraham was in turmoil. He did not seem to be tortured with thoughts of *What will Sarah say?* or *How will Isaac react?* or *Why is this necessary?* He seemed to have laid down … sacrificed … his own logic and reasoning and thinking. He was just trusting. But before they reached the summit, Abraham's trust in God was tested … again.

The whisper of the mountain breeze in the trees, the breaking twigs underneath the weight of their steps, the rattle of small stones displaced by their feet, the plaintive cry of a bird, the labored breathing of Abraham were the only sounds until Isaac spoke up:

"Father?"

"Yes, my son?" Abraham replied.

"The fire and wood are here, … but where is the lamb for the burnt offering?" (22:6 – 7).

Isaac's words must have been like daggers to Abraham's heart!

Isaac had lived with his father for years as an only child. He must have known his father well. He surely observed during the three-day journey that the lines in Abraham's face were deeper, that his shoulders were more stooped, that his step was slower, that there was unmistakable pain in his eyes. He must have felt the heaviness in Abraham's heart as though it were his own. As he pondered what his father's burden could be, I wonder if he began to suspect. Did Isaac rightly guess that *he himself* was to be the sacrifice?

If Abraham had been dreading the moment of Isaac's discovery, if Isaac's question was emotional torture to Abraham, there was no outward indication of it. "Abraham answered, 'God himself will provide the lamb for the burnt offering, my son.'[11] And the two of them went on together" (22:8). Abraham seemed to be at total peace, his confidence in God intact as he laid down his feelings and just trusted that somehow, some way, provision would be made.

Abraham had been walking by obedient faith for forty years. He simply continued walking by faith as "they reached the place God had told him about" (22:9). The journey had ended. The waiting was over. The time had come to lay everything down, to fully surrender . . .

> All of his longings for the future,
> All of his hopes and dreams for his family,
> All of his expectations of blessing,
> The fulfillment of God's promises,
> His most precious possession,
> And *just lay Isaac down.*

So "Abraham built an altar there and arranged the wood on it. He bound his son Isaac and laid him on the altar, on top of the wood" (22:9).

I wonder what Isaac thought. Surely, as a teenager, he could easily have overpowered his aged father. He could have fought and cried and verbally assaulted the old man for daring to even think such a thing, much less do it. But Isaac obediently submitted and allowed his father to bind him to the altar. Maybe he braced himself and tightly squeezed his eyes closed when Abraham "reached out his hand and took the knife to slay his son" (22:10). It was obvious not only to Isaac but even to me, as I read the account four thousand years later, that Abraham fully intended to bring that knife down. The sacrifice was complete in his heart, mind, and will. All that was left was the physical act.

Are you still counting the cost of laying it all down? Are you still focused on the pain and the cross? Are you still wrestling with God's will? It's time to stop struggling! Surrender everything to Him. Lay it all down. That's the condition: if you want to receive the fullness of His blessing, you must lay it all down. *Lay it down!*

It's a choice. It's a commitment. And it's a condition for receiving all that God wants to give you. It's time to sacrifice your most precious possession ... lay everything down ...

It's a Condition

Abraham's desire for the fullness of God's blessing had not lessened over the years. Not one little bit. But this ultimate test must have stretched his faith until it was strained almost to the snapping point. As he reached for the knife and raised it high above his head, ready to plunge it into his son, I imagine his hand trembled so violently the knife almost slipped from his grip. Did he feel faint? Were his knees about to buckle before he could complete what God had told him to do? Was his focus blurring when, to his astonishment, he heard his name called?

"Abraham!"

He must have paused with his brow furrowed, his hand trembling, yet his ears alert to an unmistakable sound. Someone had called his name. But who? The voice was not coming from the top of the altar. It was not coming from Isaac. It was coming from above! It was a voice from heaven! It was a *familiar* voice ...

> *the same voice* that had called him out of Ur,
> *the same voice* that had told him to walk the length and breadth
>   of the land because it would be his,
> *the same voice* that had brought peace and comfort after his battle
>   with the eastern kings,
> *the same voice* that had promised him descendants more numerous
>   than the stars of the sky,
> *the same voice* that had sworn by Himself to keep His covenant,
> *the same voice* that had confirmed the covenant with the sign of
>   circumcision,
> *the same voice* that had promised Sarah she would be the mother
>   of their son,
> *the same voice* that had so patiently conversed with him about
>   the pending judgment of Sodom,
> *the same voice* that had told him to send Hagar and Ishmael away
>   because Isaac was the son through whom all the blessings would flow,

the same voice that had told him to sacrifice Isaac as a burnt offering on the mountain ...

Now he heard the same voice calling him again!

When he heard the voice, Abraham must have frozen with the knife in midair, sucking in his breath as he listened intently with every fiber of his being. I wonder if he thought his imagination had been playing tricks on him. But he quickly knew it had not! He heard the voice calling insistently yet again, "Abraham!" (22:11) It was the voice of the angel of the Lord. *It was the voice of God!*

A Condition to Receive God's Pleasure

What a welcome, beloved voice! It was the voice of the One who was becoming Abraham's familiar Friend.[12] Abraham immediately answered from a throat that must have been husky with emotion: "Here I am" (22:11). He seemed to be saying, in effect, "I'm still listening, Lord, still available for whatever You command. I'm Your man for whatever You want."

That in itself is pretty amazing. Abraham had been available earlier to hear the Word of the Lord, and he remained available to hear from God. How long do *you* make yourself available to God? My tendency is to want to do one assignment at a time. I have difficulty multitasking. What if Abraham had been more like me and, when he heard his name called, he had resisted, saying, "God, just a minute. I'm busy. Let me finish what You've told me to do, then I'll be ready to hear what You want me to do next"?

How available are you to hear from the Lord when He speaks ... *again*? Especially if the last time He spoke to you He convicted you or challenged you or gave you a hard assignment or a painful command.

Abraham could have said, "God, I really don't want to hear from You again. Last time You spoke to me, You gave me the most painful command imaginable. So I'm not that open to hearing from You again." Disaster would have followed!

Thank God, Abraham was still available to hear the voice of God! Disaster was avoided because he was still listening! The next words he heard must have wrapped around him like a warm embrace, filling him with relief and then with overwhelming, overflowing, overawed joy. I can almost hear a release of emotion in God's voice as it rang out clearly in the mountain air: "Do not lay a hand on the boy.... Do not do anything to him. Now I know that you fear God, because you have not withheld from me your son, your only son" (22:12). God revealed that He *knew* now that Abraham feared Him. Because God is not bound by our time and space, because He is the great I AM — fully present in every age the same — He *knew* personally what this sacrifice had cost Abraham. Two thousand years before Calvary ...

> *God knew!*
> *God knew* in a way no one else ever would.
> *God knew* personally the agony of a Father's sacrifice of an only
>   beloved son.
> *God knew* the pain of giving up His most precious possession.
> *God knew* the inestimable cost of laying everything down!

Why would I ever think God is indifferent to my pain? What about you? Do you think He commands you to sacrifice, then steps back to coldly or casually calculate how well you carry out His command? He doesn't. He is right there with you, knowing every shard of suffering, every flicker of feeling, every tear on your face as though it were His own. He knows! He knows firsthand all about painful sacrifice. He knows when you have surrendered everything to Him, with nothing held back. He knows the price you have paid. He understands the costliness of your sacrifice. And with a smile on His face and tenderness in His eyes and love in His heart, the words on His lips express His pleasure... *with you!*[13]

Recently I talked with a successful young businessman who is also a leader in his church and an influential supporter of ministries outside of the church. He is very active in sharing his faith publicly as well as one-on-one. He has even led others to place their faith in Jesus. But he confessed to an emptiness inside, a spiritual restlessness robbing him of joy. When I gently probed, he revealed with disarming honesty that he had surrendered to God only about 90 percent of his life. He confessed he had not been willing to lay down one major area of his life.

I told him he could continue serving the Lord, and God would continue to bless what he did as it lined up with God's Word, but he would reap no personal benefit from it. He would be like a financial adviser who gives great advice to his clients to make them rich but becomes bankrupt himself because he doesn't take his own advice. I challenged him to lay *everything* down. And I pray he will, because total surrender is a prerequisite — a hard-and-fast condition — to experiencing the deep-down peace and satisfaction of knowing that God is pleased with your life.

Until you know God is pleased, you too will have a nagging uncertainty, an emptiness, a restlessness, and an absence of unhindered and uninhibited joy. This is one reason the apostle Paul urged Christians to "make it our goal to please him."[14] If that goal is not your own, then you have yet to embrace the magnificent obsession. And the goal is attainable only when you lay everything down.

A Condition to Receive God's Provision

Abraham's ears were still ringing with the sound of God's voice and the dramatic impact of His words when his attention was caught by sudden movement near the altar. Through what must have been tear-filled eyes, "Abraham looked up and there in a thicket he saw a ram caught by its horns" (22:13). Where had the ram been up until that moment? Without any hesitation or doubt, Abraham immediately knew that the ram was God's provision. He quickly untied Isaac, who must have climbed off the altar with knees that knocked and legs that trembled. As Abraham seized the ram to sacrifice "as a burnt offering instead of his son" (22:13), I wonder if Isaac, with tears of overwhelming gratitude streaming down his young face, embraced the ram God had provided to die in his place on the altar. I know that neither father nor son would ever forget the sight of that ram.

"So Abraham called that place The LORD Will Provide. And to this day it is said, 'On the mountain of the LORD it will be provided' " (22:14).

Abraham's experience reminds me of a story told by Corrie ten Boom, a Dutch woman who spent time in a Nazi concentration camp for helping Jews escape the Holocaust. Corrie said she had been terrified of being captured by the Germans and of dying. When she expressed this fear to her wise father, he inquired, "Corrie, when you and I go to Amsterdam — when do I give you your ticket?"

"Why, just before we get on the train."

"Exactly. And our Father in heaven knows when we're going to need things too. Don't run out ahead of Him, Corrie. When the time comes that some of us will have to die, you will look into your heart and find the strength you need — just in time."[15]

What do *you* need?

Strength to go through another day, not just somehow, but triumphantly?

Wisdom to make critical health decisions for your loved one?

Patience to endure one more painful injustice?

Forgiveness for the person who is perpetrating the injustice?

Hope for a child who has made a life-altering mistake?

Grace for a coworker who has defied you?

Love for a rude, belligerent family member?

Joy when your life seems to be unraveling?

These are some of the tickets I've needed in the past. Like Abraham, I can bear witness to the truth that when I lay it all down and surrender everything to Him — my emotions and how I feel, my mind and what I think, my will and what I decide, my actions and how I respond, my goals and what I want — He gives me the ticket "on the mountain," at the foot of the cross, where He laid it all down for me.

As I surrender all, God wraps His arms of love around me, fills me with Himself, draws me near to His heart, and holds me close until I can hear His own heartbeat. The warmth of His love and the sweetness of His presence make everything else fade away. All I care about is Him. And provision is made.

What is the one thing hindering you from receiving all that God wants to give you? You will have no idea how God will provide for you, or what God will do for you, or the blessings He will pour out upon you, until you lay it down! So ... *lay it down*!

A Condition to Receive God's Praise

As Abraham absorbed what he had just experienced — the sacrifice of his only son that had not ended in death, but in figurative resurrection power and the joyous celebration of God's provision — "the angel of the LORD called to Abraham from heaven a second time and said, 'I swear by myself, declares the LORD, that because you have done this and have not withheld your son, your only son, I will surely bless you and ... through your offspring all nations on earth will be blessed, because you have obeyed me" (22:15 – 18).

Four thousand years later I can still hear heaven rocking as God poured out His heartfelt, passionate praise, saying, in essence, "Abraham, well done! Well done! I am surely going to bless you to be a blessing to the whole world for all time! Well done, good and faithful friend!" I know the courts of heaven rang with the thunderous, reverberating applause of God Himself! The vaults of heaven were opened, and blessing upon blessing upon blessing was poured out on Abraham and his descendants forever. He received all God wanted to give him, and so much more. Because he received God Himself!

Abraham had emphatically confirmed once and for all that his obsession with knowing God was the *magnificent* obsession that lasted a lifetime. God meant more to him than any gift or blessing he would ever receive, including his most precious possession, his only son. The blessing Abraham longed for more than the son of his dreams, more than descendants as numerous as the stars, more than the Promised Land that stretched out farther than the eye could see or his old feet could walk — the blessing Abraham was obsessed with possessing ... was God Himself! Abraham had ...

made the choice and left everything behind,
kept the commitment and let everything go,
satisfied the criteria and trusted everything completely,
accepted the challenge and pursued everything patiently,
resolved the conflict and cast everything out,
effectively communicated and lifted everything up,
and he paid the cost and laid everything down ...

... to embrace God!

Are you obsessed with knowing God and making Him known?
Are you obsessed with being blessed that you might be a blessing?
Are you obsessed with receiving everything God has for you?
Then ...

Lay it down!

Lay it down!

Lay everything down, including ... *especially* ...

your most precious possession!

Why? Why would you and I lay everything down and withhold nothing from God? Why would you embrace the magnificent obsession? Because, wonder of wonders, *you* are *His* magnificent obsession! And He laid everything down for you! Demonstrating the greatness of His love, God laid down His life for His friends ... for you and for me!

Abraham had distinctly told Isaac that God would provide Himself a lamb, not a ram. Had Abraham been mistaken? Was it just a question of semantics? Or was this ram, like Isaac, just a foreshadowing of the Lamb God would one day provide to die in our place, the Lamb who is also the Father's only beloved Son?

Because two thousand years after the life of Abraham, another Father laid down all He had on the altar. The Father took the wood and laid it on the shoulders of His Son. He carried the fire of His judgment for sin and the knife of His wrath, and the two of them went together up Calvary's mountain so that God might provide Himself as a Lamb for the sacrifice.

They came together to the determined place. The Father arranged the wood of the altar in the shape of a cross, then He laid His Son on the altar and bound Him there with nails. And His Son, who was well able to resist, said, "Shall I not drink the cup the Father has given me?"[16] Then the Father reached out His hand and took the knife of the fierceness of His wrath against your sin and mine. He raised it to slay His Son. But there was no voice from heaven to interrupt or stay His hand. Instead, He freely gave up His Son, sacrificing Him for you and for me.[17]

To this day it is said that on the mountain, on Calvary, on the altar of the cross, God provided a Lamb who died in your place that you might have life. It was on the cross that God the Father laid down heaven's treasure for you and for me.

Words fail me at this point. What more can be said ... or needs to be said? In fact, I don't think the Father is looking for my words. He's looking for my response. For my choice to lay down my life for Him. So I want to borrow the words of George Matheson, a blind Scottish preacher.

> O Love that wilt not let me go,
> I rest my weary soul in thee;
> I give thee back the life I owe,
> That in Thine ocean depths its flow
> May richer, fuller be.
>
> O Joy that seekest me through pain,
> I cannot close my heart to thee;
> I trace the rainbow thro' the rain,

And feel the promise is not vain
That morn shall tearless be.

O Cross that liftest up my head,
I dare not ask to hide from thee;
I lay in dust life's glory dead,
And from the ground there blossoms red
Life that shall endless be.[18]

If you truly want to know God as Abraham did — and to make Him known . . .

If you want to receive the fullness of His blessing . . .

If you want to be a channel of His blessing to others . . .

If you want everything He wants to give you . . .

If you want to not just embrace the magnificent obsession but experience the God-filled life for yourself . . .

If you want to know God as Abraham did, *lay down your Isaac.* The Father's love will not let you go. He will be with you every moment. So . . . *Lay Everything Down . . . Now!*

EIGHT

Mourn Everything Hopefully

Genesis 23

My friend Amy tells the story of her uncle who was killed during World War II and buried in the Philippines. After the war, her heartbroken farm family paid to have the body shipped home to the family burial ground. But when her grandfather and two other sons went to the funeral home to identify the body, they received the shock of their lives. As her grandfather peered at the body, he blurted out, "This ain't him!"[1]

Amy says when she replays this old family story in her memory, she hears God whispering into her grandfather's heart, "You're right! That ain't him! He came home a long time ago. Since he caught that bullet, he's been up here with Me."

As Abraham faced the end of Sarah's earthly life, he mourned with the hope of a heavenly home to come. The Bible tells us that he looked beyond the grave "to the city with foundations, whose architect and builder is God."[2]

HOPE BRINGS COMFORT

Without doubt, Sarah is the most important woman in the Old Testament. She is the equivalent in the Old Testament of the Virgin Mary in the New Testament. She expressed her pursuit of the magnificent obsession in a supporting role. I don't believe for a minute that Abraham would have become the man he did without her support and encouragement.

Imagine with me for a moment how radically different things would have been if, when Abraham announced that God had called him to leave everything behind, Sarah had retorted, "Well, I'm not going." Or, as he moved from place to place in Canaan, she had dug in her heels and resisted, "I'm tired of moving. I'm staying put." Or if, after Abraham had betrayed her in Egypt, she had become bitter, deciding, *I can never forgive him for what he did.* Or if, at the age of ninety, she had told Abraham she didn't care about his dreams anymore, she was too tired and too old to conceive a baby, much less give birth to one.

If her attitude had been any of these, I, for one, would have understood. What makes Sarah remarkable is that she devoted her life to Abraham, giving him her support and encouragement through good times and bad so that he could wholeheartedly abandon himself to God and His call.

Then Sarah died.

Death is the great equalizer, isn't it? It doesn't matter if we have lived on this earth as ...

> young or old,
> rich or poor,
> famous or unknown,
> educated or ignorant,
> powerful or weak,
> good or evil,
> servant or king,
> honored or reviled,
> religious or atheistic,
> athletic or crippled,
> healthy or sickly,
> happy or depressed ...
> *we all die.*[3]

Comfort in Grief

I wonder if Sarah had become ill. Maybe she had caught a summer fever that went into pneumonia, then lapsed into a coma from which she never awoke. Maybe she simply collapsed beside the fire one day as she was baking bread. Maybe one morning she just didn't wake up. Her death must not have been entirely unexpected because she "lived to be a hundred and twenty-seven years old" (Genesis 23:1). What a long, full, rich, eventful life she'd had. If she had a few lucid moments before death, maybe she reflected back over all she had experienced. I suspect she had few regrets.

My own dearly beloved mother embraced the magnificent obsession for herself as a young girl and pursued God in a personal relationship all of her life. More than any other person, she made that pursuit contagious to me. Her unwavering encouragement and support of my father enabled him to answer God's call in his life with abandon and become the man God intended him to be. Without Ruth Bell Graham, there would not have been a Billy Graham whose incredible life, worldwide ministry, and faithfulness to the gospel of Jesus Christ impacted the lives of millions.

But as I observed my mother trapped in a slowly fading body — first she was unable to walk, then unable to see, then unable to sit, then unable to speak clearly, then unable to hear well, then unable to move at all — I saw the sparkle in her eyes and the smile on her lips and the joy in her heart undimmed. Her humor was also intact, and I heard her remark on more than one occasion that she felt like "a little mouse stuck on a glue board."

A few months before she died, I sat by her bedside and read to her the words of her own prayer that help to explain so clearly her remarkable attitude:

> And when I die
> I hope my soul ascends
> slowly, so that I
> may watch the earth receding
> out of sight,
> its vastness growing smaller
> as I rise,
> savoring its recession
> with delight.
> Anticipating joy
> is itself a joy.
> And joy unspeakable

> and full of glory
> needs more
> than "in the twinkling of an eye,"
> more than "in a moment."
>
> Lord, who am I to disagree?
> It's only we
> have much to leave behind;
> so much ... Before.
> These moments of transition
> will, for me, be
> time to adore.[4]

While a body that slowly gives out or a death that tarries can be extremely difficult, it also can be a time filled with dignity and delight for the person, like my mother, who so enthusiastically embraced the magnificent obsession. I wonder if Sarah also had "time to adore" before "she died at Kiriath Arba (that is, Hebron) in the land of Canaan, and Abraham went to mourn for Sarah and to weep over her" (23:2).

Abraham must have been a white-haired old man with long flowing beard and noble, rugged face. I can imagine him as he gazed for the last time on his life's companion. His heart must have broken. Tears must have streamed down his weather-lined cheeks and run down his beard as his shoulders shook and his chest heaved with sobs of sorrow.

Did he remember ...

  the first time he had laid eyes on her ...

  the first time he had been aware that she was shyly looking
  back at him ...

  the way her eyes had flashed beneath her wedding veil ...

 her gorgeous figure swaying with the rhythm of the camel, making
their long journeys a feast for his eyes ...

  the panicked look of fear she had thrown him over her shoulder as she
  had disappeared with the Egyptian officials into Pharaoh's harem ...

  the thrill of her presence when she had returned unharmed ...

  the tenderness on her face as she had watched him build
  his altars and speak with his God ...

the energy she displayed as she supervised the servants
and cared for the household ...
the sweet willingness to bake bread over a hot fire in the noonday
heat for three unexpected visitors ...
the sound of her laughter when Isaac was born ...
the sound of her rage when Ishmael was caught mocking ...?

Did the scenes of a lifetime together replay in Abraham's mind as he bent over Sarah's limp, lifeless body? Memories were all he had left.

Sarah was gone forever. She was dead. And Abraham wept.

Have you recently wept over the grave of a loved one? Who is *your* Sarah? A precious family member or friend who is gone from you? Weep, if you must. Weep if you want. Don't hold back the tears. I haven't. My tears have flowed like an unending fountain, day after day, night after night, as the absence of my beloved mother, who died in the summer of 2007, has been almost unbearable.[5]

While I may weep, I also know I've been instructed not "to grieve like the rest of men, who have no hope."[6] I *have* hope! And one primary reason for it is that this life is not all there is. There is *so* much more to come.

A woman who was on her deathbed was very literal and practical as she thought ahead to all that was to come. The story of her funeral arrangements is a familiar one, but it bears repeating here. Apparently the woman called her young minister to come to her side, then began to give him instructions regarding her funeral and her burial ...

"Preacher," she said.

"Yes, ma'am."

"Preacher, I want you to have the people sing 'Amazing Grace' at my funeral."

"Yes, ma'am," the preacher said, as he carefully recorded the name of the hymn in his small leather notebook.

"And I want to wear my new silk dress and straw bonnet."

"Silk dress and straw bonnet, yes, ma'am. I've got it."

"And, Preacher, I want you to place a fork in my hand."

The preacher stared hard at the old lady. "Ma'am, I can understand the special hymn and the dress and the bonnet. But why would you want a fork in your hand?"

"Preacher, you know when we have church suppers — when we finish the meal and we're told to throw away our paper plates but to keep our forks 'cause the best is yet to come? Well, Preacher, I want a fork in my hand because I want everyone to know the best is yet to come!"

I don't want to grieve like those who have nothing to look forward to! I want to keep my fork in my hand! When Jesus sought to comfort His disciples who were beginning to spiral downward in a vortex of hopelessness at the thought of His leaving them, He commanded them with quiet authority, "Do not let your hearts be troubled. Trust in God; trust also in me. In my Father's house are many rooms; if it were not so, I would have told you. I am going there to prepare a place for you. And if I go and prepare a place for you, I will come back and take you to be with me that you also may be where I am."[7]

Jesus was telling His disciples, "Keep your fork. The best is yet to come!" He described heaven as His Father's house.[8] It's a home that is being prepared as a place for you and me to dwell with the Lord and our loved ones who have "fallen asleep" in Jesus.[9]

Sometimes I have to remind myself that our lives here are temporary. They are like the narthex to a grand cathedral. Several years ago I went to London's Westminster Abbey — the cathedral where kings and queens are crowned, where members of the royal family are married, and where dignitaries are buried. The door to the cathedral was small and insignificant, and once I walked through it, I entered another insignificant place: a dark, cramped narthex where I bought my ticket and guidebook.

On the opposite side of the narthex, another door led to the magnificent, cavernous sanctuary of the cathedral itself. I can't imagine anyone being satisfied with staying in the narthex of Westminster Abbey, clutching a ticket and studying the guidebook! The whole purpose of the narthex is to provide a place to get the ticket and make the transition into the cathedral itself.

Why do we cling so tightly to the narthex of this life? Why do we get our ticket to heaven, read the guidebook of God's Word, and then grieve and mourn at the thought of leaving the narthex and entering the extraordinary sanctuary of our Father's house?

Although I know Abraham would not have fully understood the promises of a heavenly home yet to be given, I know he believed God could raise the dead, and we know he was looking forward to heaven.[10] Surely his faith upheld him with comfort during his time of grief. There is no denying his grief — grief that every single person, regardless of how strong that person's faith may be, experiences at the death of a loved one.

My own father is a person of strong faith, which has been lived out over a lifetime. Yet it may have been easier for my mother to move out of the narthex into the sanctuary of her heavenly home than it was for my father, who watched her move. As long as I live, that moment will be forever emblazoned in my mind's eye.

Our family had gathered at our parents' home in Montreat, North Carolina, responding to the word that Mother had been taken off all life support. For weeks, Mother had clung to life. She seemed torn between wanting to remain here, with Daddy and the rest of the family, and wanting to be with Jesus. We all felt her struggle.

On June 14, 2007, as her time to go "home" drew near, we gathered around her bed, singing and praying and reading Scripture. Daddy had excused himself for a brief rest. But as Mother's breathing became more labored, he returned to her side. She gazed in his direction, took two breaths, and entered into the presence of Jesus.

My tears, which had been held in check for weeks, flowed freely. My sorrow and grief were great. I couldn't help but reflect at that very moment that the only person my mother would leave my Daddy for ... was Jesus.

I was standing beside Daddy, and I put my hand gently on his shoulder and whispered softly, "Daddy, Mother is in heaven." And she was! Praise God! *But we weren't!* We were left in the narthex, which to this day seems emptier, darker, lonelier, sadder, and more cramped without her vibrant presence.

About four months after Mother's move, Daddy and I were sitting on the front porch of the home in Montreat. I asked him how he was doing. He looked off into the distance, as though looking into another world, and replied, "Anne, it's getting harder."

And so it is ... for him and for me. The daily routine without her is like a hammer pounding a spike into our hearts, reminding us that while we will certainly see her again one day in heaven, she is never coming back here to earth as we knew her.

Death is so final. So excruciatingly painful. So ... *deadly*.

Comfort in Guilt

Might there have been more to Abraham's grief than just mourning the death of a loved one? After the interrupted sacrifice of Isaac, "Abraham returned to his servants, and they set off together for Beersheba. And Abraham stayed in Beersheba" (22:19). Yet Sarah died in Hebron, and Abraham went to mourn for her there (see 23:2). Could it possibly be that Abraham was not with Sarah when she died? Could it be that he was overcome, not only with grief but with guilt? She had been there for him all of their married life, and in her final moments, had he not been there for her?

Have you too felt grief intensified because you felt guilty? Now that your friend or family member is gone, are you flogging yourself with the if onlys?

> If only you had gone to see her that last week.
> If only you had told him you had forgiven him.
> If only you had said you were sorry for your failure.
> If only you had told her you loved her.
> If only you had appreciated him more.
> If only you had made more of an effort to restore your broken relationship.

But now it's too late. Death is so final. Are you tormenting yourself with memories of your past actions and attitudes that hurt your relationship but now can never be explained or set right?

As Abraham faced Sarah's death, did he also face his own lies, failures, shortcomings, insensitivity, selfishness, and sinfulness? Was he tormented, knowing he hadn't been the husband he should have been, hadn't done all he could have done for her? Did he appreciate Sarah in her death in a way he never really had in her life? I have no way of knowing, but I wonder if there was more to his tears than grief.

If my guessing is right and Abraham did feel guilty, he surely was comforted by the fact that God had counted him as righteous. After all, his hope was in God.[11]

When I've been tormented by guilt, I've found that I have to talk to God about the reasons for it. I have to get to the bottom of my feelings by confessing my sin specifically by name. I have to confess my failures and mistakes and shortcomings to Him. Would you do the same? And remember: don't talk to God in generalities. Be specific. Ask God to forgive you. He promises He will.[12] Then you must — it's not an option, you *must* — forgive yourself.

Think through this with me for a moment: if God says He forgives you, who are you to say, "God, thank You for forgiving me, but I just can't forgive myself"? Are you greater than God? Are you more righteous than He is? Are your standards higher than His? If He says He forgives us, then you and I have no option but to respond by simply saying, "Thank You. I don't deserve Your forgiveness, but I accept it. And for Your sake, I *will* forgive myself."

If Abraham was feeling guilty, he didn't wallow in that guilt. He accepted the comfort God gave him, then he got up and continued walking by faith ...

Hope Brings Clarity

When Sarah died, it's obvious that Abraham was acutely aware that he had many flocks and herds and servants and tents but nothing truly permanent. He owned no buildings or homes or businesses. Everything he had was of a temporary, portable, transitory nature as he "rose from beside his dead wife and spoke to the Hittites. He said, 'I am an alien and a stranger among you'" (23:3 – 4).

Clarity Concerning the Present

The older I get, the more life seems not only fragile but also very brief. When I have faced the death of a loved one or stood by the casket of a close friend, the temporariness of life has come into clear focus. One moment the person was thinking and feeling and speaking and hearing and loving. The next moment he or she is silent and still ... gone. The sorrow is magnified when we realize that, unless there are people who make an effort to keep the memories alive, that person will soon be forgotten. I am left almost numb by the thought that my own grandchildren will never really know my mother, except through the stories I tell them and pictures I show them and her writings I read to them.

What a sobering realization! As I observe people working so hard, achieving so much, living so frantically, accumulating so abundantly, indebted so deeply, known so famously, and acclaimed so highly, King David's reflections come to mind: "As for man, his days are like grass, he flourishes like a flower of the field; the wind blows over it and it is gone, and its place remembers it no more."[13] Death has seemed to bring life more into focus for me. Has it done the same for you? If life is not about more than just living at the present, it's basically meaningless.

Abraham's perspective on life was incredibly accurate when he described himself to the Hittites as "an alien and a stranger." He might have been speaking of the fact that he was not a Canaanite, but his words are quoted in the New Testament as describing his philosophy of life in general.[14] He wisely lived with heaven on his mind.

As you examine your life — your daily, weekly, and monthly schedule; your priorities, activities, and goals — how much of it has eternal value? How much of the way you spend the majority of your time and attention and thoughts and money and energy will last beyond your lifetime? As I have asked myself that question, the answer has been very eye-opening. Jesus, who certainly knew we would have the tendency to waste our lives, urged His followers not to "store up for yourselves treasures on earth, where moth and rust destroy, and where thieves break in and steal. But store up for yourselves treasures in heaven."[15]

As Abraham said good-bye to Sarah, he must have been overwhelmed with gratitude that he had not wasted his life. In light of her passing, he seemed to see not only the present more clearly but also the future.

Clarity Concerning the Future

Abraham's confident hope was firmly rooted in the promises God had given him more than sixty years earlier. God had said, then later confirmed with an oath, that He would give to Abraham all the land he saw and walked over.[16] At Sarah's death, Abraham made his first claim on that land. He asked the Hittities, "Sell me some property for a burial site here so I can bury my dead" (23:4). "So Ephron's field in Machpelah near Mamre — both the field and the cave in it, and all the trees within the borders of the field — was deeded to Abraham as his property" (23:17 – 18). After years of wandering, Abraham's purchase of the burial site expressed his absolute, unwavering faith in God's Word that the land would ultimately belong to him and to his descendants forever.

As I thought about it, I realized Abraham could have gone back to Ur in order to bury Sarah among his own "people." He could have gone back to Haran, where he still had some family, and buried her there. But Abraham had embraced the magnificent obsession. God was now "his people," his "family." His life on earth was just a journey to the Father's house.

So Abraham buried Sarah "in the cave in the field of Machpelah near Mamre (which is at Hebron) in the land of Canaan" (23:19).[17] As Abraham laid the body of his beloved wife in the cave, then sealed the opening against invading predators, I wonder if a tear trickled down his cheek as he sighed deeply. Did he take a moment to look at the dusty cave and the trees that dotted the rock-strewn grassy field and thank God, not only for Sarah's life and all that had been but also for all that was to come? Did he thank God one more time for the covenant promises that guaranteed him ownership of the land, confident that Isaac and his children and his children's children for generations to come would also live and be buried there?[18]

When he bought the cave of Machpelah from Ephron the Hittite, Abraham was driving down his stake of confident hope for the future.[19]

As you face death, your own or that of a beloved family member or friend, is your focus clouded because your eyes are on the grave and all that *was*, instead of on the glory and all that *will be*? My mother's own words come back to me. When I asked her how she could stand being so alive on the inside and so helpless, like a little mouse stuck on a glue board, on the outside, she replied, "Anne, it's because I have so many wonderful memories — and I have so much to look forward to."

The apostle Paul said that the physical body of a child of God is like a tent.[20] In other words, all that I am in my personality, emotions, will, and intellect — all of that which is "me" — lives inside the tent. When I die, I simply fold up my tent, but I continue to live more fully and abundantly than ever before! When I embrace the magnificent obsession, living my daily life by obedient faith as I walk step-by-step with God, death does not interrupt my walk! Death is just the transition from walking by faith to walking by sight!

And I want to remember this: the death of my physical body, or that of my mother, or yours . . . is not the end of our bodies. We have the resurrection to look forward to! I'm reminded of that fact by another Old Testament giant of the faith. Job was a man who also embraced the magnificent obsession, even when his faith was tested to the utmost in a dramatic series of events and conversations recorded in the oldest book of the Bible, which bears his name. The dates for his life indicate that he was very possibly a contemporary of Abraham,[21] and his testimony of faith has been a source of strength to believers throughout the ages.

In the midst of horrendous trials and troubles, Job said, "I know that my Redeemer lives, and that in the end he will stand upon the earth. And after my skin has been destroyed, yet in my flesh I will see God; I myself will see him with my own eyes — I, and not another. How my heart yearns within me!"[22]

Job's confident hope was echoed by the apostle Paul, who revealed an amazing truth to the Corinthians when he confided, "Listen, I tell you a mystery:... For the trumpet will sound, the dead will be raised imperishable, and we will be changed."[23]

Your body ... my body ... Mother's body ... our bodies will be changed! We will have *no more...*

> aching heads, aching joints, aching hearts.

No more...

> dim eyes, dim wits, dim hopes.

No more...

> deafness, lameness, weakness.

No more...

> comas, cardiac arrests, coughing, choking.

No more...

> 911 calls, ICUs, IVs.

No more...

> PMS, STDs, HIV.

No more...

> operating theaters, respirators, ventilators.

No more...

> wheelchairs, artificial limbs, pacemakers.

Praise God! One day we will have brand-new bodies! There are days when I can hardly wait.

Paul shared this intense expectation as he declared, "Our citizenship is in heaven. And we eagerly await a Savior from there, the Lord Jesus Christ, who, by the power that enables him to bring everything under his control, will transform our lowly bodies so that they will be like his glorious body."[24] Hallelujah! Relief is coming! There is a new day — and a new body — on its way!

What a comfort to any of us who are suffering ... or who love someone who is. Jesus, as He comforted Martha following Lazarus's death, promised, "Your brother will rise again." When her response indicated her faith was small and she didn't quite get it, Jesus catapulted her faith beyond the boundaries of her own reasoning into the infinite sphere of the eternal when He placed her hope and focus squarely on Himself: "I am the resurrection and the life. He who believes in me will live, even though he dies; and whoever lives and believes in me will never die. Do you believe this?"[25] I've had to ask myself that same question: Anne ...

Do you believe this ...

> when your loved one closes her eyes and breathes her last breath?

Do you believe this ...

> when the funeral director places the beloved body on a gurney and
> > wheels her out of her room and her beloved mountain cove?

Do you believe this ...

> when the casket is lowered into the ground?

Do you believe this ...

> when the grave is filled with dirt and the sod is placed over it?

Do you believe this ...

> when your loved one's life is just a memory?

Do you believe this?

—∞∞—

Do you believe, with Job and Abraham and Martha and Paul, that in your flesh you will one day *see God*? And that you will one day see your family members and friends who had placed their faith in Him and who have already moved to the Father's house? And I have answered yes. Yes! *YES! I believe!* Praise God for the living hope of the resurrection![26]

So ... go ahead and weep. I do. But take comfort in knowing that your tears are on His face. Mourn if you must. Mourn if you want. But mourn with the confident hope that the best is yet to come!

NINE

Pass Everything On

Genesis 24

When my children were small, on the weekends my husband would take them to athletic events on the campus of a nearby university. One of their favorite events was the relay race in which runners compete as a team. As each race begins, the first runner from each team crouches at the starting block, gripping the baton in his hand. When the signal to begin is given, the runner explodes out of the starting block and runs the first leg of the race as swiftly as he can. As he completes his portion of the race, he is met by the second runner on his team. In full stride, the first runner shifts the baton to his right hand, stretches out his arm, and, with his teammate running full speed alongside him, he passes the baton into the outstretched hand of the second runner. The second runner then runs his portion of the race and passes the baton to the number three runner, who also takes it in full stride, and so on until the last runner on the team crosses the finish line, tightly clutching the all-important baton.

Winning a relay race depends not only on the speed of the runners but also on their skillful ability to transfer the baton. If the baton is dropped, precious seconds are wasted, and the race may be lost. If the runner fails to pass the baton, he is disqualified from the race altogether.

The race of life is very similar to the relay race. The "baton" is the truth that leads to personal faith in God. Each person, or even each generation, that receives the baton runs the race to the best of his or her ability, then is challenged to pass on the baton smoothly and securely to others.[1]

Why do the revival fires of one generation burn out in the next?

Why do the children and grandchildren of believers leave the church?

Why does each generation need to be re-evangelized?

Why is our world getting morally and spiritually worse instead of better?

Why are those who pursue the magnificent obsession *rare*?

I've concluded that one answer lies in the failure to pass everything on.

At the very end of his life, Abraham was determined to pass the "baton" to his son Isaac and to his unborn grandchildren. One practical, necessary course of action was to secure a godly bride for Isaac, because Abraham knew the strong influence a wife wields over a husband and a mother wields over her children. So Abraham sent his trusted servant to find a bride for his son.

This concluding story in Abraham's life has held a tremendous challenge for me, not only to continue living the magnificent obsession but also to pass it on to my children, grandchildren, ministry staff, church, and others with whom I come in contact. I can't help but question myself: Who will pursue God because I do?

And what about you? Who will make it the priority of their lives to know God as Abraham did, and make Him known to others, because you have? Who will refuse to settle for anything less than everything God wants to give them because you've refused to settle for less? To whom are you and I passing the baton? We need to be as intentional as Abraham was about passing everything on because we have also been commissioned by the Father to find a bride for the Son . . .[2]

THE CHARGE

Do you have married children? Is your son-in-law or daughter-in-law a positive or negative spiritual influence on your child? Either way, your grandchildren are impacted, aren't they? This is reinforced every time I talk with my friends and hear stories of a daughter-in-law who refuses to let her children go to church or a son-in-law who ridicules Bible reading in the home. The solemn reality is that the blessing of God in the next generation can be either hindered or enlarged by the influence of a spouse.[3]

Abraham knew that God had "chosen him, so that he will direct his children and his household after him to keep the way of the Lord by doing what is right and just, so that the Lord will bring about for Abraham what he has promised him" (Genesis 18:19).

Would God choose me for the same reason? Will God bring about for me what He has promised because He knows I will direct my children to keep His ways? Think this through in application to your own life. What are you actively, intentionally doing to direct your children *after you* to keep the way of the Lord?

The Father Took the Initiative

Abraham directed his household after him to keep the way of the Lord by living a life that modeled righteousness and justice. But he also took the bold initiative to find a bride for Isaac.

At the age when some elderly people are content to take naps, play bridge, watch TV, baby-sit grandchildren, talk about their surgeries, complain about their health, bag groceries, clip coupons, wander the malls, reminisce about the old days, Abraham was preoccupied with passing the baton. As someone who is approaching the ranks of senior citizenship, that's a lesson I want to wrap my old age around!

Following Sarah's death, Abraham, if he was like my own father, must have felt an ache of loneliness and emptiness. They had been together so long that to be without her hour after hour, day after day, must have been almost greater than he could bear. I imagine that each day was harder than the last.

I'm sure he must have taken some time to reflect on all they had experienced together. I wonder if he once again sat in the doorway of his tent, trying to catch any slight breeze that might blow in from the desert. I can almost see him smiling with a knowing, faraway expression as he shook his head with secret thoughts and drummed his fingers to the sound of Sarah's now-silent laughter.

Did the shimmering desert mirages and the little dust devils dancing in the distance bring back to his mind the day when the Lord had come for lunch? Certainly he would never forget the momentous announcement given quietly and rather matter-of-factly that day: "I will return to you at the appointed time next year and Sarah will have a son" (18:14). I imagine he could almost hear Sarah's voice again, muted yet distinct, from behind the tent flap, denying her laughter.

And did that memory remind him of his conversation with the Lord as they walked together toward Sodom when God revealed He had chosen Abraham to direct his children in the way of the Lord? As Abraham thought it over, did he suddenly sit upright, with eyes narrowed and brow furrowed, struck by the realization that directing his children after him was a condition to receiving the fulfillment of God's promises?

Whatever it was that actually prompted Abraham, who "was now old and well advanced in years ... [and] blessed ... in every way" (24:1), he must have insistently clapped his hands or rung a gong or blown a horn, whatever was necessary to summon his servant.

Abraham's age alone was enough to alert him to the fact that his death very likely would not be that far off.[4] And his death would cut him off from direct influence in his son's life. When he was gone, it would be up to Isaac to pursue God, claiming the promises and the covenant. I think that Abraham was suddenly confronted by the conscious realization that he needed to do something. He couldn't leave this to chance. He needed to make sure Isaac had all the support and encouragement necessary to pursue the magnificent obsession.

Abraham knew what you and I should also know, that our sons and daughters will need godly spouses to help them rear godly children who will in turn pass on the baton of faith to succeeding generations.[5]

Abraham had probably been thinking about Isaac's need for a wife for a long time. Isaac was approximately forty years old by this time. Singleness wasn't an option, because God had promised a multitude of descendants, which implied Isaac would have children and would therefore need a wife. But in the land of the Canaanites, where would he find a godly woman, someone who would share the magnificent obsession?

Sometime after Abraham had laid Isaac on the altar, Abraham received word about his family in Haran.[6] That information must have come back to his mind as he continued to ponder Isaac's need. The answer to finding a suitable bride seemed to lie within his extended family, and he concluded that this would be a good place to start looking. He was too old to go to Haran himself, so Abraham called for "the chief servant in his household, the one in charge of all that he had" (24:2).

The Father Gave the Instructions

I imagine the servant entering through the open door into the maze of connecting tents that was Abraham's home, walking over plush, thick woven carpets, past comfortable overstuffed seats and tables laden with figs, fruit, and pitchers of cool water until he stood before his greatly beloved master. But he found no customary gracious greeting, no friendly comment on the weather, no inquiry about the status of the flocks and herds and investments, just a very serious, solemn charge from Abraham: "I want you to swear by the LORD, the God of heaven and the God of earth, that you will not get a wife for my son from the daughters of the Canaanites, among whom I am living, but will go to my country and my own relatives and get a wife for my son Isaac" (24:3 – 4).

If the servant was stunned by this request, or even taken aback by it, he gave no evidence. His mind must have already begun to sort through the many details of how he would carry out such an assignment. "What if the woman is unwilling to come back with me to this land?" he respectfully asked. "Shall I then take your son back to the country you came from?" (24:5).

His questions seemed very logical. It was highly improbable that a marriageable young woman suitable to be Isaac's wife would accept an unknown relative's proposal, forsake her own friends, her own father's house, her own country, and all that was familiar, and travel more than five hundred miles with a servant to marry someone she knew nothing about. The idea was almost preposterous!

But Abraham was insistent. He told his servant that God would "send his angel before you so that you can get a wife for my son from there" (24:7).

Abraham exuded complete confidence in the fact that God would help the servant on this critical mission. He was also completely confident God had a godly wife out there, waiting for his son. Abraham made it clear that if the servant found the woman, and for any reason she was unwilling to accept Abraham's offer of his son, then the servant was released from his obligation and oath to bring her back (24:8).

But Abraham mandated that under no circumstances was the servant to take Isaac to the woman. He already knew what would later become apparent to others — Isaac was placid and submissive. Abraham wisely foresaw the possibility that Isaac could be swayed in Haran, as Lot had been swayed in Egypt, with all the comforts, conveniences, and temptations there. He must have shuddered at the thought that if Isaac fell in love with a girl in Haran, and she refused to leave, he might never return to Canaan to lay claim to all that God had promised. I don't think Abraham wanted to risk losing Isaac the way he had lost Lot.

Abraham's bold leadership and instructions, as well as the insight he had into the personality of his son, were truly remarkable.

His example stirred my own heart over thirty years ago to direct my children in the same way. And as a Christian parent, you need to direct your children to connect with Christian friends[7] (since they will likely choose a friend to date); to limit their dating to Christians (since most likely they will marry someone they have dated); to not go to certain places (where the temptations may be more than they can handle); to marry someone who shares not just their religion, or their denomination, or their traditions, or their education, but their passion — someone who also has embraced the magnificent obsession!

What priorities have you helped your children set for selecting their spouses?

The sad thing is that sometimes even Christian parents secretly want their children to marry for the parents' advantage. Do you? Are you steering them to make friends of families from certain backgrounds, certain neighborhoods, certain education levels, certain financial means, certain political views, certain social status because it would make *you* look good? Are you silently instructing your children by your actions that these things are more important than their life of obedient faith and their relationship with God?

I'm sure Abraham could have married off Isaac to the daughter of Abimelech and secured political advantage for himself, Isaac, and his children. He could have married Isaac off to the daughter of a local chieftain, doubling his assets in one marriage ceremony and thus guaranteeing financial security for his grandchildren. But Abraham's priority was spiritual. It was unthinkable to him that Isaac might marry someone who wouldn't share the magnificent obsession.

What initiative have you taken to instruct your children to marry godly spouses? If you don't give them parental guidance in this area, who will guide them? And if they don't get it at all and end up with someone who is not truly godly, how will your faith, and your personal relationship with God, be passed on to your grandchildren? *Don't drop the baton!*[8]

Abraham's leadership is not only exemplary to me as a parent but is striking in its beautiful parallels to the heavenly Father's desire to secure a bride for His Son. Think about it with me for a moment. Just as Abraham sent his servant to look for a godly bride, God the Father sends you and me into the world to not only seek and save those who are lost[9] but to bring them into a love relationship with His Son.[10]

We are to pass the baton not only from generation to generation within our own families but we are to pass it to others outside of our homes as well.

God the Father so loved everyone of every generation in the whole world that even before creation, He took counsel with Himself and decided to create each person for the purpose of knowing Him in a personal, permanent love relationship.[11] Yet even as He brought us into existence, He knew we would sin and fall short of His purpose for our lives; therefore, He took the initiative and made preparations to send His own Son to be our Savior, who would give His life as a sacrifice to make atonement for our sin.[12] Through faith in His death and resurrection, we can be forgiven of our sin, be reconciled to the Father, and come back into the purpose for which we were originally created. But that sacrifice is effective only for those who claim it for themselves by faith. And how will anyone know to do that unless they are told?[13]

There are millions of people in the world who long to know God, who long to be a member of His family, who long to be in a love relationship with His Son, who long to have eternal life and the hope of a heavenly home, but who have never had God's offer presented to them. In fact, many of them don't even know of the existence of God's Son, much less the fact that they can belong to Him in a personal, permanent love relationship. I'm convinced that there are millions of people who would embrace the magnificent obsession for themselves — if they just knew about Jesus!

That's why the Father has instructed you and me to "go into all the world and preach the good news to all creation."[14] If the people we tell are not interested — if they reject the Father's offer of His Son — then we are released from our obligation. We are not to force or coerce anyone to accept Jesus as his or her personal Savior and Lord. We just move on and tell someone else.

The thrilling prospect that fills me with expectancy as I go into all the world is that I will find the "bride," those whose hearts God has prepared to come into a personal relationship with His Son. But finding them requires steadfast, persevering, prayerful, sensitive, daily commitment ...

THE COMMITMENT

When Abraham finished giving the instructions and his servant had sworn an oath to follow them, his servant "took ten of his master's camels and left, taking with him all kinds of good things from his master" (24:9 – 10).[15] The "good things" that were packed carefully into those trunks loaded onto the backs of the camels would have included gold, jewelry, linens, silks, spices, and other costly items. Once the servant found the right person, he would want to make Isaac attractive to her, so he planned to shower her with gifts to give her some idea of the greatness of the son and his father.

Even though he faced almost insurmountable difficulties and overwhelming odds of traveling safely through five hundred miles of forsaken bandit-riddled territory with a virtual fortune on the backs of the camels, finding the right girl in the right family in the right city, convincing the girl to return with him as Isaac's bride, convincing the girl's parents to allow her to return with him, pleasing both Abraham and Isaac with the girl of his choosing when he returned with her, I detected nothing other than the servant's total commitment to the success of his mission.

The Commitment to Search

After the long journey through desert wasteland and rock-strewn wilderness, the servant arrived in the city of Nahor, a suburb of Haran. Instead of checking into the nearest hotel, taking a hot shower, having a fine meal, and getting a good night's sleep before poring over a city map and beginning his search, neighborhood by neighborhood and street by street, the servant was so committed to his task that he wasted no time at all.

"He had the camels kneel down near the well outside the town; it was toward evening, the time the women go out to draw water" (24:11). The servant was so practical and wise! What better place to find the woman he was looking for than the place where women gathered — in the evening at the well?

As you and I go into all the world to seek those who would come into a love relationship with the Father's Son, the task is formidable. The world is a great big place, and the journey can be filled with hazardous dangers.[16] How can we find those whose hearts are inclined to respond to the Father's invitation?

Instead of going to seminars and conferences and meetings that talk about how to find them, we need to commit ourselves to go to the "wells" where they are . . .

working next to us in the office,

sitting next to us at school,

living next door to us at home,

shopping in the stores,

packing out the sporting events,

eating at the next table,

serving us at the restaurant,

waiting on us at the agency,

teaching us in the classroom,

standing in the food line,

huddled in a doorway,

locked behind bars.

Can you think with me of other places where they can be found in the world that's beneath your own two feet? Don't get discouraged in your commitment even before you get started. Follow the servant's example. Before going out into your day, take a moment to pray first and ask God to lead you.

Search Prayerfully

Instead of plunging headlong into dozens of different interviews or staring rudely at each woman who came to the well, trying to see which one might match the type of bride he was looking for, the servant prayed: "O LORD, God of my master Abraham, give me success today, and show kindness to my master Abraham. See, I am standing beside this spring, and the daughters of the townspeople are coming out to draw water. May it be that when I say to a girl, 'Please let down your jar that I may have a drink,' and she says, 'Drink, and I'll water your camels too' — let her be the one you have chosen for your servant Isaac. By this I will know that you have shown kindness to my master" (24:12 – 14).

Abraham's servant didn't ask God, "Help me find the right girl." How would he know if God had done so? His prayer was very personal, specific, and to the point.

The servant teaches us by his example that when we pray for God to lead us to the person whose heart He has prepared, we need to be specific. Neither of us should generalize, saying, "Lord, help me be a good witness for You today." We won't know if He has answered our prayer, and we'll be confused about whom to speak to. We need to be specific: "Lord, as I go into the office this morning, open my eyes to those sitting around me. If I see someone with a sad or faraway expression on her face, I will take that as a sign from You that she's the person I'm to speak to." Or, "Lord, I know my neighbor is having trouble in his marriage. If You want me to speak to him today, have him out in the yard this afternoon when I come home from work." Or, "Lord, my roommate is really floundering. If you want me to speak to her, have her come in early tonight from class."

The servant's request was specific — and it almost seemed unreasonable to me. Many girls who came to draw water would possibly have given a hot, dusty, thirsty traveler a drink of water if he had asked. But I would think it highly unlikely for anyone to have offered to also water his camels ... unless God intervened and touched her heart to do so.

For instance, you and I could pray something like, "Lord, as I go into the office this morning, open my eyes to those sitting around me. If I see someone with a sad or faraway expression on her face, I will take that as a sign from You that she's the person I'm to speak to." And then we could add, "And, Lord, have a tear slip down her cheek. Then I'll know she's the one." Or, if our prayer is, "Lord, I know my neighbor is having trouble in his marriage. If You want me to speak to him today, have him out in the yard this afternoon when I come home from work." And we could add, "And, Lord, have him come to my door and ask to borrow a tool." The additional request is not beyond the realm of possibility since people do weep, just usually not publicly in the office. Neighbors do borrow tools, but the guy next door to you has never asked before. The more specific the prayer, the more thrilling it is when God answers.

In the case of Abraham's servant, he was in for the thrill of a lifetime!

The spring of water on the outskirts of Nahor most likely was located within a well that was accessed by a circular stairway. Whoever watered the camels would have to walk down the steps, fill the bucket with water, walk back up the steps, pour it into the watering trough, turn around, go back down the steps, fill up the bucket, walk back up the steps, pour it out ... again and again and again. Camels drink from between five to twenty-five gallons of water each! The servant was praying for a girl who was willing not only to get the water she needed for herself but also to spend at least an hour of hard work getting water for his camels! A prayer like that took more faith than I would have had!

But before the servant had even finished praying, God answered. I wonder how he prayed. Did he pray with his eyes open, so expectant that God would answer that he didn't want to miss one person who might slip by him? Or maybe he prayed with his eyes shut, and when he did open them, Rebekah was the first person he saw. Out of all the women coming to the well, I'd love to know what it was that made her stand out. Did she have beautiful dark, flashing eyes? Or did she give him a quick friendly yet respectful smile as she passed by? Was it the fresh innocence of her countenance? Or her graceful movements as she descended the stairs? Or her physical strength as she lowered her jar, filled it with water, and climbed effortlessly back up the steps?

Search Purposefully

The servant's heart must have beat a little faster as he "hurried to meet her and said, 'Please give me a little water from your jar'" (24:17). Rebekah quickly lowered the jar and graciously gave him a drink. I can almost hear his heart pounding under his robe! Did he take a sip of water, then wait expectantly? Did he take another sip, pause, look casually around, then take another ... waiting until the tension mounted unbearably? He must have involuntarily sucked in his breath when finally she offered, "I'll draw water for your camels too, until they have finished drinking" (24:19).

Even though her offer was exactly what he had asked the Lord for, he still must have been almost overcome by the exact answer to his prayer. I'm sure his excitement and anticipation rose with every step that she took and every bucket of water she poured out, but he didn't say a word. He just "watched her closely to learn whether or not the LORD had made his journey successful" (24:21). The servant's enormous self-control was extraordinary. He was so careful not to manipulate the circumstances or inject something into the situation to make it fit his need. He simply stood back and watched.

As the servant observed Rebekah's obvious thoughtfulness and kindness and the strength of her resolve to follow through and finish the very arduous task she had begun, he must have been filled with admiration. I wonder if he saw her face flush red and her brow bead with moisture and strands of sweat-dampened hair begin to curl around her neck as she went up and down the steps ... perhaps as many as *fifty times!*[17] I wonder if he was silently rooting for her, *Don't quit. Don't quit. Keep going. Just one more trip down. One more trip back up the stairs.* The servant must have begun to longingly hope that this very special girl was the one for his master's son.

When finally the last camel had thoroughly satisfied its thirst, the servant took out a gold ring and heavy gold bracelets to give to Rebekah in appreciation for what she had done. Finally he knew the time had come for him to speak to her. With hands that surely shook and a voice that must have trembled, he inquired, "Whose daughter are you? Please tell me, is there room in your father's house for us to spend the night?" (24:23). He knew it wasn't enough to find a phenomenally beautiful, hardworking girl for Isaac, even if she had seemed to be a specific answer to his prayer. Abraham had instructed him not to choose a Canaanite, but to find a girl from among his own family living in Haran.

I wonder if he held his breath, waiting for what would be the last vital piece of information that would confirm whether or not Rebekah was the one he was searching for. He didn't have to wait long, because her straightforward answer put the last piece of the puzzle in place: "I am the daughter of Bethuel, the son that Milcah bore to Nahor" (24:24). The servant didn't seem to hear her add that he would be welcome to spend the night in her father's house. A flourish of trumpets must have been going off in his head! All he seemed to think about was that Nahor was Abraham's brother! This girl who had offered him a drink, then watered all of his camels, was from the very family his master Abraham had directed him to find. This was the girl! God had answered his very specific prayer! God had led him to the right person!

The servant's knees must have buckled as he fell to the ground in amazement and in unrestrained worship. He exclaimed, "Praise be to the LORD, the God of my master Abraham, who has not abandoned his kindness and faithfulness to my master. As for me, the LORD has led me on the journey to the house of my master's relatives" (24:27).

The Commitment to Speak

God will lead you and me to those He has prepared to belong to His Son, just as He led Abraham's servant to Rebekah. One of the most exciting aspects of living a God-filled life has been to discover the "divine appointments" He places in my path.

Recently, as I was traveling home after a series of engagements, the airport security agent who examined my travel documents commented loudly on my destination, then waved me through. I smiled weakly, walked through the scanner, then continued down the concourse to my gate, where I had about a forty-five-minute wait. I was weary and didn't want to be bothered by anyone, so I seated myself at the end of a long row of empty chairs that were against the wall, facing the rest of the gate area. Beyond the other end of the row of chairs was the desk and the boarding gate for the plane.

I buried my face in a newspaper, then was somewhat startled to realize someone was talking loudly about my hometown. I looked up to see the security agent now standing behind the desk at the gate — to this day I have no idea why he had left his post and was now standing there at my gate. I actually believe God must have placed him there. He looked directly at me as he began what I'm sure he felt was a friendly conversation about where I was going. Something just clicked in my spirit, and I knew this was someone the Father had sent me to find. So I began to tell the man — I'll call him Brad — where I was *really* going.[18] I told him about heaven and my Father's house.

We talked for the full forty-five-minute wait as he asked hard questions about hell and judgment and sin and salvation. The interesting thing was that Brad was fairly far from where I was sitting, and I was too tired to move, which meant both of us had to speak loudly. Because I was actually facing the gate area, everyone there easily heard every word we said to each other.

To this day I can still see in my mind's eye the gate agent who was standing next to Brad, staring at me in astonishment and apprehension. I'm sure she thought the political-correctness police were going to show up any moment and take us both off in handcuffs.

I got Brad's contact information and, when I returned home, sent him one of my books. Two months later, I received a beautiful note from his wife, who related that Brad had come home from work after speaking with me and has been a different person ever since. She revealed that he had placed his faith in Jesus years before but because of problems she didn't go into, he had rejected his faith and become bitter. Following our conversation, he started going to church again.

And I will never forget Helena.[19] She was one of the two security guards assigned to me during a "Just Give Me Jesus" revival in another country. Her manner was very tough and professional. If I sat by the pool to relax, Helena sat across from me dressed in her dark pants suit, white shirt, and necktie with her gun in a holster on her hip. When our car had to cross a busy street, Helena would quickly jump out into the middle of the traffic, hold up her hand, and shake her fingers in the face of the oncoming cars to make them stop so our car could get safely to the other side of the road. When I led an all-day pastors' conference, Helena sat by the platform and kept her eyes on the crowd. When I "just gave them Jesus" in the large arena, surrounded by thousands of women, Helena sat at the steps to the platform, alert for any possible emergency.

Helena didn't speak fluent English, so I never had an in-depth conversation with her. But I went out of my way to take her a cool drink at the pool, to thank her for her attentiveness during a meeting, to applaud her efforts when she got back into the car after having stopped the traffic, and just to give her a hug when she took me to my room at night. Increasingly, I sensed, along with other members of my team, that Helena was someone God was drawing to Himself.

On the last day we were in the city, Helena was with various members of my traveling party and me in the hotel elevator. When we reached my floor, we all got out and went into my room, where we were going to order room service for a quick bite to eat before crashing for the night. I noticed that neither Helena nor my interpreter had come into the room. After ten or fifteen minutes, I became concerned because I knew they had been in the elevator with us.

Just when I was about to go look for them, my interpreter came in. Her face was glowing, her eyes were sparkling, her hands were clapping, and her feet were almost floating off the floor. Then she told us what had happened. She had held back to speak with Helena. And Helena had prayed with her to receive Jesus as her personal Savior and Lord! We all praised the Lord for leading us not just to the thousands in the arena but to the one who was assigned to our security.

The next day, Helena's last assignment was to escort me to the airport. When she met me at the car, the hardness of her face had melted into a soft radiance, her eyes were moist and sparkling, and her hug for me was warm and tender. Before leaving the country, I prayed with her and for her . . . and still do.

And then there is Jack.[20] He was my driver in a large American city where I was speaking at a sizable event. His father was from Colombia, his mother was from Sicily, and Jack was as tough as they come. He had arrived in America when he was sixteen and had been fighting for survival ever since. He had been a champion welterweight boxer and a longtime worker on the oil platforms off the Louisiana coast. He had even attended a theological seminary but had been expelled when he had taken a strong unpopular stand on certain issues. When I met him, he owned his own security company and limousine service. He had a successful career, but his personal life was filled with pain. He had been separated from his wife for seventeen years, had one son who was the apple of his eye, and still had a stormy relationship with his own very controlling father.

Jack gave me most of these details as he drove me from the airport to the hotel. Because I'm a bottom-line kind of person, I bluntly told him the first thing he needed to do was to get right with God, that his obedience to his heavenly Father took priority over his earthly father or any other of the many problem areas in his life.

The night I spoke, Jack said later that something compelled him to park his armor-plated SUV on the busy street outside the church, telling God, *If You want me to hear this lady, You take care of my truck. But even if You don't, I'm still going to hear her.*

That night, God touched his heart. Jack responded to the Father's invitation and totally committed his life to Jesus. When he went back outside, his truck was undisturbed, right where he had left it. Even I knew that was a miracle!

When I returned home from that trip, I sent Jack some materials, including my book *Heaven: My Father's House*, which had been the subject of the message I had given that had so impacted his life.[21] The next time I saw Jack, to my amazement, he quoted passage after passage of the book to me. He had practically memorized the entire contents and had given dozens of copies to family members, associates, and friends. He was overwhelmed to know with confident assurance that he was as loved and accepted by the Father as Jesus is.

Jack has since become a friend of our entire family. He has driven us almost every time we have returned to his city, and his stories of God's grace in his life are thrilling. He and his wife reconciled, he is teaching a men's Bible class at his church, and he publicly apologized to his father for the pain he had caused.

When my husband and I recently went through an almost unbearably difficult time involving his health, the phone rang. It was Jack, who said God had put it on his heart to call us, find out how we were, and to pray for us. My husband put him on the speakerphone so that his prayer would be a blessing to both of us as well as to my daughter and grandchildren, who were in the room at the time. What an indescribable thrill it was to have someone God had sent me to find become a person who, in turn, is sent by the Father to find and encourage *me*! It doesn't get much better than that!

What thrill are you missing because you are not searching for those whose hearts are prepared by God to belong to His Son? Do you say you can't find them ... or you don't know who they are? Is it because you are huddled safely in your church group or Bible study or Christian family and never venture to the wells where the people are? What is keeping you so preoccupied that you don't open your eyes to the ones He places in your path? Why are you so afraid to open your mouth and say something? Are you trying to make it more complicated than it is? Is it because you are afraid of failure?

I'm sure Abraham must have recognized that failure was a possibility when he told his servant "to get a wife for my son," but "if the woman is unwilling to come back with you, then you will be released from this oath." Abraham was acknowledging the fact that even if the servant would find the woman, and even if he represented Isaac perfectly to her when he did, she had free choice and might refuse to accept the invitation to be Isaac's bride. Likewise, God has never commanded you and me to be successful in actually leading someone to faith in Christ. He only commands us to be faithful to represent Him to the best of our ability. Many, many times I have spoken to someone only to have him or her turn away, or become hostile, or change the subject, or walk out. In fact, I would say I have failed many more times to "bring home the bride" than I have succeeded. But when that happens, I know the Father releases me from my responsibility as far as that person is concerned, and I just go on to the next encounter He has arranged for me.

Could it be that you are willing to search for those whose hearts have been prepared by God to accept His invitation, but you're afraid to speak out, not so much because of the fear of failure but because you don't know what to say? Look closely at the servant's example. He kept his appeal very simple. He was not pushy. He patiently waited for the right time to tell his story.

Speak Patiently

After traveling such a long way, after searching for the bride so diligently and prayerfully, after finding Rebekah so miraculously, when the servant finished praising God and rose from the ground, he discovered she had run off! But I saw no evidence that he panicked. He simply waited, knowing that if God had brought her to him once, He could bring her to him again.

My friend Joe is also the Father's servant, and he loves to find "brides" for God's Son. On one occasion, Joe dropped into a local café packed with the noontime lunch crowd. He struck up a conversation with another customer, but before he could really present the gospel, he was interrupted, the customer left, and the moment was lost. Still, Joe was convinced that God was working in the heart of the guy he had spoken with. A week later, on the other side of the city, Joe popped into a pizza parlor to grab a bite to eat, and there was the same guy! This time, Joe made sure there were no interruptions, and before lunch was over, the man had accepted the heavenly Father's offer and established a personal relationship with the Son!

Have you lost contact with someone you have shared the gospel with? Just pray and ask God to reconnect you in some way. If He doesn't, then trust that He will send another one of His servants to make the offer again and bring it to a conclusion.

While the servant was praising God, Rebekah had run back and told her family about a remarkable man who had given her some pretty spectacular and valuable jewelry. As her brother Laban viewed the expensive gifts, I can almost see his eyes light up with little dollar signs. He was a conniving, shrewd man who "hurried out to the man at the spring" to greet the servant — more in greed, I suspect, than in hospitality (24:29). I imagine Laban dashing through the city streets, dodging stray dogs and playing children, until he came to the road on the outskirts of town that led to the well. Even as his heart raced, he must have deliberately slowed his pace to a dignified walk while his eyes frantically scoured the surrounding area, looking for the stranger his sister had described. He found the servant "standing by the camels near the spring," obviously waiting very patiently for the next step to unfold (24:30).

Laban gushed as he greeted the servant, "Come, you who are blessed by the LORD.... Why are you standing out here? I have prepared the house and a place

for the camels" (24:31). Abraham's servant accepted the invitation and followed
Laban to the house. Immediately the camels were unloaded and fed, a bath was
prepared for the servant and the men who had traveled with him, and refresh-
ments were set before them. Through it all, the servant appeared to me to be very
dignified and patient as he waited for the perfect time to tell his story.

Timing is so important, isn't it? The servant had an amazing story to tell and
an astounding invitation to offer, but he was not pushy in his presentation or offensive in his manner. He was patient as he waited for the right time to speak.
But he did not procrastinate. When the food was set before him, he resisted. "He
said, 'I will not eat until I have told you what I have to say'" (24:33). He couldn't
and wouldn't wait one more minute. He had to tell them the story about why he
had come.

There are times in a conversation or a relationship when I know I can't wait
one more minute to speak up. My heart quickens its beat, or my knees feel weak
and wobbly, or the pressure to say something builds inside of me until I *have* to
say something.[22]

Speak Persuasively

I was interested to note that the servant never spoke of himself. He spoke of the
greatness of Abraham, the father, when he began. "The LORD has blessed my master abundantly, and he has become wealthy. He has given him sheep and cattle, silver and gold, menservants and maidservants, and camels and donkeys" (24:35).
He spoke of Isaac as the only beloved son of the father, to whom Abraham "has
given ... everything he owns" (24:36). He persuaded Rebekah and her family, not
by bringing attention to himself, but by speaking of Abraham and Isaac in such
glowing terms that although they were not visibly present, those listening were
drawn to them.

When you present to someone the heavenly Father's offer to be part of His family by coming into a love relationship with His Son, how do you approach that person? While a word of personal testimony is very valid, we need to be careful that
the focus stays on Jesus. Even an interesting and powerful testimony can draw
an unhealthy attention to ourselves by going into unnecessary details as we talk
of our sin, our doubts, and our struggles to the extent that we direct the person's
focus on ourselves, not on the Lord.[23] I want to make God the heavenly Father and

Jesus Christ His only beloved Son attractive to others. I want to draw others, not to me, but to them. Jesus said if that's our aim, then we must lift Him up.[24] So lift Him up! Speak of His glory and His greatness, His power and His love. Speak of who He is, then what He has done for you. Keep the focus on Him.

With Rebekah and her family hanging on every word, the servant explained how Abraham had given him the trusted charge of finding a bride for Isaac, telling him, "You must not get a wife for my son from the daughters of the Canaanites,... but go to my father's family and to my own clan, and get a wife for my son" (24:37–38). Even as the servant recalled Abraham's exact words, the tone of his voice must have conveyed the seriousness with which he had accepted the responsibility and the overwhelming task that had faced him.

I wonder if his face broke into a warm smile at the memory of Abraham's encouraging words of faith that had given birth to genuine expectancy in his heart. Abraham had told him, "The LORD, before whom I have walked, will send his angel with you and make your journey a success" (24:40). Rebekah's family must have noticed the sparkle of excitement in his eyes as he began to unfold for them his side of the meeting at the well. He described how he had come to the spring, how he had prayed specifically for God to give him success by leading him to the bride for Isaac, how he had looked up even before the prayer had left his lips and had seen Rebekah! His admiring gaze must have turned on her as he related their interaction and shared the dramatic answer to his prayer as she not only offered him a drink but also watered his camels.

I noticed that the servant didn't go into minute details that would have been boring or tedious. And he didn't embellish the story to make it more dramatic than it was. He just briefly gave the facts, but in such a way that those listening were caught up in the wonder of his story. His gratitude to God and the praise that filled his heart were fresh from his encounter with Rebekah and must have permeated his expression and spilled out in his tone of voice as he related that she had identified herself as none other than a member of Abraham's father's family!

With confident assurance, he boldly stated that he knew God had led him "on the right road to get the granddaughter of my master's brother for his son" (24:48). Everyone who had gathered around to listen was convinced that there was no doubt in the servant's mind that Rebekah was God's choice of a bride for Isaac.

What has God done for you lately? What specific prayer has He answered?

When have you told someone else about it in such a way that he or she could almost visualize His faithfulness to you?

While I was writing this very chapter, my daughter called to share with me how God almost supernaturally brought someone to her to help her with her three little girls. She didn't go into great detail, but I could hear the gratitude in her voice and the excited anticipation of having someone nearby she could call on. As I listened to her, there was no doubt in my mind that God had answered her prayer . . . and it made me love the Father more.

You and I can tell others about the Father's greatness and glory, about the Son's love and beauty, about the offer to be part of the Father's family through a personal relationship with the Son. We can describe our own relationship with the Father and the Son and tell others about all the things God has done for us. We can state with conviction that we believe God has a plan and purpose for their lives that includes accepting that offer . . . that they have been chosen by the Father to belong to the Son. We can be as persuasive as the servant was in his presentation, but we also need to get to the point.

Speak Pointedly

The servant concluded what he had to say by presenting the family with a choice. He had said all he knew to say. Nothing was left except for them to decide. "Now if you will show kindness and faithfulness to my master, tell me; and if not, tell me, so I may know which way to turn" (24:49). He didn't try to manipulate them or coerce them or pressure them to make the decision of his choosing. He simply laid the offer on the table and asked them to take it or leave it.

When you tell others about the Father's offer, do you beat around the bush? There have been so many times when I have done exactly that. And later I've wondered why. I think there may be several factors that cause you and me to struggle with getting to the point:

First, we need to be convinced beyond any doubt that our God is God, that His one and only Son is Jesus.

Second, we must personally accept the charge He has given us to tell others that He has invited them to be members of His family, that they can be born again.

Third, we must believe that the Father's offer is genuine. And don't be confused. The Father is not offering a religion, or a denomination, or an institution, or an organization. He is offering a personal relationship with Himself through faith in His Son, Jesus. He is inviting us to become a member of His own family.

Fourth, we must care about the people to whom we speak to the extent that we tell them the truth. It is not loving to tell others what they want to hear or what will make them feel good if it's not true, no matter how politically correct it may be.

Fifth, we have to be willing to risk failure and rejection if the offer is not accepted. We need to keep in mind that the choice is theirs. If they refuse the Father's offer, we will still have been successful by virtue of the fact that we have been faithful to present it to them.

Would you take a moment to examine your heart? If any of the above reasons for beating around the bush are yours, would you talk to God about it? Then ... *get to the point*! Tell others that God so loves them that if they would choose to place their faith in His only beloved Son, Jesus, they would not perish in a life of separation from Him, but they would enter into a personal, permanent relationship with Him.[25] Go ahead. Let them see the joy you feel as you tell them God's love story. Then ask them to make a decision ...

THE CHOICE

When the servant finished speaking, I wonder if there were a few moments of collective silence as everyone stared at him, almost afraid to breathe for fear of breaking the powerful sense of God's presence. Did Rebekah's eyes fill with tears as the reality of what had been said pierced her heart? Finally, did someone shift his position and someone else clear her throat as Laban, Rebekah's brother, and Bethuel, her father, both spoke in total unity and agreement, saying, "This is from the LORD" (24:50)? They both seemed to be deeply moved by the obvious evidence of God's leading. There was nothing else they could say, so they responded, "Here is Rebekah; take her and go, and let her become the wife of your master's son, as the LORD has directed" (24:51).

The Choice Was Pursued

The servant was so overcome once again with gratitude to God that before he made any response to the family, "he bowed down to the ground before the LORD" (24:52). His heart must have melted with amazement at God's goodness and faithfulness to him. His words had been received, his mission had been understood, the offer had been accepted. He had no words to express how he felt, only the intensely meaningful and poignant gesture of humble worship.

What sheer delight it must have been for the servant then to go to the big, heavy trunks he had brought such a long way, open them up, and distribute sparkling jewels, gleaming gold and silver necklaces, bracelets, and rings, along with shimmering silks, fine linen clothing, and other "costly gifts" for Rebekah and her family (24:53). I can imagine their eyes widening with astonishment as each treasure was brought out, displayed for all to admire, then given to Rebekah and Laban and Rebekah's mother.

There were so many gifts! And such a variety of gifts! If the gifts were any indication, Abraham must have been wealthier than their wildest dreams. Surely the abundance and the extravagance of the treasures themselves confirmed the choice Laban and Bethuel had made for Rebekah to become Isaac's bride.

But something was missing. The wise servant had not yet heard from Rebekah. She had yet to say what her choice would be. So I wonder if the display of gifts and jewels was partially his way of pursuing her, without pressure. Maybe he was just letting her glimpse a little of what would one day be hers if she chose to become Isaac's bride.

When I am presenting the Father's offer to someone, one way I pursue them is by displaying the "jewels":

- His joy that is unspeakable and full of glory. [26]
- His peace that passes all understanding.[27]
- His love that will not let me go.[28]
- His compassion that never fails.[29]
- His forgiveness of every sin and all sin.[30]
- His life that is abundant and free.[31]
- His blessings that are unlimited.[32]
- His mercy in my failure.[33]
- His strength that is made perfect in my weakness.[34]
- His grace that is sufficient for my every need.[35]
- His family that surrounds me with support and encouragement.[36]
- His Word that is so personal and powerful and true.[37]
- His faithfulness that continues to all generations.[38]

- His Spirit that will never leave me nor forsake me.[39]
- And the blessed hope of one day seeing Him face-to-face![40]

Praise God! *Praise God!* He has promised that these "jewels" are just the down payment. There is much more to come![41] He has tantalizingly revealed that no human "eye has seen, no ear has heard, no mind has conceived what God has prepared for those who" enter into a love relationship with His Son.[42] He has given His Word that He "is able to do immeasurably more than all we ask or imagine, according to his power that is at work within us, to him be glory."[43] Praise God!

The "jewels" displayed in my life ought to make others want to know God as I do. Others ought to look at me and listen to me and want to love Jesus as I do. The magnificent obsession should be contagious simply by the way others see me embrace it for myself.

God knows that I am obsessed, not only with knowing Him more and more each day but also with making Him known. He desires that the "jewels" in my treasure trove would not only increase in number but would increase in beauty and visibility. So He arranges them in my life the way the British crown jewels are displayed in the Tower of London ... on black velvet. As spectacular as the crown jewels are — emeralds as big as walnuts, diamonds as big as eggs — their brilliant clarity and color would not be nearly as noticeable if it were not for the contrast against the black velvet.

God carefully, personally arranges the black velvet in the display case of my life. What black velvet has He carefully draped in your life? Do you have the "black velvet" of ...

Migraine headaches against which to display His joy?

Financial reversal against which to display His peace?

Rejection by a spouse against which to display His love?

Betrayal by a friend against which to display His forgiveness?

Overwhelming demands against which to display His strength?

Unanswered prayer against which to display your trust in His Word?

One hundred interruptions against which to display His patience?

While I was writing this chapter, my wretched computer crashed, taking half of what I had written into the never-never land of cyberspace. In spite of automatic backups and meticulous attention to saving each page, the document vanished irretrievably.[44] And it disappeared at the moment when I had just finished describing the "jewels" — and expressing my desire that they would attract others to Jesus by the way they were displayed in my life!

The lesson was not lost on me. The black velvet was a backdrop for displaying my godly treasures: for my computer guru to observe my patience, for my husband to observe my humility as I apologized for taking out my frustration on him, for my children to observe my joy in spite of the crisis, for my friends to observe my faith that God would bring the fresh water of ideas out of the rocks in my head, and for my readers to indirectly "observe" my perseverance as I switched to another computer, booted it up, and started rewriting everything all over again![45]

It wouldn't be surprising to me at all if Abraham's servant had spread out yards of soft heavy black velvet on which to display the father's treasures. As Laban, Bethuel, Rebekah, and her mother marveled at the silver and the gold and the jewelry and the clothing, they must have been amazed to realize that the beauty, the richness, the magnificence of the treasures belonged to them. And that if Rebekah agreed to be Isaac's wife, there would be much more to come for her.

Following the servant's presentation and the display of treasures, I wonder if the shrewd and crafty Laban slept well that night. I doubt it! I expect he lay in his bed, eyes wide open and mind spinning as he tried to come up with a plan to get his hands on more of the treasure for himself. Finally, he seemed to think of something brilliant. He would agree to Rebekah's becoming Isaac's bride, but he would delay her departure for ten days. During those ten days, he knew she would have second thoughts about the amazing turn of events in her life. In the meantime, he would send the servant back and force Isaac to come to Haran . . . and that would be the beginning of his extortion scheme.[46]

So when everyone else got up the next morning and Abraham's servant said, "Let's go," Laban said, "Not so fast." Laban was resisting Rebekah's commitment by trying to delay it.

The Choice Was Pressed

I've noticed again and again as I present the Father's offer to someone, that's when the interruptions and distractions come. It's at the moment I'm presenting the Father's invitation that the flight attendant comes to ask if I want something else to drink, or the person's cell phone vibrates, or other people begin talking loudly at another table.

Probably the most vivid example of this kind of distraction came as I was speaking from a platform in the center of one of the nation's largest arenas. After I had presented the gospel to approximately 20,000 women and just as I began to issue the Father's invitation for them to come to the cross, repent of their sin, and place their faith in Jesus as their Savior, a dog began to bark! I'm serious! And then another dog began to bark! Then these two dogs began chasing each other around the platform with a woman chasing them and a security guard chasing her! To this day, when I listen to the CD of that message, I can hear the barking dogs in the background.

I laugh about it now, but at that moment I knew I was in a battle for the hearts and minds of hundreds of women in that arena whom the enemy was trying to distract. God is so good. The outlandish commotion seemed to make the audience listen even more closely, and when I finally invited them to come to the cross, hundreds of women streamed down to the platform to accept the Father's offer!

Have you had the experience of presenting the Father's offer to someone and, just as you sense he or she is on the verge of agreeing to make a commitment, the telephone rings? Or the UPS guy shows up at your door? Or the baby starts to cry? Or you are suddenly seized with a coughing fit? Be alert! Our very crafty and shrewd enemy will do all he can to delay a final decision, knowing if he can get the person to put it off, he or she will be less likely to finalize it.[47]

Abraham's servant was wise. He insisted, "Do not detain me, now that the LORD has granted success to my journey. Send me on my way so I may go to my master" (24:56). He knew the decision needed to be made at that moment and then acted on if it was going to be made at all. Postponing the decision would only serve to weaken Rebekah's resolve to make it.

So ... you and I need to be reminded: don't stop short of pressing for a decision. Don't be afraid to ask the person to make a commitment to Jesus *now*. A fisherman doesn't catch a fish by throwing a line into the lake and hooking the fish, only to leave it dangling in the water. He doesn't influence or inspire the fish to jump into his boat. He reels it in! You and I need to reel in our "fish." Just ask, "Would you like to pray with me now and accept the Father's offer?" Or, "Would you commit your life to Jesus by repenting of your sin and inviting Him into your heart right now?"

I remember sitting across from a young man with whom I had shared the gospel as he struggled with the decision to commit his life to Christ. When I gently asked him if he would like to pray with me then and there, he was silent. After a few moments, I asked him if he had heard me, and he answered that he had and he was just thinking about it. The next few minutes seemed like a lifetime. Finally, I pressed him, "George, are you all right?"[48] His response gave me incredible insight into what goes on in the hearts of those in an audience when I extend an invitation from the platform, because he said, "I'm all right. I just have a lot of issues to work through." The muscles in his face were working hard, as though he was in a fierce battle . . . and I knew that he was.

Silently, I began to pray for God to give him the will to repent of his sin and the strength to make the decision. I didn't want to push him, but I didn't want him to procrastinate either. Finally, he nodded he was ready. When he prayed with me, the barriers of a lifetime broke, and the tears flowed as he confessed his sin, told God he was sorry, asked for forgiveness, and invited Jesus into his heart. When we finished praying, he threw his arms around me, and we both sobbed and sobbed. Twenty minutes later, when I left him, he was joyfully sharing his decision with his boss.

The Choice Was Personal

Neither Laban nor the servant would have forced his will on Rebekah. The decision was hers to make. "So they called Rebekah and asked her, 'Will you go with this man?'" I imagine that all eyes were on her. Did she look almost longingly at her mother, and respectfully at her father, and knowingly at her brother? I think her gaze must have been clear and level as she then looked at the servant and replied firmly, "I will go" (24:58).

Hearing her answer, I want to applaud! Good for you, Rebekah! You've chosen well! You have no idea the blessings that will be yours for generations to come! Four thousand years later you will still be respected and admired and emulated. Other mothers and fathers will measure the spouses of their own children by you. Well done! Your decision is just the beginning of a lifetime adventure of being a member of the Father's family.

Her choice was very personal as well as voluntary. No one could make it for her. She had to make it for herself. In fact, it was the only way she could become Isaac's bride. The servant never would have accepted a forced arrangement. He wanted her to come with him of her own free will.

As we conclude the story of Abraham's life, would you examine whether you have ever made the choice to go with "this Man Jesus"? When did you make the personal choice to accept the Father's offer to come into a love relationship with His Son? The gospel of John states that the only way you and I can come into the heavenly Father's family is by an individual decision to believe in the Lord Jesus Christ and receive Him by faith.[49]

The incredible truth is that God the Father not only extends an offer to you to belong to His Son, He has *chosen* you for that purpose.[50] Out of all of the daughters of Eve and the sons of Adam, the Father took the initiative and sent His Holy Spirit, His Servant, into the world to search for you. When the Servant found you, He began to convince you to accept the Father's offer.[51]

Did you think it was your friend who was so persistent when she kept telling you about Jesus? Did you think it was just your own random curiosity that caused you to go to the conference? As you have read this book, did you think your heart was stirred only because of the words on the page? Could it be in each case that it's God's Holy Servant who is drawing you to the Father's Son?

Your choice to either receive or reject the Father's offer will determine where you spend eternity. You can ...

resist the choice,

ignore the choice,

procrastinate in making the choice,

deny you have the choice,

assume you have made the choice,

close this book and forget about the choice,

ridicule the choice,

but it's still your personal choice. No one can make it for you.

Have you accepted the Father's invitation to be the bride of His Son? Are you unsure whether you have accepted it? If you are doubting, there could be several reasons ...

unconfessed sin in your life,

disobedience to His Word,
      resistance to His will,
           neglect of prayer and Bible reading.

But the biggest reason of all for lacking assurance is that although the Father has invited you to come into His family, you may never have RSVP'd to His invitation. So if you are plagued by doubt, I suggest you slip down on your knees right now and pray this simple prayer:

> Dear heavenly Father,
> Right now, I want to RSVP to your invitation to become a member of Your family. I confess that I'm not worthy. I'm a sinner, and I'm sorry. But I am willing to repent of my sin, to turn away from it and trust in Jesus alone as my atoning sacrifice. I open the door of my heart and invite Him to come into the center of my life in a covenant, permanent love relationship. I am personally choosing to accept Your offer to be the bride of Your Son. I want to go with this Man. Amen.

Are you at this moment even more unsure and discouraged because you have prayed a similar prayer on other occasions but still doubt your relationship to God's Son? If so, I suggest it may be you have never prayed this prayer even once *by faith*. Faith says ...

> Father God,
> You have said if I confess my sin, You will forgive me.[52]
>   I now take You at Your Word and thank You that I am forgiven.
> You have said if I believe in Jesus, You will give me eternal life.[53]
>   I now take You at Your Word and thank You that I have eternal life.
> You have said if I open my heart, You will come to live within me.[54]
>   I now take You at Your Word and thank You for living inside of me.
> You have said if I receive Jesus into my life, I am Your child.[55]
>   I now take You at Your Word and thank You that I am now Your
>   child.
> I choose to place my faith, not in how I feel at this moment or in what anyone else says, but in Your Word alone. Amen.

At the moment you thank Him by faith, taking Him at His Word, you may still lack assurance. But as you read your Bible, pray, and get into fellowship with other

Christians, yielding your life to God's will and beginning to live out your journey of faith, the assurance will come. God's Holy Servant will guide you and guard you and keep you and deliver you safely to the Father's Son.

It would take days, weeks, and even months for Rebekah to "feel" she was a member of Abraham's family. But once she made the decision, she knew she was blessed. "Then Rebekah and her maids got ready and mounted their camels and went back with the man. So the servant took Rebekah and left" (24:61).

The servant had to transport Rebekah back over the difficult and dangerous five-hundred-mile journey to Canaan. He had to protect her and guard her and keep her and deliver her safely to Isaac ...

THE CONTINUATION

Abraham's servant and Rebekah, and the men and the maids who were with them, had miles and miles to go. Day after day. Week after week. Month after month. But as monotonous as it may have been, the anticipation must have mounted. Rebekah had to be consumed with thoughts of Isaac. During the long hours of riding the camel, I would imagine she must have peppered the servant with hundreds of questions about Isaac.

Was he tall or short? Was he skinny or fat? Was his hair straight or curly? Did he *have* hair or was he balding? What were his hobbies? What was his favorite food? Was he kind? Did he have a temper? Was he thoughtful? Was he sensitive? Would he love her? And what was his father like?

The servant must have thoroughly enjoyed talking to the beautiful young Rebekah about the greatness of the father and the glory of the son. He must have told Rebekah about Isaac's miraculous conception and birth. He may have told her about Ishmael's jealousy of Isaac, his voice dropping as he described the painful scene of Ishmael's removal from the home. Did he tell her about Mount Moriah, when Isaac was spared death at the last moment because God Himself had provided a ram to die on the altar in his place?

As Rebekah learned more and more about Isaac, she must have fallen in love with him before she even saw him. She must have longed for him and begun to look for him, especially as she knew her journey was coming to an end and she was drawing near to the place where he was.

As I journey through life, I know the Holy Servant is teaching me about the Father's Son.[56] He has told me about His miraculous conception and birth[57] ... about His life on earth[58] ... about His sacrifice on the cross when the Father provided Himself as the Lamb[59] ... about His resurrection[60] ... about His ascension into heaven.[61] I have learned that He is the Father's sole heir[62] and that as His bride, I will share in His wealth and power and glory.[63] I have learned that He is seated right now at the Father's right hand, thinking of me and praying for me.[64] And I have been told that He is looking for me! That one day I will look up and see Him coming to receive me to Himself so I can live with Him in His heavenly home forever![65] It's no wonder that, even though I've yet to see Him visibly, I already love Him! I believe in Him! And I'm filled with inexpressible and glorious joy at the very thought of Him![66]

As my journey draws to an end because I'm growing older, and also because I believe the time for His second coming is near, the expectation of seeing Him is intensifying. I long to see His face. I long to see the expression on His face when He sees me ... and my children. I long to hear the sound of His voice calling my name. And I long to feel His touch. My longing to visibly, physically see Him and hear Him and feel Him at times is almost a tangible ache.

In a similar way, Rebekah's anticipation must have reached a crescendo as her journey neared its end. After weeks of travel, on an evening that probably looked like many previous ones, Rebekah would have been swaying on the back of the camel in its unique side to side movement. Her eyes must have scanned the distant rolling terrain. If it had been a clear, cloudless day, the edge of the earth and the sky would have seemed to blend into one as the sun melted into a huge red fireball that slipped from sight, leaving streaks of glory in the heavens. As she searched the horizon, her attention was caught by movement. Someone was coming toward her.

Instinctively, she knew. It was Isaac! He was coming for her! The climax of her entire journey was wrapped up in this encounter. She hastily slipped off the camel. Then, just to make sure, she asked the servant in a voice that must have quivered with excitement, "Who is that man in the field coming to meet us?" (24:65). Her hope was confirmed when the servant, who was as loyal to the son as he was to the father, answered, "He is my master" (24:65).

I wonder if it suddenly occurred to her that while she had been learning all about Isaac, he knew nothing about her! I wonder if she was in love with him but suddenly was afraid he wouldn't love her. Would she be pleasing in his eyes? Would she be what he was looking for and longing for? Would she be what he expected her to be?

She suddenly seemed to me to be overcome with shyness; "she took her veil and covered herself" (24:65). She knew Isaac was the father's sole heir.[67] As his bride, she would share in all that was his. She was walking toward one who would transform her life into one of vast wealth, and power, and position. But would their marriage be an "official" arrangement? Or would they have a personal love relationship?

Do you ever wonder the same things Rebekah must have wondered? Do you wonder if your relationship is just an "official" arrangement between Savior and sinner ... or is it really a personal love relationship? Does Jesus really want to see you? Will you be what He's looking for? Will you be pleasing to Him? When the moment comes for you to see Him face-to-face, will you want to hide? To cover yourself? The thrilling truth is that there will be no need to fear. Because *you are the bride* the Father has chosen. You have been cared for by the Servant, who is perfectly preparing you for the day when you will be presented to the Son, holy and blameless.[68]

As Rebekah saw Isaac coming toward her, it didn't take long for her to discover his desire for her. He had gone out into the field to meditate, but I wonder if he had been watching for her too. After almost forty years of being single, his mind must have been filled with thoughts of his bride and what she would be like. As she drew near, he too must have felt his heart skip a beat.

All he would have been able to see was a female form swathed in the fine linen clothing he had provided for her. There must have been introductions, then, as Isaac and Rebekah gazed on each other for the first time, "the servant told Isaac all he had done" (24:66). What overflowing joy must have welled up in the servant's heart as he related the details of his journey and told once again of God's extraordinary faithfulness in leading him to exactly the right person. How thrilled he must have been to present the bride to Abraham's son.

The father's charge had been kept. The servant had been totally committed to find a bride for Isaac who would be pleasing to both the father and the son, and God had led him to exactly the right person. The bride had agreed to come, and she followed through on her choice by traveling with the servant until they safely reached Isaac. What celebration there must have been when "Isaac brought her into the tent of his mother Sarah, and he married Rebekah. So she became his wife, and he loved her" (24:67).

There is no indication that Isaac saw Rebekah's face before he claimed her as his bride, since she had covered herself with her veil. Yet even in conversation, he must have found himself captivated by the godliness of her character surely transmitted by a gentle, quiet spirit.[69] In our culture, where so much emphasis is placed on physical beauty and sexual attraction, we need to remind our children that their choice of a spouse should not be based on outward appearance, but on inward character. They need to seek God's choice of a mate. Yet God knows the desires of our hearts, just as He knew the desire of Isaac's heart. Even as God had chosen Eve for Adam, He had chosen someone for Isaac that Isaac could get excited about!

When Isaac finally did see Rebekah, I wonder if he caught his breath, then found that he couldn't take his eyes off of her! She was more physically beautiful than he could have imagined! She was the answer to his prayers and the fulfillment of his dreams. *"And he loved her"* (24:67, emphasis mine).

The Bible doesn't tell us what Abraham thought about his new daughter-in-law. But I know. Without any doubt, he loved her because she loved his son. And if you ever have reason to question what the heavenly Father thinks about you, just remember . . . love His Son and you can be absolutely assured that the Father will love you.[70]

Isaac and Rebekah were faithfully married to each other for a very long time in a loving relationship. They were perhaps even more wealthy than the kings of their day, since "Abraham left everything he owned to Isaac" (25:5). But they embraced the magnificent obsession, adopting Abraham's nomadic lifestyle as pilgrims who were just passing through this life on the way to a heavenly home.

They gave Abraham twin grandsons, Jacob and Esau. Jacob was the younger twin who passionately pursued knowing God and making Him known. His desire to embrace the magnificent obsession and all that God had for him was so strong that he manipulated circumstances and stole the birthright from Esau. His brother was so enraged, he threatened to murder Jacob! With that threat ringing in his ears, Jacob was exiled to the school of hard knocks under Rebekah's conniving brother Laban for twenty years. When he returned to Canaan to claim all that God had for him, he had twelve sons of his own. His sons became the twelve founding fathers of the nation of Israel. And the rest is history, as the pursuit of knowing God as Abraham did in the magnificent obsession continued.

Abraham had effectively passed on everything . . .

to his son Isaac,

who passed it to his son Jacob,

who passed it to his twelve sons,

who passed it to Moses, whom the Lord uniquely knew face-to-face.[71]

Moses passed the magnificent obsession on to . . .

Joshua,

Deborah,

Gideon,

Samson,

Ruth,

Samuel,

David,

Solomon,

Josiah,

Hezekiah,

Elijah,

Elisha,

Ezra,

Haggai,

Zechariah,

Nehemiah,

Malachi . . .

. . . to John the Baptist . . .

who received the baton and passed everything on by bearing witness to "the Lamb of God, who takes away the sin of the world!"[72] For a short while, the magnificent obsession was lived not only by faith but also face-to-face! The descendant through whom the world was to be blessed . . . the One God had promised to Abraham . . . *came*! His name was Jesus! He was embraced by the apostle John, who rejoiced as he exclaimed that he had "seen his glory, . . . full of grace and truth . . .

the only begotten of the Father ... which was from the beginning, which we have heard, which we have seen with our eyes.... No one has ever seen God, but God the only Son, who is at the Father's side, has made him known."[73]

John passed everything on to Polycarp, an early church leader who heard John say he had seen for himself the Father's only Son, the promised Seed of Abraham. Polycarp received the baton, embraced the magnificent obsession, and passed it to ...

Ambrose,

Augustine,

Anselm,

John Wycliffe,

John Huss,

Martin Luther,

John Knox,

John Calvin,

John Bunyan,

Jonathan Edwards,

John Wesley,

George Whitefield,

Francis Asbury,

William Carey,

Charles Haddon Spurgeon,

Dwight L. Moody,

I. M. Haldeman,

Billy Sunday ...

... to Billy Graham ...

And my father passed on to me an authentic, God-filled life by his example as well as his preaching. For over sixty-five years, my father's message has been consistent: that anyone and everyone can know God in a personal, permanent relationship when we confess that we're sinners, ask God to forgive us, claim His Son as our only Savior, and surrender the control of our lives to Him. My father and my mother both embraced the magnificent obsession of knowing God and making Him known ... and it has become my own. I now have the privilege of passing it on ... *to you*!

Now it's your turn. Don't drop the baton! Once you have embraced the magnificent obsession for yourself . . . once you have embraced a truly God-filled life by . . .

> leaving everything behind,
>> letting everything go,
>>> trusting everything completely,
>>>> pursuing everything patiently,
>>>>> casting everything out,
>>>>>> lifting everything up,
>>>>>>> laying everything down,
>>>>>>>> mourning everything hopefully.

Pass everything on . . . until your faith becomes sight and you see the only beloved Son of the Father face-to-face. On that day, you are going to see His desire for you as though you're the only one He loves. You will see the delight in His eyes as He takes you into His heavenly tent, and loves you forever and ever. And all that is His will be yours.

> *Because you are His magnificent obsession!*

Epilogue

Altogether, Abraham lived a hundred and seventy-five years. Then Abraham breathed his last and died at a good old age, an old man and full of years; and he was gathered to his people. His sons Isaac and Ishmael buried him in the cave of Machpelah near Mamre, in the field of Ephron son of Zohar the Hittite, the field Abraham had bought from the Hittites. There Abraham was buried with his wife Sarah" (Genesis 25:7 – 10).[1]

Abraham had embraced the magnificent obsession for one hundred years! He had begun his journey of faith in order to claim the promise of God's blessings. In the end, the greatest, most coveted blessing was ...

> more than just the promise of a son,
> more than just the promise of descendants as numerous as the stars,
> more than just the land he walked on,
> more than just being a blessing....

The ultimate blessing was that Abraham didn't just embrace the magnificent obsession of a God-filled life, he actually experienced it. Quite simply, Abraham knew God.

Praise God! *Praise God!* You and I have been redeemed "in order that the blessing given to Abraham might come to [us] through Christ Jesus.... So those who have faith are blessed along with Abraham."[2] We can experience the God-filled life too. We can know God too!

Modus Operandi

I praise God for people outside my family who share Abraham's MO ... his magnificent obsession. Their vibrant faith and authentic personal relationship with God have been contagious ... *to me.*

Sheila Bailey ... whose pursuit of God seemed to intensify, instead of falter, when her life's companion, Dr. E. K. Bailey, moved to our Father's house.

Henry Blackaby ... whose experience of the God-filled life has brought it out of the mystical and down into the practical for millions of people.

Jill Briscoe ... whose warm, intimate relationship with God has led me to conclude if she can have a relationship like that, so can I.

Stuart Briscoe ... whose words are like "apples of gold in settings of silver,"* and whose sprint to the finish line of obedient service remains focused, faithful, and fired up.

R. V. Brown ... the size of his giant triceps is exceeded only by his great heart for the kingdom of God.

Robert Cunville ... whose power-filled preaching has been life-saving and life-changing to hundreds of thousands of his countrymen in India,

---

*Proverbs 25:11.

and whose personal life brings glory to God and honor to my father whom he has served faithfully for over thirty-one years.

A. *Wetherell Johnson* ... whose journey of faith led her to Europe, China, a Japanese concentration camp, America, and into my life ... and whose love for God was mirrored in her love for His Word, her love for His Son, and her love for His people.

Crawford Loritts ... whose work for God has never seemed to come before his worship of God.

Mike MacIntosh ... whose abundantly fruitful ministry bears witness that God can use broken pieces.

Steven Olford ... whose passionate, powerful dissection of God's Word could set even the coldest, hardest heart on fire.

Joe Stowell ... whose journey on the Glory Road has challenged me not to take an exit ramp.

Notes

My Magnificent Obsession
1. See Isaiah 41:8 and 2 Chronicles 20:7.
2. Hebrews 13:8.

Chapter 1: Leave Everything Behind
1. See Acts 7:2 – 4.
2. John 4:24.
3. See Romans 1:19 – 20.
4. See Exodus 14:21; Daniel 5:5 – 6; Exodus 19:16 – 19; and Mark 9:2 – 3.
5. See Exodus 3:1 – 2.
6. See Revelation 3:8.
7. See 1 Samuel 16:11 – 12.
8. Following the covenant of circumcision described in Genesis 17:5, God changed Abram's name to Abraham.
9. See Acts 7:2.
10. Isaiah 40:6 – 8, quoted in 1 Peter 1:24 – 25.
11. Luke 14:33.
12. See Hebrews 11:8.
13. See Psalm 31:15.
14. See Leviticus 18, in particular verses 3 and 27.
15. See 1 Kings 18.
16. See Matthew 26:1 – 5.
17. See Acts 7:54 – 60; 12:2.
18. For help in learning how to listen to the voice of God, please go to my website, *www.annegrahamlotz.com*. There you will find many resources available, including Bible studies

in print and on CD and DVD that will help you learn how to listen to God's voice as you read your Bible.

19. 1 John 1:5 – 7.

20. John 14:6.

21. See John 20:19 – 29.

22. See Luke 24:13 – 31.

23. See John 21:4 – 14.

24. Sarah was Abraham's half sister, the daughter of his father but not of his mother (see Genesis 20:12). What Abraham said was a half-truth, but a half-truth is a whole lie.

25. See Proverbs 6:16 – 17.

26. The New Testament instructs you and me to follow Sarah's example as one "who obeyed Abraham and called him her master. You are her daughters if you do what is right and do not give way to fear" (1 Peter 3:6). I believe Peter is encouraging wives that when they are submissive to their husbands and the husbands abuse them in any way, the husbands will have to deal with God. God defends women who are right with Him and are trying to be right with others.

Chapter 2: Let Everything Go

1. See Genesis 11:31; 12:4.

2. See 2 Peter 2:7 – 8.

3. Luke 3:21 – 22. Based on this passage, I've asked myself a searching question: Does heaven open when I pray?

4. Luke 5:16. Prayer has been described as the language of loneliness.

5. Luke 6:12. By His own example, Jesus teaches us the importance of prayer before making a big decision.

6. Luke 9:18. It's interesting to note that Jesus prayed in private ... with His disciples. In other words, He could be alone in a crowd.

7. Luke 9:28 – 29. Prayer can transform the person who is praying ... even facial expressions can be different.

8. Luke 11:1. At this stage in my life, I don't think I need to be taught to pray as much as I need to just pray!

9. Revelation 3:1.

10. Revelation 3:2.

11. Revelation 3:2.

12. My husband is extremely grateful for this growth in my spiritual life.

13. Anne Graham Lotz, *Daily Light* (Nashville: Countryman, 1998), March 4, evening. This is my adaptation of a little book of Scripture quotations first published in 1794 by Samuel Bagster, a forerunner of Marshall Pickering.

14. James 5:10; Job 2:10; Leviticus 10:3; 1 Samuel 3:18; Psalm 55:22; Isaiah 53:4; Matthew 11:28 (all NKJV).

15. See Ephesians 1:3.

16. 1 Kings 17:2 – 4 NKJV, cited in Lotz, *Daily Light*, March 7, evening.

17. Although my wise mother encouraged me to "be ready" to serve Jesus outside my home, she had reservations when I felt called to lead the weekly BSF class. As I explained in chapter 1, those reservations quickly evaporated when she and my father visited our home — after surprising me one morning.

18. See 1 Peter 1:6 – 7.

19. 2 Corinthians 6:17.

20. Galatians 6:7 – 8.

21. 2 Peter 2:7 – 8.

22. See Hebrews 11:25.

23. See Galatians 6:7.

24. See Genesis 18:20 – 22; 19:1.

25. Luke 17:32 – 33.

26. See 2 Peter 3:7.

27. Matthew 6:19.

28. See Deuteronomy 23:3.

29. God's grace is evident in Lot's descendants because Ruth, great-grandmother of King David and in the lineage of Jesus Christ, was a Moabite.

30. Mark 8:36 – 37.

31. Matthew 19:29 – 30.

Chapter 3: Entrust Everything Completely

1. Hebron was located approximately twenty miles south of the city that later became Jerusalem. While no one knows for certain where Sodom was situated, it is believed that it was located in the Dead Sea area at the southern end of the Jordan Valley. All three sites are assumed to have been in the same province, one of the five attacked by the four kings of the East.

2. One can only imagine how large Abraham's household was if he had "318 trained men" (Genesis 14:14), because that number would not have included the young men, old men, women, and children.

3. Years later, the city of Salem was taken from the Jebusites by King David and became the capital of Israel, Jerusalem.

4. Melchizedek is an intriguing figure because the New Testament describes him as an illustration, or type, of Christ (see Hebrews 5:6, 10; 6:20; 7:1 – 21). He was a king, a priest, who had no known beginning or end. Abraham received his blessing, then tithed to him, acknowledging he was the greater.

I find it fascinating that Melchizedek obviously was a godly, righteous man who served the Lord and knew Him in a personal way. Yet Melchizedek was not connected to Abraham. This seems to indicate that there were others in Abraham's day who knew God and were in a right relationship with Him who are not recorded in the Bible.

5. Amy Carmichael, *Edges of His Ways* (London: SPCK, 1955), 148.

6. I read these verses from my *Daily Light* (Nashville: Countryman), Deuteronomy 33:25; Isaiah 40:29; 2 Corinthians 12:9; Philippians 4:13; and Judges 5:21.

7. This is the first time this particular familiar phrase is used in the Bible and it is distinctly different from "the angel of the Lord" who appears for the first time in Genesis 16.

8. See John 1:1 – 2, 14; Revelation 19:13.

9. There are other beautiful examples of God initiating contact with His children when they are in need. Some of the ones that come readily to mind are Adam and Eve in Genesis 3:8 – 9; Ezekiel in Ezekiel 1:2 – 3; the woman of Samaria in John 4:4 – 10; the paralyzed man in John 5:1 – 8; the man born blind in John 9:1 – 7; Mary Magdalene in John 20:10 – 18; the apostle John in Revelation 1:9 – 13; and, of course, you and me in John 3:16 with Romans 8:6 – 9.

10. See John 10:1 – 4.

11. Isaiah 43:1.

12. See 1 John 4:1.

13. See 2 Peter 1:16 – 21.

14. Psalm 139:2, 4.

15. Luke 2:10, 14.

16. Psalm 119:165.

17. Philippians 4:6 – 7.

18. See Ezekiel 1:24; Revelation 1:15.

19. Exodus 3:14.

20. See Malachi 3:6.

21. See Lamentations 3:22 – 23.

22. See Hebrews 13:8.

23. See Joshua 1:5.

24. See Psalm 139:7 – 12.

25. See Romans 8:38 – 39.

26. See Hebrews 13:5.

27. See Joshua 1:9.

28. See Psalm 46:10.

29. See Psalm 119:114.

30. See Psalm 32:7.

31. See 2 Samuel 22:2.

32. See Psalm 140:7.

33. See Psalm 18:2.

34. See Matthew 26:56.

35. See 1 Corinthians 2:9; John 14:2.

36. See Ephesians 2:8 – 9; Isaiah 64:6; Romans 3:10.

37. See 2 Peter 3:9; Revelation 22:17.

38. See John 14:6. The interview continued for over an hour. At the most, only about

thirty seconds was actually used on air. I was tempted to think, *What a waste of time*, except that after the taping, I continued talking to the film crew members, who listened attentively, with one actually saying he found himself fascinated by what I had said. A week later, I received an email that let me know they were still thinking about it.

39. See Ephesians 3:20.

40. Mark 9:24.

41. See Psalm 8:3.

42. See Psalm 147:4.

43. See Jeremiah 31:35.

44. Romans 4:20 – 21.

45. This verse is quoted five other times in the Bible: Romans 4:3, 9, 22; Galatians 3:6; James 2:23.

46. See Galatians 3:16.

47. See Genesis 3:15.

48. John 8:56.

49. John 8:57.

50. John 8:58 – 59.

51. See Matthew 11:27; John 1:14, 18; 5:23 – 24; 6:40; 10:27 – 30.

52. See 1 Peter 2:9.

53. See 1 Peter 1:18.

54. See John 3:16.

55. See Ephesians 2:1 – 10.

56. See 1 John 1:9; Ephesians 1:7.

57. See John 17:2 – 3; 1 John 5:11 – 13.

58. See Revelation 3:20; Luke 11:13.

59. John 14:2 – 3; Revelation 21:1 – 4.

60. *Eerdmans Handbook to the Bible* (Grand Rapids, Mich.: Eerdmans, 1973), 138.

61. The despair and depression that gripped Abraham as he saw into the future may be one reason God doesn't let us know more about what has yet to take place.

62. See Genesis 50:20.

63. The story can be found in Genesis 37, 39 – 50.

64. See Hebrews 12:29.

65. See John 9:5.

66. See Ephesians 1:13 – 14.

67. Hebrews 6:13.

68. See Romans 8:32.

Chapter 4: Pursue Everything Patiently

1. Gene Stratton-Porter, *Freckles* (New York: Grosset & Dunlap, 1916).

2. "Pavonia pavonia," Emperor Moth. *Wikipedia. http://en.wikipedia.org/wiki/Pavonia_pavonia.*

3. Mrs. Charles E. Cowman, *Streams in the Desert* (Grand Rapids, Mich.: Zondervan, 1977), January 9.

4. See Genesis 18:10–12.

5. John MacArthur, ed., *The MacArthur Study Bible*, NKJV (Nashville: Word Bibles, 1997), 37, note 16:3.

6. See Genesis 2:24.

7. Jesus confirmed this creation principle in Matthew 19:5–6.

8. This is an illustration. I understand that with radar equipment and other high-tech advantages, landing a plane safely today involves much more than just runway lights.

9. These principles are not listed in the Bible as such, but a careful examination of decisions made by people in Scripture reveals that they are there. One clear example of the use of these principles is in the New Testament, when the apostle Peter explained to the church leaders his decision to make the gospel available to Gentiles without first making them become Jews (see Acts 11:1–18). Peter related that as he was praying and asking God's direction, God spoke to him from heaven, preparing his heart and mind to make a decision so radical, it was confirmed by God's Word. At that moment, the practical circumstances fell into place as three men showed up at his door asking him to come present the gospel to their Gentile employer, Cornelius. Peter immediately had the inner conviction to do so as the Spirit of God assured him he was to go. When he consulted with six other Christian brothers, they affirmed his decision. As a result of Peter's bold obedience to the will of God as it was revealed to him, the church as we know it today was established.

10. Matthew 14:28.

11. During the two years of frustrating failure and delay, I experienced stress and pressure in many areas of my life. The result was that my personal heart's cry was for revival. I studied the gospel of John, seeking a fresh encounter with Jesus through His Word, and I found Him! And I wrote down my personal studies that I published in the book *Just Give Me Jesus* (Nashville: Word, 2000). Only God could have timed the publication of the book and the arena events to coincide.

12. Psalm 25:9.

13. Isaiah 30:15.

14. See Matthew 10:14.

15. God used this difficult experience to open my eyes to the fact that there are legions of other believers in exile, people who have been saved through faith in Jesus Christ, who read their Bibles and pray faithfully, who long to know God better, but who have been burned by their experience in organized Christianity. It was this experience, as much as any other single factor, that prompted me to write *The Magnificent Obsession* ... now.

16. See Genesis 3:8–9.

17. John MacArthur, ed., *MacArthur Study Bible*, NKJV, 37, note 16:7.

18. Luke 19:10.

19. See Ephesians 3:18.

20. Acts 3:19 – 20.

21. Hagar's descendants through Ishmael are the Arabs … too numerous to count, just as the Angel of the Lord promised. He also said in verse 12 that Ishmael would "be a wild donkey of a man; his hand will be against everyone and everyone's hand against him, and he will live in hostility toward all his brothers." This was not a curse but a prophecy regarding Ishmael's personality. In Ishmael's lifetime, this was partially fulfilled as conflict arose between himself and his half brother, Isaac. Even today we see the Arabs continuing to live in hostility to Israel (Isaac's descendants) and to each other.

22. Romans 8:28.

23. Romans 8:28.

24. This is King David's prayer (Psalm 51:1 – 4) after he was confronted about his sin with Bathsheba.

25. *MacArthur Study Bible*, NKJV, 37, note 16:11.

26. See Mark 14:30 – 31.

27. See Mark 14:66 – 72.

28. See John 20:19 – 20.

29. 1 Peter 1:3.

30. "God Almighty," in Hebrew, is El Shaddai.

31. See 2 Corinthians 12:9 – 10.

32. Matthew 6:10.

33. For a brief but helpful explanation of the symbolism of circumcision, see *MacArthur Study Bible*, NKJV, 38, note 17:11.

34. See Genesis 18:10 – 15.

35. See Matthew 17:20.

Chapter 5: Lift Everything Up

1. 2 Timothy 4:5.

2. Like Abraham, it takes us a little while to understand, from reading this passage, who these three visitors were. From later verses, we see that one of these visitors was the Lord and the other two were angels: After the three visitors left Abraham's tent, Genesis 18:22 says, "The men turned away and went toward Sodom, but Abraham remained standing before the LORD." Then, a few verses later, Genesis 19:1 says, "The two angels arrived at Sodom in the evening." The conclusion is that two of the visitors were angels, while the third was the Lord Himself.

3. The text of the 1978 copyright version of the New International Bible I use says "they inquired." Did they speak in unison? Did they speak in harmony like a trio singing a gospel chorus? Did the voices sound like one? Like the voice of rushing waters? See Revelation 1:15.

4. To give Sarah the benefit of the doubt, maybe she meant she had not laughed out loud.

5. See John 2:24 – 25 and Psalm 139:2, 4.

6. See 1 John 1:6 – 7; 2:5 – 6.

7. See Genesis 3:8. The implication is that walking with God in the evening was a daily habit for Adam and Eve.

8. See Genesis 5:24.

9. See Genesis 6:9.

10. John 15:15.

11. John 1:1 – 2, 14, 18.

12. See Luke 19:40.

13. Psalm 34:15, 17.

14. See Galatians 3:24 KJV.

15. See Amos 7:7 – 8. Interestingly, the word *canon*, which we use to refer to the Bible, means "plumb line."

16. See John 1:14.

17. Romans 3:23; 3:10 KJV; 6:23.

18. Philippians 2:7 – 8.

19. This powerful thought was inspired by Arthur Bennett, ed., *The Valley of Vision* (Edinburgh: Banner of Truth Trust, 2002), 74.

20. John 12:13.

21. Luke 24:15 – 16.

22. Luke 24:27.

23. See James 4:8.

24. Hebrews 10:22; 1 John 5:14; Hebrews 11:6.

25. Operation Daily Light, P.O. Box 37434, Charlotte, NC 28237; *ODL@angelministries. org.*

26. I wrote down my questions and the answers God gave me, then published them in a book entitled *Why? Trusting God When You Don't Understand* (Nashville: W, 2004).

27. John 11:15.

28. See 2 Corinthians 4:6 – 7.

29. See Habakkuk 3:2.

30. See John 14:13 – 14; 15:16; 16:23 – 24.

31. This conversation was based on Exodus 15:13.

32. See Isaiah 43:2.

33. See Hebrews 13:5.

34. Two of my very favorite books that are filled with conversations with God are Jill Briscoe, *God's Front Door: Private Conversations* (London: Monarch, 2004) and Jill Briscoe, *The Deep Place, Where Nobody Goes: Conversations with God on the Steps of My Soul* (Oxford: Monarch, 2005).

35. The ten people were Lot, his wife, his two daughters and their husbands, his two unmarried daughters, and I assume two sons since the angels referred to them in the plural.

36. Daniel 9:2.

37. Daniel 9:20 – 23.

38. 1 Thessalonians 5:17.

39. Habakkuk 2:1.

40. See James 5:16.

41. See Ezekiel 22:30.

Chapter 6: Cast Everything Out

1. Not all species of cuckoos are parasites, but some are. While their nest of choice is a lark's nest, I've used the sparrow here to emphasize the contrast.

2. See Hebrews 12:1 KJV.

3. See Genesis 20:11.

4. See Deuteronomy 12:31; Psalm 11:5; Proverbs 6:16; Isaiah 1:14; Revelation 2:6.

5. It is hard to imagine that Sarah, at ninety years of age, would have been so desirable. It may be that Abimelech, who had heard of Abraham's military exploits with the kings of the East and who observed Abraham moving into his territory, was seeking to build an alliance with Abraham to forestall any threat to himself.

6. God's threat to Abimelech indicates that Abimelech may have been planning some sort of retaliation against Abraham.

7. Isaiah 42:3.

8. See Romans 3:23.

9. The name Isaac, appropriately, means "laughter."

10. Genesis 16:16 says Abraham was eighty-six years old when Ishmael was born. Genesis 21:5 says he was one hundred years old when Isaac was born. That means Ishmael was fourteen when Isaac was born. Children in Abraham's day were weaned between two and five years of age, the average age being approximately three, which would make Ishmael sixteen to nineteen years old when the incident in Genesis 21 occurred.

11. See Galatians 4:29.

12. See James 2:10.

13. See Romans 3:23.

14. Ephesians 4:22.

15. Romans 8:8 KJV.

16. Galatians 5:17, 19 – 21; Romans 7:18.

17. See 1 Corinthians 15:22.

18. See Galatians 4:22 – 30.

19. See Romans 8:8.

20. John 3:7.

21. See Luke 1:30 – 38.

22. See Colossians 1:27; John 14:7; Revelation 3:20.

23. 2 Corinthians 5:17.

24. Ephesians 4:22 – 24.

25. See Galatians 4:23, 28.

26. Fanny Crosby, "Blessed Assurance," 1873.

27. Galatians 5:17.

28. Romans 7:14 – 19.

29. See Isaiah 64:6.

30. Romans 7:24.

31. John MacArthur, ed., *The MacArthur Study Bible*, NKJV (Nashville: Word Bibles, 1997), 1706.

32. Romans 7:24.

33. See Revelation 3:1 – 6, 14 – 22.

34. Ephesians 4:22 – 24.

35. Colossians 3:5, 8 – 10.

36. Although Ishmael represents an old nature, he also can represent something else worth noting. Ishmael was Abraham's greatest mistake, his greatest sin and failure. God told Abraham to let Ishmael go if Abraham wanted to experience God's blessing on himself, his home, and his sons. What is your Ishmael? Is it an abortion or involvement in one? Is your Ishmael an illegitimate child? What is the biggest mistake in your life? How are you still clinging to it? While you should not throw out an illegitimate child, are you clinging to and dwelling on memories through your attitude of self-pity, regret, or guilt? Maybe your Ishmael is a live-in lover to whom you are not married. Is God saying to you, "Get rid of your Ishmael"? Before you truly can enjoy your new life in Christ, do you need to acknowledge and confess your mistake, sin, or failure to God? Accept His cleansing and forgiveness (see 1 John 1:9). Put out of your life the sin, memories, guilt, and self-pity. Forgive yourself because God, for Christ's sake, has forgiven you.

37. Galatians 4:28 – 31.

38. Romans 8:1 – 2.

39. See Romans 8:8.

40. See 1 Peter 1:24; Romans 8:13; 1 Corinthians 15:50.

41. See 1 Corinthians 3:12 – 15.

Chapter 7: Lay Everything Down

1. Revelation 12:11.

2. Marcus Luttrell survived to tell the story of what took place in that remote mountain region on June 28, 2005. As a result, on October 22, 2007, President George W. Bush awarded Lt. Michael Murphy the Medal of Honor, our nation's supreme applause for the bravest of the brave in our armed forces. See the website *www.cmohs.org*.

3. John 15:13.

4. This principle reminds me of one that Jesus taught His disciples five days before He laid everything down at the cross. When Jesus taught this principle, I imagine He was walking through the city surrounded by His disciples. Perhaps as they were passing a vendor with large baskets of grain for sale, He stopped, seizing the opportunity to give an object lesson. I wonder if He scooped up a handful of grain, letting the seeds flow through His fingers until only one was left. Then, holding up that one seed, He explained, "I tell

you the truth, unless a kernel of wheat falls to the ground and dies, it remains only a single seed. But if it dies, it produces many seeds" (John 12:24). In other words, the single grain of wheat would never fulfill the potential it had to sprout with life and cover an entire field with wheat unless it was planted. But if it was laid down, the ground would press down upon it, rain would fall and soften it, and the shell, or chaff, would break. The seed would then be released to press upward, sprout, and grow into a stalk of wheat with dozens of seeds of grain in its head.

From our perspective on this side of the cross, we can look back and see the truth of this principle worked out in Jesus' own life. It was not on the throne of world rulership that Jesus came into power, as the disciples had imagined, but on the cross where He was broken. Like the grain of wheat, He had to die in order to be raised up with the power to reproduce His life hundreds of thousands of times over — in the lives of you and me and believers all through the centuries. He laid everything down in order to be raised up to receive the fullness of all that His Father wanted to give Him as the Son of God and the Son of Man.

And it's this same principle that I see in Abraham's life as he embraced the magnificent obsession. He had to lay everything down, including ... and especially ... his most precious possession if he wanted to receive everything God wanted to give him.

5. See 1 Corinthians 10:13.

6. Exodus 16:10.

7. Our Isaac may be like Mary's alabaster jar, described in John 12. The ointment it contained was the equivalent of her life's savings. While people today invest in fine art, antiques, or jewelry as a way to increase the value of their holdings, Mary, as was the custom in her day, collected perfumed ointment, adding to her cache as her savings would allow. The ointment never spoiled and actually increased in value as time passed. It may even have served as Mary's dowry, collected not only by herself but also contributed to by family members in order to insure a secure future for her. Without question, the alabaster jar of perfumed ointment was Mary's most precious possession.

As John described the scene that took place during the week preceding Jesus' death on the cross, Mary clutched her alabaster jar, gliding quietly through the banquet hall in Simon's house where Jesus, His disciples, and other friends were enjoying dinner. I doubt that anyone noticed her at first ... except Jesus. Surely He had watched her enter, fully aware of her intentions. He must have ceased eating, the expression on His face softening into one of total acceptance and love. Feeling His eyes on her, she must have glanced at His face and seen the welcome that was there.

Without any hesitation or embarrassment, Mary took the gleaming alabaster jar containing a veritable fortune of perfumed ointment, broke the seal, and extravagantly poured the contents on Jesus' head and feet (see Mark 14:3; John 12:3). Because she loved Him.

In this simple, profound act of devotion, Mary gave Jesus *everything* — her future, her hope for a future, her financial security, her status in society, her reputation, her pride, her self. By pouring out her ointment, she withheld nothing from Him and expected nothing in return.

8. The King James Version says, "Abraham rose up early in the morning."

9. In Genesis 3:1 – 5, the serpent's response to the woman was to contradict God's Word — "You will not surely die" — when God had said, "You will surely die" (Genesis 2:17), and to cast doubt on God's character: "For God knows that when you eat of it … you will be like God," leading her to think God was holding out on her.

10. See Hebrews 11:17 – 19.

11. The King James Version translates this verse very meaningfully: "My son, God will provide himself a lamb for a burnt offering."

12. See Psalm 139:3.

13. See Psalm 51:19 KJV.

14. 2 Corinthians 5:9.

15. Corrie ten Boom and John and Elizabeth Sherrill, *The Hiding Place* (Uhrichsville, Ohio: Barbour, 1971), 33.

16. John 18:11.

17. Romans 8:32.

18. George Matheson, "O Love That Wilt Not Let Me Go," 1882.

Chapter 8: Mourn Everything Hopefully

1. Incredibly, Amy's grandfather looked at the stranger lying in the casket and said, "Bury him. Ma's been through enough." Amy's grandmother, the soldier's mother, never knew that the body they buried was not her son. (This story is true, but the name has been changed.)

2. Hebrews 11:10.

3. See Hebrews 9:27.

4. Ruth Bell Graham, *Ruth Bell Graham's Collected Poems* (Grand Rapids, Mich.: Baker, 1998). Used by permission.

5. I have been greatly comforted by the fact that Jesus understands tears of grief. He went to Bethany to draw near to those who were mourning the death of Lazarus, a friend whom He loved (see John 11:3). He asked those who had gathered, "Where have you laid him?" (John 11:34). Jesus knew exactly where Lazarus was buried, but He wanted those who were grieving to invite Him to share their sorrow and to feel their pain. When they showed Him their grief, which was focused on the tomb of Lazarus, Jesus … the Creator of the Universe, the eternal I AM, the Lord of life, the One who knew Lazarus would be raised from the dead within moments … stood there with tears running down His cheeks! *Jesus wept!* (John 11:35).

He doesn't blame you and me for weeping. When have you invited Jesus to feel your pain? To come and see your tears? To enter into your grief and hurt and brokenness? If you had eyes to see, you would know that in a very tender way, your tears are on His face. He enters into your suffering if for no other reason than it's yours. And He loves you!

6. 1 Thessalonians 4:13.

7. John 14:1 – 3.

8. For a more detailed look at what Jesus said and what the apostle John saw, see Anne Graham Lotz, *Heaven: My Father's House* (Nashville: Word, 2001).

9. 1 Thessalonians 4:14. See also John 11:11.

10. See Hebrews 11:10, 19.

11. See Hebrews 12:2.

12. See 1 John 1:9.

13. Psalm 103:15 – 16.

14. See Hebrews 11:9 – 10.

15. Matthew 6:19 – 20.

16. See Genesis 13:15, 17; 15:18.

17. Today a mosque covers this site.

18. Not only Sarah but also Abraham and their son Isaac and Isaac's wife, Rebekah, were buried at this site, along with Isaac and Rebekah's son Jacob and one of Jacob's wives, Leah. See Genesis 25:9; 49:31; 50:13.

19. Abraham's purchase of the cave of Machpelah gives us a fascinating glimpse into the typical haggling in business transactions of that day. As Abraham and Ephron bargained over the price of the field, Abraham seems to have allowed himself to be cheated. I've seen estimates that say the average price for the land could have been approximately forty shekels, but Abraham paid four hundred shekels. In his grief, maybe he just wanted to close the deal. Or maybe he didn't care because he knew money was temporary, but the promises of God, symbolized by the cave, were eternal. See Genesis 23:14 – 16.

20. See 2 Corinthians 5:1.

21. Although Genesis is the first book in the Bible and describes the creation, it is believed to have been written by Moses, who came after Abraham and Job. See *MacArthur Study Bible, NKJV* (Nashville: Word Bibles, 1997), 693.

22. Job 19:25 – 27.

23. 1 Corinthians 15:51 – 52.

24. Philippians 3:20 – 21.

25. John 11:23, 25 – 26.

26. See 1 Peter 1:3.

Chapter 9: Pass Everything On

1. Adapted from Anne Graham Lotz, *Daily Light* (Nashville: Countryman, 1988), v.

2. See John 3:29; Ephesians 5:25 – 27; Revelation 19:7.

3. If your children are small, start praying now for whomever they will marry. And teach them to do the same. If it's too late to pray for the spouses of your children because they are already married, then join me in praying for the spouses of our grandchildren.

4. Abraham actually outlived Sarah by forty-eight years.

5. See Genesis 25:20.

6. See Genesis 22:20 – 24.

7. One reason it's vital for us to belong to a strong Bible-believing, Jesus-loving, gospel-preaching church is that our children need the reinforcement of a strong youth group. But since they are only in church one or two days a week and are in school five days a week, help get your children into a Christian organization on campus such as Youth for Christ, InterVarsity, Campus Crusade for Christ, Fellowship of Christian Athletes, or others. If there is not one at your child's school, see what you can do to start one. These organizations are a wonderful resource, not only for fellowship but for friendships that will help your children set their standards, maintain their values, and, in time, make their choice of a spouse. Interestingly, I found my husband (or he found me) through the Fellowship of Christian Athletes, as did two of our children.

8. In Abraham's day, parents often arranged marriages for their children. Even as I write this, I am painfully aware that in our culture, our children make their own choices. And in spite of our clear instructions, they have the freedom to make the wrong choices.

9. See Luke 19:10.

10. See John 14:21; 17:25 – 26.

11. See Ephesians 1:4.

12. See 1 Peter 1:20; Revelation 13:8.

13. See Romans 10:17.

14. Mark 16:15.

15. The actual oath-taking seems strange to us but was an ancient custom that emphasized the extreme importance of the mission.

16. See John 15:18 – 21.

17. Camels can drink from five to twenty-five gallons of water at a time, so Rebekah drew between 50 and 250 gallons from that well to water the servants' ten camels … no small feat! If her jar held five gallons, she went up and down those steps anywhere from ten to fifty times!

18. The story is true, but the name has been changed.

19. The story is true, but the name has been changed.

20. The story is true, but the name has been changed.

21. Anne Graham Lotz, *Heaven: My Father's House* (Nashville: W, 2001).

22. Peter and John, the two leaders of the disciples who helped establish the early church, were arrested for preaching about Jesus. When they were forbidden by the authorities to speak or teach in the name of Jesus, they boldly replied, "We cannot help speaking about what we have seen and heard" (Acts 4:20). Like the disciples, the servant could no longer hold back.

23. The apostle Peter challenges us, that "if anyone speaks, he should do it as one speaking the very words of God … so that in all things God may be praised through Jesus Christ. To him be the glory and the power for ever and ever. Amen" (1 Peter 4:11).

24. See John 12:32.

25. See John 3:16.

26. See 1 Peter 1:8.

27. See Philippians 4:7.

28. See Romans 8:38 – 39.

29. See Lamentations 3:22.

30. See 1 John 1:7, 9.

31. See John 10:10.

32. See John 1:16.

33. See 1 Timothy 1:16.

34. See 2 Corinthians 12:9.

35. See 2 Corinthians 12:9; Ephesians 1:6.

36. See Ephesians 1:18.

37. See 2 Timothy 3:16 – 17.

38. See Psalm 119:90.

39. See John 14:16.

40. See Titus 2:13; Revelation 22:4.

41. See Ephesians 1:13 – 14.

42. 1 Corinthians 2:9.

43. Ephesians 3:20 – 21.

44. I have been using a computer for about fifteen years, and this was only the second time I had had this experience. But both experiences occurred during the writing of this book!

45. The morning after my computer crashed, my daily Bible reading was Exodus 17:1 – 7. God seemed to speak to me through it verse by verse, promising that He would give me water from the rock for people to drink (see verse 6).

46. This is purely my conjecture, but it fits Laban's character as we see him in Genesis 29 – 31.

47. This is such a common tactic of the enemy that one evangelism training course warns participants to expect the interruption and be prepared to press through it.

48. The story is true, but the name has been changed.

49. See John 1:12.

50. See Ephesians 1:4.

51. See John 16:6 – 15.

52. See 1 John 1:9.

53. See John 3:16.

54. See Revelation 3:20.

55. See John 1:12.

56. See John 14:26.

57. See Luke 1:26 – 38; 2:6 – 7.

58. See Luke 7:22.

59. See John 19:17 – 37.

60. See Matthew 28:1 – 7.

61. See Acts 1:9 – 11.

62. See Hebrews 1:2.

63. See 2 Thessalonians 2:14.

64. See Hebrews 7:25.

65. See John 14:3.

66. See 1 Peter 1:8.

67. See Genesis 25:5.

68. See Ephesians 5:27.

69. See 1 Peter 3:3 – 4.

70. See John 14:23.

71. See Deuteronomy 34:10.

72. John 1:29.

73. John 1:14; 1 John 1:1; John 1:18. "The only begotten of the Father" is from the King James Version.

Epilogue

1. Abraham had one wife, Sarah. He had a concubine, Hagar, and he had a second wife, Keturah. I don't know why Genesis 25:6 and 1 Chronicles 1:32 refer to Keturah as a concubine, since Genesis 25:1 clearly says Abraham took her as his wife. It may be that second wives were considered subordinate. Certainly Keturah was secondary to Sarah in God's ultimate promise, which would come through Sarah's son, Isaac.

Also, it's worth noting the beautiful reconciliation that must have taken place between Isaac and Ishmael as they were united in grief over their father. It seems to underscore something I've experienced: funerals can be a very tender time for those who mourn.

2. Galatians 3:14, 9.

A Very Special
Thank-You

To
Bob Chandler
President of MacVantage, Inc.,
who saw me through two computer crashes
and several technical panic attacks
during the writing of this book.
Thank you, Bob, for …
your patience,
your calm demeanor,
your comforting kindness,
and your availability 24/7.
You are a true brother in Christ.

—◦◦—

To
Sue Ann Jones
the beloved freelance editor of seven of my books,
who worked on this manuscript while confronted
with personal, life-altering challenges …
Thank you for your perseverance under pressure
and for always working from your heart as well as your head.

—◦◦—

And to my
Zondervan team ...

Moe Girkins: Thank you for your personal "ownership" of this book
in the midst of assuming your broader responsibilities as president.

Dudley Delffs: Thank you for not only wielding
your editorial knife with skillful wisdom and respectful insight
but also for adjusting the timing of publication
so that the book's release was poised for maximum impact.

Sandra Vander Zicht: Thank you for your grasp of the message
underneath the words and for your brilliant word-smithing
that has enabled the message to come through more clearly.

Ginia Hairston: Thank you for your commitment to get this book
into as many hands as possible and, to that end,
giving it your undivided attention in the midst of personal transition.

And to all who've read this book ...
thank you for embracing this Magnificent Obsession
with me.

I Saw the Lord

A Wake-Up Call for Your Heart

Anne Graham Lotz

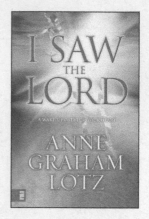

When we call ourselves Christians, we expect that our love for Jesus, our hunger for His presence, our urgent longing to see Him again will be a constant, motivating force in our lives, writes Anne Graham Lotz. Yet sometimes ... in the busyness of our days or the duties of our jobs or the familiar habits of our worship or the everyday routine of our homes, the longing becomes complacency, and we sleep through opportunities to be with Him.

Anne knows from personal experience that it's then, as we're drifting in comfortable complacency, that we most need a wake-up call—a jolt that pushes us to seek out a revival of our passion for Jesus that began as a blazing fire but somehow has died down to an ineffective glow.

The revival we need now is not a tent meeting or a series of church services designed to save the lost. It's something completely different: authentic, personal revival.

In *I Saw the Lord*, Anne shares the revival lessons she has carried to audiences throughout the world, showing you how you can experience an authentic, deeper, richer relationship with God in a life-changing, fire-blazing revival.

It begins here. Now. Open this book and hear the wake-up call. Then get ready for the fire of revival to fall ... on you!

Available in stores and online!

I Saw the Lord Curriculum

A Wake-Up Call for Your Heart

Anne Graham Lotz

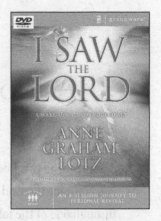

Gifted Bible teacher and international speaker Anne Graham Lotz believes that our world today is desperate for churches filled not with good Christians, but with great ones — men and women like Isaiah, the greatest of the Old Testament prophets, who have had a fresh vision of God, who enjoy a vibrant, personal relationship with Him, and whose lives are empowered to change the lives of others.

In this eight-session Zondervan Groupware, Anne, along with Crawford Lorritts and Henry Blackaby, helps guide small groups in seeing that vision so that each participant can have a genuine experience of personal life-changing revival. Drawing from the examples of key biblical characters, Anne, Crawford, and Henry share with your group the revival lessons they have learned through their lives. Here is how you can experience an authentic, deeper, richer relationship with God in a life-changing, fire-blazing revival. Also included is a Bible study workshop where Anne demonstrates her approach to studying Scripture.

The DVD and participant's guide work hand-in-hand to make this a meaningful experience for small groups and church classes.

Eight interactive sessions include: 1. Bible Study Workshop 2. You're Sleeping (Josiah) 3. Wake Up (Ezekiel) 4. Open Your Eyes (Moses) 5. Rend Your Heart (David) 6. Bend Your Knees (Ezra) 7. Just Say Yes! (Isaiah) 8. Move Your Feet (Nehemiah)

Available in stores and online!

ZONDERVAN®
.com

A Note to the Reader

After reading this book, if you need additional resources to help
you embrace the God-filled life, please contact Anne Graham Lotz
through one of the following means:

AnGeL Ministries
5115 Hollyridge Drive
Raleigh, North Carolina 27612
919.787.6606
www.AnneGrahamLotz.com.
angelmin.info@angelministries.org

ZONDERVAN®

ZONDERVAN.com /
AUTHORTRACKER
follow your favorite authors

CPSIA information can be obtained
at www.ICGtesting.com
Printed in the USA
LVHW031924150920
666066LV00003B/21